FACING THE BIG CATS

Facing the Big Cats

MY WORLD OF
LIONS AND TIGERS

by CLYDE BEATTY

with EDWARD ANTHONY

1965
Doubleday & Company, Inc.
GARDEN CITY, NEW YORK

To JANE,
my trainer,
and Clyde, Jr.,
her able assistant,
with love

COLLABORATOR'S COMMENT

IN THE spring of 1963 I was traveling with the Clyde Beatty-Cole Bros. Circus gathering material for this book. The one-night stands were over for a while and we were in Philadelphia, where the circus was playing an eleven-day engagement.

We were seated at a table in the house-trailer that is Beatty's home when he is on tour, and he was answering questions I had asked him about different aspects of his career, when there was a knock on the door.

Clyde opened the door and was greeted by a group of five or six boys ranging in age from about ten to twelve. "What can I do for you, boys?" he asked.

They had heard, they told him, that the circus sometimes admitted children free if they did a little light work around the big top. "Better see Mr. So-and-so," said Clyde. "He's in charge of that."

"We did," replied the spokesman for the group. "He said other boys had beat us to it. We should have come earlier."

"Sorry, boys. Better luck next time."

"I don't suppose you have any free tickets around," asked the spokesman hesitantly but hopefully.

"No, I'm afraid not."

"We'd love to see the show."

"Well, why don't you?" asked Clyde.

"Without tickets?"

"Sure."

Then Clyde advised them on the best way to duck in, even suggesting the exact area on the other side of the big top where they would have the best chance.

"Suppose we get thrown out, Mr. Beatty?"

"If you do, come back and we'll try to figure out something else."

The boys went on their way. I saw them inside later. They seemed to be enjoying themselves. One of them recognized me and said, "It worked. Will you please thank Mr. Beatty for us?"

Before we resumed work Clyde said, "I hate to turn kids down." He paused, then added, "If I had arranged to get them free tickets, half the kids in Philadelphia would be rapping on my door tomorrow asking for the same thing. News travels fast over the children's grapevine."

Anything is possible when you travel with Clyde Beatty.

People frequently ask me, "What sort of guy is Clyde Beatty?" The story of the boys answers that question as well as anything I can think of.

It also illustrates the weakness of the first-person technique in writing a book of this kind. Clyde couldn't very well tell an anecdote like that about himself—or a number of others as typical that come to mind.

But the first-person device has its merits too, and I suppose in the end there is not much to choose between it and the third-person approach.

At any rate, the decision was made to write this book in the first person. In putting it together I hoped it would be possible to tell it all in Clyde's easy conversational style. Wherever possible I have done this, but I have also had to do considerable paraphrasing.

In this approach there is an occasional loss of saltiness. However, the equivalent of What the Man Said frequently enables the writer to make clearer certain aspects of a subject that most people are unfamiliar with.

The paraphrasing technique also permits short cuts and results in a shorter book. And who is going to squawk about that?

E.A.

New Milford, Conn.

Contents

Illustrations

1. Big-Cat Audiences

What the Public Wants to Know – Fallacies about
the Feeding of Lions and Tigers – Clawless and Tooth-
less? – Alleged Cruel Practices in Training Wild
Animals – *Must* the Show Go On? – Recollections of
Ernest Hemingway, Animal-Training Fan, in My
Dressing Room at Madison Square Garden

I N THE approximately forty years that have elapsed since I
began training animals at the age of seventeen, I have given
over 30,000 performances and have traveled more than a million miles in the process. This has necessitated my training
almost a thousand lions and about the same number of tigers
and a very much smaller contingent of other members of the
cat family—an assortment of something like sixty leopards
(spotted and black), jaguars and pumas. Eventually I settled
down to being a lion-and-tiger man exclusively.

I once put on a show with an audience of one—yes, *one*—
solitary person in the house; the other extreme was a crowd
of 103,000 at the Nebraska State Fair.

During the many years I was with the Hagenbeck-Wallace
Circus audiences of 6500 to 8000 were not uncommon. I recall a ten-day engagement in the St. Louis Arena during
which we played to several capacity houses of 23,000. Some
days during this engagement we had to play two matinees
(one in the morning)—in other words, three shows a day.

We operated then, as we do today, on a seven-day-a-week basis. Once the season starts there are no days off.

My regular season begins early in the spring and terminates the second week in November. In addition, over the years I have played many post-season engagements—in New York, Detroit, Omaha, New Orleans, Kansas City, Cleveland, Minneapolis, St. Paul, Chicago, Boston, Milwaukee, Buffalo, Honolulu and elsewhere in Hawaii, San Juan, Puerto Rico; and in Montreal, Toronto, Ottawa, Mexico City and other large centers of population.

I have had to pass up a number of offers—some of them recently made—to appear in Europe. After a long season I consider it too wearing for all concerned to make these long hauls with as big a show as mine. While, for instance, I enjoyed touring the Hawaiian Islands under the management of the able impresario E. K. Fernandez, I found it too much of a strain to move a whole menagerie, including fifteen elephants and a few dozen lions and tigers—in addition to the vast amount of equipment of all kinds that goes with the modern circus—from the continental United States to so distant a destination.

I've been doing some digging into the records and I'm surprised to find how many times during my long career I have played three and four shows daily. The extra matinees are usually played Saturdays, Sundays and holidays, when the children are home from school.

No official attendance records are available for the early years of my career, but attendance figures appear in some of the news stories dealing with this period. These figures, plus the estimates of past and present associates, enabled me to arrive at reasonably accurate figures covering those early days.

The stacks of figures my collaborator and I have been struggling with make it amply clear that I could not have played to less than forty million since I first began. Though I don't believe that in the approximately forty years which have elapsed since I started performing I have heard from more than 1 per cent—(by mail, visits to my dressing room, pre-arranged and spur-of-the-moment autographing bees mainly involving children, and at dinners, luncheons and other affairs of circus fans' associations which I have attended over the years, etc., etc.)—I can still point to a vast number of fans who have communicated with me in one way or another.

Admittedly, some of the mail I have received over the years belongs in the files of the Crackpot Department and does not merit a reply or even a rubber-stamp acknowledgment. On the other hand, I have received many thoughtful, provocative letters. Some of the correspondence in this category—(I answer as much of it as a man almost constantly on tour has the time and the facilities for handling)—has led to lasting friendships.

In many an audience there is someone who remembers the days way back when we both were with the Such-and-such Circus. At least half the time these people are mistaken. From time to time someone calls on me—I had several such visitors as recently as 1963 and 1964—and starts talking enthusiastically about the good old days when we trouped together with the Sells-Floto Circus. I never worked for that show. If I decide that my caller, familiar with the fact that in my early days as a performer I appeared with a number of circuses, has decided to assume that Sells-Floto must have been among them, I get rid of him before he has a chance to get too reminiscent, particularly when after asking a few key questions I am convinced he was never associated with *any* circus.

Circus organizations are so large—and there is so rapid a turnover in the labor squads that erect and tear down the big top during one-night stands—that the man who says he once worked in your show has you at a disadvantage. No one, especially when the frame of reference involves some long-ago period, can remember all the circus hands he has worked with. But by the same token I have the phonies at a disadvantage, for it is hard to fake circus experience.

If obviously my visitor is an old-time circus hand whose memory is playing tricks on him, I permit him, for at least a few minutes, to draw upon his recollections of the great days when we worked together for some show I never worked for. Usually this type of caller winds up by saying, with a hopeful gleam in his eye, that he hears that my act, which, alas, he hasn't seen for years, is better than ever. I always take the hint and, unless we happen to be sold out, see that he gets a pair of tickets.

Among the questions I am asked most frequently by callers and correspondents is the inevitable: do you feed your lions and tigers before or after you put on your act?

Visitors to my dressing room are puzzled when I answer, "Both." I then explain that my animals are fed once a day, between shows. Feeding time is after the matinee and well before the animals do their stuff at night.

One of the myths that refuses to die is that the animals are fed before each performance, the theory being that a lion or tiger with a bellyful of meat will not be tempted to make a meal of his trainer.

Yes, myths die hard. One of my recent correspondents insists that he has heard "reliably" that my big cats are fed *a few minutes before they enter the arena for each performance.* If I had the time, I would write to inform him that fifteen to eighteen pounds of meat—depending on the animal's requirements, which are usually determined by its weight— leaves a lion or a tiger drowsy and ready for a nap. If I fed them just before they were due to perform, I might have to carry an alarm clock into the arena with me to wake the dozers.

There are also some people who want to know whether it is true that my animals are decrepit, old, toothless specimens. Not many have had the nerve to ask this question in person, although I have no objection to their doing so. The public has been kind to me and when a question of this type is thrown at me I like to attribute it—perhaps kidding myself in the process—to a desire to learn the facts rather than to any urge to embarrass me.

When this kind of query turns up in letters, I find that the most effective reply is what I tell newspapermen who, to draw me out, occasionally put the same question to me. I invite them to drop in when the animals are being fed. I explain that the butcher who looks after the needs of the big cats has instructions to include in each animal's daily meal a slab of meat that runs heavily to bone—usually a rib section—because I have learned from experience, and also from veterinarians, that a lion or a tiger is a happier and a healthier animal if he has a chance to swallow a certain amount of practically pulverized bone with the raw meat on which he subsists. Anyone seeing the big cats grind up those bones also has a chance to see the big powerful teeth that do the grinding. It is an awesome sight, and an unforgettable one, and those who have had a chance to witness it will never again ask whether my animals are toothless.

Frequently these same skeptics also want to know whether my lions and tigers have had their claws clipped. I can't give the answer individually to every doubter, but it is easy to do so for the benefit of the press. The newspapers from coast to coast have been more than fair to me, so whenever an interviewer tosses a controversial question at me to start me talking, I don't mind in the least. If it happens to be the old clipped-claw staple, I walk him over to the cages and, letting him select the animal whose claws he wants to see in all their glory, I make a few gestures designed to put the lion or tiger in a fighting mood. The claws, normally retracted, show up formidably when bared for action. Then, just to remind the animal that I was only fooling, I say something to him designed to get him to quiet down. If the animal happens to be Rajah, one of the most powerful and best-natured tigers

I have ever trained, I get him to purr, which is his specialty. Five hundred pounds of purring tiger is quite a sight.

One reporter thinks I throw away my case when I get Rajah to purr. "Okay, so his claws haven't been tampered with!" he exclaimed. "But how do you expect anyone to believe that a tiger that purrs like my pet cat is really dangerous?" Well, he is. No matter how much affection I lavish on him he will never lose his basic primitiveness.

I had a somewhat similar experience when I provoked a lion into a full-dress baring of his claws, this time for the benefit of a spectator who, without being too unfriendly about it, announced he was from Missouri and wanted to be shown. Well, I showed him and he was convinced. But he, too, was puzzled when the demonstration was over and it was time to pacify the animal. I achieved this by alternately whistling softly and speaking gently to my lion friend. He, to show he got the message, presented an ear for rubbing, a familiar routine with him and some of my other big cats. The reaction of the man from Missouri was the same as the reporter's when I started Rajah purring. When you see a lion presenting an ear for scratching much as a pet dog would, you can't help wondering whether despite those deadly claws the animal is really dangerous. Too bad lions don't purr. I would have liked to confuse that skeptic further by cuing this particular one to purr his head off.

In recent years wild-animal enthusiasts who have bought big-cat cubs as pets have subjected them to the surgery commonly known as declawing—usually at the age of two months. The animal is anesthetized, and while he suffers no serious discomfort, it is a practice of which I strongly disapprove.

Clawless cats—this operation involves the complete removal of the claws from the pads—have been known to undergo unfortunate personality changes. It is as natural for a big cat, especially a youngster, to sharpen its claws on trees or heavy underbrush as it is for it to breathe. I recall a lion cub that had been declawed, a practice which seems to be on the increase, that changed the animal from a happy-go-lucky, cheerful character to a chronically irritable one. Some of the things he did seemed to indicate frustration, and though he couldn't very well try to sharpen claws he didn't possess, he began behaving oddly, somehow suggesting that he sensed he was missing something, although he wasn't sure what. It is one of those phenomena that is difficult to describe satisfactorily. But that the animal's disposition and behavioral pattern had changed was unmistakable.

It is hard to condone a practice as unnatural as declawing. I have never trained an animal that has undergone this operation nor would I consider doing so.

A woman who professes to love tiger cubs offered me a handsome price for one during the spring of 1964. I turned her down for two reasons: I did not want to part with the animal, nor did I approve of her plan to declaw it.

This woman, whose knowledge of wild animals was sadly deficient, apparently believed that declawing would render the animal harmless. She had overlooked the fact that a big cat—a cub or a full-grown one—can do more damage with his teeth than with his claws.

From the animal psychologist's standpoint it would be interesting to turn loose in a wooded area, where they could be regularly observed, a big-cat cub—say, a lion, tiger or leopard—that had been declawed, and one of the same species and approximate age that had not undergone this operation. Instinctively the one with the claws would, sooner or later, start sharpening them on a tree. What the other's reaction to this would be is anybody's guess. It is quite possible that such an experiment would yield information so disturbing that it would start a trend away from declawing, which I would like to see happen.

Skepticism makes better reading than commendation. Most of the circus-going public who have written me over the years have expressed themselves favorably, even enthusiastically,

2.

about my work. But nothing could be duller reading, I imagine, than a cross-section of complimentary comments—especially those that are uncomfortably loaded with over-praise.

I find the skeptics far more interesting and I imagine the reading public does too. I don't know how many times I have been asked by correspondents whether it is true that unless the trainer resorts to cruel practices he cannot hope to train a wild animal. Such queries are relatively infrequent today because of the expanding literature of circusdom, which in dealing with animal training focuses attention on the essentiality of the kindly approach by the trainer who is teaching animals —wild or otherwise—to perform.

In the late 1920s and in the 1930s and 1940s, this was not understood except by a scattering of perceptive mammalogists and people who had had circus experience.

I always welcome questions that give me a chance to clear up misconceptions. It is a simple matter to explain that for years I have made a practice of inviting the public to see me break in new animals. Most of these training sessions take place in winter quarters between seasons. There is no better way of getting a lion or a tiger accustomed to an audience than to have people watching from the very beginning of the training period. In fact, getting an animal used to crowds is part of its training—so the bigger the audience when I conduct these big-cat classes the better I like it. People react at these training sessions pretty much as they do under the big top. For instance, they applaud when something happens that appeals to them. They chat with one another as they watch me work, and this steady buzz of conversation is something my animals have to get accustomed to. They will hear plenty of it when they are working under the big top, and it is best not to have this almost continuous hum of voices come as a surprise to them.

I shall always be grateful to the late Raymond L. Ditmars, former curator of mammals and reptiles of the New York Zoological Society, for debunking a charge made by an organization dedicated to fair play for animals, that I employed "cruel practices" in training my lions and tigers (which information, I might add, they had "on good authority," although the authority's name was not given).

It would take dozens of pages to tell all the weird stories that have gained currency over the years about cruel practices to which trainers have allegedly resorted in breaking in animals. There is one that was once common gossip, although it is seldom heard any longer. It had to do with trainers who, in order to get animals to perform, indulged in the quaint practice of jabbing them with sharply pointed steel rods.

Another that once had quite a vogue had to do with trainers who exacted compliance from their trainees by searing them with red-hot irons. Such cock-and-bull stories never completely die out, although in the long history of animal training there is no record of anyone having ever seen a trainer resort to the methods described.

Only a trainer anxious to get himself killed would attempt such cruelties. There are pleasanter ways of committing suicide.

Myths have always fascinated me, and when possible I like to trace them back to their earliest beginnings. As far as I can determine, the story of the red-hot irons originated in the early 1900s when a visitor to the training quarters of the great English trainer Frank C. Bostock saw some irons being heated in a coke fire. The visitor did not contend that he had seen Bostock apply any of these red-hot irons to an animal (which, had he done so, would have burned unpretty holes in the creature's coat in addition to broiling the flesh underneath). All he said was that he had seen these irons heating. With nothing more than this to go on, the overzealous critic accused Bostock of cruel practices. In his book, *The Training of Wild Animals*, Bostock explained: "It is my practice in cold weather to put hot irons into the drinking-water of my animals. This practice is always observed in my show during the winter months. It has the value of taking the chill off the water, and also imparts some of the beneficial qualities of the iron, thus giving an iron tonic and drinkable water at the same time."

I disagree with Bostock's theory about the "iron tonic," as I do with a few of his other beliefs about how to keep wild animals healthy, but there is no doubt in my mind that the accusation against him was absurb. Even if his had been a cruel nature—(no trainer ever handled his animals more gently or patiently)—Frank Bostock had too much sense to poke an animal with a hot iron and then expect it to perform. He knew, as all successful trainers know, that aside from a basic knowledge of animals, the two greatest factors in securing results in our little-understood profession are the kindly approach and a capacity for taking pains, plus a reasonably cheerful disposition, which helps absorb the inevitable disappointments one suffers in teaching certain types of animals that are very slow, deliberate learners.

Not since 1937—and that was twenty-eight years ago—have I had a complaint from any of the organizations dedicated to seeing that animals are decently treated. Which is not surprising, as my big cats—and all the other animals connected with our show—are so well cared for.

I have a great respect for the people who love animals sufficiently to make a career of seeing that they get a square deal. Understandably the organizations which they represent have made some mistakes, but there is no doubt in my mind that they perform an essential service and deserve the support of the public.

In May of 1964 our show was playing its annual eleven-day engagement in Philadelphia. I arrived in town with an assortment of aches and pains and had to see a doctor. During the next few days I was X-rayed until I thought the radiologist in charge would run out of film.

Fortunately the physician who had ordered these pictures was able to report to me that he could find nothing wrong. However, he was convinced that I was suffering from exhaustion as a result of performing for a few weeks prior to the Philadelphia engagement while battling a heavy cold, and he suggested that my understudy take over. He was surprised when I explained that I didn't have one and would have to carry on, as best I could, with my aches and pains.

Why don't I have a substitute to fill in for me when I don't feel fit enough to go on myself? This is a difficult subject to discuss, as it is easy to give the reader the impression that I consider myself "the indispensable man." There are some performers—I am one of them—whose work is so highly individualistic that it is hard to find replacements for them. I have tried for years to get someone to act as my understudy to avoid the necessity of working when the demons of fatigue remind me how nice it would be to step out for a day or two and get some rest.

Once I thought I had found the right replacement. But in rehearsal he proved too excitable and this excitability communicated itself to the animals, who will not respond as they should unless handled by someone who is calm and collected—and confident. There are times when even the most confident-seeming trainer has his worried moments, but he must bluff his way through the tough spots in which he finds himself—at least, he must *try* to. Occasionally there is a situation from which he cannot extricate himself—one of those inevitable crises when he is marked for injury—but then more than ever he cannot afford to panic. In fire-department language, he must walk, not run, to the nearest—and only—exit: the safety cage. That is, if after he is attacked he still has the power of locomotion.

Sophisticated writers sometimes kid the familiar circus platitude that "the show must go on," and I don't blame them. Undoubtedly this do-or-die business has been overworked.

Nevertheless, when visitors to my dressing room, or newspaper, radio or television interviewers, want to know how much validity there is to this show-must-go-on philosophy, there is only one answer I can give them: that many of my fellow performers and I have given performances when we had excellent excuses for not appearing. Serious illness is all that prevents a big percentage of us from doing our stuff.

Of course, in all walks of life, there are exceptions, the people who take advantage of opportunities to avoid working. I recall the day—it was not so long ago—a performer connected with our show decided he could not appear because there was "too much gravity," whatever he meant by that. He used the word in so peculiar a context that I wasn't sure he knew what gravity meant.

This performer's act, which I'd rather not identify, involved propulsion through space—and how he had arrived at the conclusion that there was "too much gravity" on that particular day was a mystery to all of us. It must have been a mystery to him too, since he offered no factual explanation, just his opinion. This imaginative and entertaining excuse earned him a day off.

There are some very basic reasons why so many of us ignore indisposition, such nuisances as backaches and other aches and pains and an assortment of other discomforts. The public sometimes demands refunds when a featured performer fails to appear, so, for this and other reasons, we circus performers —most of us—take this show-must-go-on business seriously. One of the other reasons is that while no one ever mentions it, we of the circus have a Pike's-Peak-or-Bust feeling that almost amounts to a compulsion. You're supposed to be out there in one of those three rings doing your stuff, so you do unless you have a broken leg or a raging fever.

In my own case this compulsion to carry on in the face of physical handicaps goes back many years. For instance, on January 13, 1932, I was giving my big cats a workout at the winter quarters of the Hagenbeck-Wallace Circus in Peru, Indiana. Nero, a big, powerful lion who had established himself as the arena boss, was about to go over a hurdle. Instead of making a clean jump he suddenly swerved in his course and came straight at me. It was one of those determined charges that an experienced trainer recognizes instantly. But though I knew it for what it was, I didn't have a chance to get set for it.

The first thing I knew I was flat on my back on the floor of the arena with the lion standing over me.

It was the worst moment I had ever known. And I haven't experienced one quite as bad since.

As the big cat bent over me and bared the teeth with which he seemed about to mess up my features, I reached up with my right hand and planted it against his upper lip and nose. Then, with strength born of desperation, I shoved him away from me, actually succeeding in working him back as far as my arm could reach. He gave his head a snap to release himself from my palm-hold, and as he did I found my hand in his mouth up to the wrist! This gave me a chance to gag him with my fingers. I needed that hand in my business and I was able to yank it out before he could recover his breath. The skin was scuffed where my hand and wrist had scraped against his teeth.

Nero did not make for my face again, but seized what was nearest him. That happened to be the upper part of my leg. He grabbed it midway between the hip and the knee and tightened his jaws as if determined to snap the member in two. Having dug his teeth in deeply enough to satisfy himself (it developed later that they had sunk right into the bone), he began to drag me around the arena, bumping my head on the floor. Then he suddenly let go, made for a nearby lioness and began licking her face with his tongue. The attack was over as fast as it had begun.

What saved me was the fact that he happened to move in the direction of a lioness that was on his mind. He had forgotten her momentarily in his determination to get me, but now that he was near her again he remembered that she was his main concern. It was only this that saved me from being torn to pieces. The attendants outside the cage, frantically working their poles and yelling in an effort to distract the beast, had little effect on him. There was nothing else they could do. It would have amounted to suicide to enter the ring and try to fight him off.

It is my belief that the animal's attack on me was related to my having been standing near the female that had captured his interest. She was in heat and her presence had excited him. In a situation of this kind an animal is capable of honest-to-goodness jealousy. If I had been another male lion, Nero could not have regarded my closeness to his mate more suspiciously.

Although antitoxin was immediately administered, a serious infection resulted. Later that day I had a temperature of 105°.

I was taken to the Duke Memorial Hospital, where the prevailing opinion was that to save my life my leg would have to be amputated. In fact, I had been taken to the operating room and it was there I heard this grim news.

Dr. Stephen D. Malouf, who is still practicing medicine in Peru, Indiana, voiced a strongly held dissenting opinion. He recommended a probing operation designed to locate the pus sac that was causing the trouble. His advice was followed, the sac was located somewhere between the knee and the hip, and this less drastic surgery started me on the road to recovery. I was on my back for three months, and at one time my wound was draining through six tubes.

After that long hospitalization I was once again back on the job, having opened the spring season at Madison Square Garden. I was still wearing bandages, but my doctor had approved my return to work. The wound was healing nicely and he thought that at this stage exercise would be beneficial.

In those days I had so many lions and tigers in my act—forty-three—that I sometimes had to fight my way into the arena. I have since learned that it is possible to put on as spectacular a show with fewer animals. "Now the audience can see you," an old-time newspaper friend—an inveterate kidder—observed a few years ago. "In the old days at the Garden you worked so many cats that people seated at a certain angle would be unable to see you, and they would say,

'Where's Beatty? Is he hiding, or what?'" Some of the photographs taken in those days support this bit of joshing.

Well, one day during that engagement a group of lions blocked the door of the safety cage through which I enter and leave the arena. After battling my way in I found myself dueling with one of the lions I had driven away from the door. He kept lunging at me, and I stopped him with my chair several times. Without realizing it, I was favoring my injured leg, and when the big cat dealt the chair a tremendous blow—the heaviest of the series—the leg buckled and I fell backward and hit the side of the arena.

I maneuvered my way forward to keep from being pinned against the bars, and in my subsequent skirmishing with the animal he hit the chair another wallop that freakishly drove it against the blank-cartridge gun in the holster at my waist. The force of the blow somehow activated the trigger and the gun went off. The wadding ripped into my trousers, dislodging my bandage and setting me on fire.

Fred Bradna, the show's equestrian director, who blew the whistle for all acts and was standing alertly by, called for a bucket of water, and when I got close enough to the bars he let fly and doused the flame. I hobbled through the rest of the act, and when it was over the circus doctor ordered me to a hospital for treatment and rebandaging.

That old wound gave me considerable trouble throughout the rest of the engagement but, having lost none of my show-must-go-on stubbornness, I didn't miss a performance.

During one of my engagements at Madison Square Garden in New York in the 1930s Ernest Hemingway called on me and presented me with an autographed copy of *Death in the Afternoon*. At that time I knew Mr. Hemingway by reputation but had not yet had a chance to read any of his books. Needless to say, I was impressed by the interest in my work displayed by so distinguished a visitor, and his kindness in presenting me with a generously inscribed copy of his book on bullfighting.

I don't recall how many times Hemingway had seen my act, but I do know that he had made a study of it and I found that in itself exciting. He was a shrewd observer and had almost a professional animal trainer's awareness of the significance of certain aspects of my work that even experienced circus men took more or less for granted. My footwork, for instance. He thought it was fast—(Gene Tunney and Jack Dempsey have pointed that out, for which I am grateful)—but Hemingway did not emphasize speed and agility so much as he did the fact that my movements were based on a knowledge of how to accommodate myself to the footwork of animals as fast as lions and tigers as I slipped in and out, advanced, side-stepped or retreated. He agreed speed was important, but realized that what made it count was a familiarity with big-cat behavior that told me almost instinctively in which direction to move.

Hemingway also told me—and of course he was right—that I put on my best show when I drew an animal as close to me as possible and "fought" him at close range.

I have never tried to "tame" a lion or a tiger or any other animal I have used in my act; I teach them to perform, and when that process is over they are basically as wild as ever. When Hemingway spoke of the animals fighting me he was referring to the resistance they frequently put up before they decide to perform the particular trick I call for. The fighting spirit is instinctive with the big cats; in the arena it develops into a sort of game for them. It's as if they are proclaiming, "I'll make Clyde sweat a little before I do the next stunt." This resistance enables me to put on a more exciting performance; and it is good for the animals because it caters to their natural urge to play rough, besides providing a nice supplement to their daily exercise period.

So I don't try to discourage this resistance, although I must be able to control it. Hemingway was one of the first to notice that my footwork—not the so-called "hypnotic eye" with which some writers have generously endowed me—is the key to keeping the animals sufficiently off balance to prevent them from making a heavy spring for me—that is, one that is solidly based —if they are so inclined.

It is because of the basic savagery that causes them to revert to type when you least expect it that I have to play this game of keeping them off balance. For as fond as I am of these rough, tough, wonderfully endowed playmates of mine, I simply cannot afford to trust them fully.

Some people never cease to be puzzled (no matter how many explanations I make) by my position that, although I do not place complete reliance in my big cats, I love them. Nature has endowed them with certain Jekyll-Hyde qualities, and that is something the animal trainer must accept. It is not unusual for a lion or a tiger that tries to wreck me one day to show affection for me the next. There are those who believe that an animal that behaves this way is "two-faced" and should be removed from the act. To me it merely reaffirms the to-be-expected mercurial characteristics of basically savage creatures. This was familiar ground to Ernest Hemingway, who was fully aware—expertly so, I might add—of the psychological unpredictability of the big cats and understood this form of "treachery."

To put together what Hemingway told me years ago—and to find all the passages in *Death in the Afternoon* which he thought had some bearing on his remarks about my work— would be a tough job. But I do remember vividly his saying— though I don't recall just how he put it—that when I let an animal get away and wander off, I lose my audience. It's the same with bullfighting, he observed. When a matador is fighting a bull at close range and the animal trots away just as he is making a pass with his cape, the matador is at once in trouble with the crowd.

I have heard people say that they couldn't understand how a man of Hemingway's stature could regard bullfighting as a sport. This puzzles me because I distinctly remember Hemingway saying that bullfighting was not a sport and that Americans get confused when they try to interpret it as such.

I have been prowling through *Death in the Afternoon* in an effort to find passages reminiscent of that conversation. In the very first chapter I found a reference to "the obvious moral wrongness of the bullfight."

Elsewhere I found this: "The bullfight is not a sport in the Anglo-Saxon sense of the word, that is, it is not an equal contest or an attempt at an equal contest between a bull and a man."

I gather from other passages in the book that Hemingway felt—of course this is only *one* of his slants on bullfighting— that you couldn't fully understand the Spanish and their "instinctive identification of themselves with the tragic" unless you understood what went on in the bull rings in Madrid, Barcelona, Valencia, Sevilla, Malaga, Granada, Bilbao, Toledo, Cordoba, Placencia, Avila and elsewhere in Spain.

Hemingway viewed the bullfight as a "tragedy in three acts," which is how the bullfight was viewed by many of his Spanish friends. I do not mean to imply by any of the foregoing that Hemingway didn't love bullfights. He did. He loved the Spanish people; and the bullfight and all its ramifications provided a key that unlocked the Spanish character and helped him to a better understanding of these people for whom he had so deep an affection.

These are impressions I got when we chatted in my dressing room in Madison Square Garden. Although the visit made a lasting impression on me, it happened so long ago that I am hesitant to try to reconstruct our conversation in terms of actual dialogue.

Hemingway thought there were times when fear was understandable in a bullfighter. In such a situation the matador's feet gave him away. There would be "nervous uncontrollable retreats," as he states in his book. He supported the Spanish idea that these retreats were "honorable" if the matador followed them up by a resumption of close work with the cape. Then he made an observation whose meaning I recall, though not the terminology. In his book he puts it this way: "It was preferable that he [the matador] be gored rather than run from the bull."

When I thought over our conversation afterward it occurred to me that in praising my work and comparing aspects of it with situations in the bullring, Hemingway had implied that *I* never ran. This was a generous appraisal, but I found myself thinking of the times animals I was breaking in at my training quarters had chased me clear out of the arena into the safety cage. I also recalled sudden crises during performances that necessitated my maneuvering my way to the safety of that same sanctuary—it was either that or get killed.

By maneuvering I don't mean actually running, although I would not have hesitated to run if it had been the wise thing to do. You simply can't take to your heels in an arena full of lions and tigers; it's as dangerous as the basic situation that gives you the urge to run. In training quarters, where you break in one animal at a time, it is sometimes indicated—if you are fairly close to the safety cage and there are pedestals and other equipment in the path of an attacking animal—that you actually make a dash for it.

The point I am trying to make is that I do not quite fit Hemingway's category of those who cannot resist the temptation of flirting with death—not because they have to, but because they get some kind of thrill out of it. I have never consciously flirted with death. When I was in my twenties I took needless risks, but not because I was trying to see how close I could come to death without getting killed. Actually I didn't know any better. I love to please audiences and was just young enough to be somewhat reckless. With the passing of the years this tendency toward a type of daredeviltry that borders on show-offism corrects itself.

Early in this chapter I referred to having once played to an audience of one. This was in the days when I operated a between-seasons circus at Fort Lauderdale.

We ran from December through March, when the weather is usually so dependable we made a practice of putting on our show outdoors without using the big top. We had a grandstand that seated three thousand, and did considerable business. Our chief patronage came from visitors to Florida from different parts of the country.

One day there was a heavy downpour and we called off the show. Only one person appeared at the box office to buy a ticket, a little old lady with a big umbrella and an even bigger voice. When she was told that the performance had been canceled, she asked to see the manager. When he appeared she told him that she had paid her money and insisted on seeing our circus. When he tried to refund her money, she refused to accept it.

Her next move was to ask for me. When I appeared she said she had tried to catch my act several times and had never been in the grandstand at the right time. This was our fault, she insisted, as the advertisements were not clear about the time I would appear on the program. I had never heard of a circus announcing in its ads or publicity when specific performers would do their stuff. When I made this point she had a ready reply and I let the matter rest there.

There was something about that old lady's determination that appealed to me. She was returning to her home in Indianapolis the next day and, by all that was good and holy, she had no intention of leaving until she had seen my act. "It's your own fault, young man," she said. (I *was* young at the time.) "You people put out all those stories saying how wonderful you and your lions and tigers are and you get a person's curiosity aroused, and then you call off the show because there's a light sprinkle."

Some "light sprinkle"! It had been raining steadily for hours and the whole performing area was soggy; and in some places little pools of water had formed.

Emulating our manager, I tried to return this scrappy old gal's money. She repeated, as she dug the point of her umbrella into the water-logged turf, that she was not interested in a refund. She wanted to see the show. Although she was standing under an overhang, water was forming under her shoes, but even that didn't seem to bother her.

For added emphasis she mentioned that she had read in the local newspaper that we performed "rain or shine." Such a story might have appeared, although I didn't recall seeing it.

But the situation had gotten beyond the point where it would be possible to get that woman to back down. Of course, I could have walked away and left her standing there. But I just couldn't bring myself to do that. Besides, her antics were beginning to amuse me, and, as unreasonable as she was, I found myself secretly admiring her. It would probably take a psychiatrist to figure out my reactions and the reasons behind them.

At any rate, her don't-take-no-for-an-answer philosophy got results. Before I realized what I was saying I announced that we would put on the show for her. (Of course, we would have to cut corners on account of the weather, but I said nothing about that.)

"I knew you'd come to your senses, young man!" exclaimed our lone ticket-buyer. "And now go get your show started."

With which she headed for the grandstand, where she dried a wet seat as well as she could with her handkerchief and sat down as the rain splashed off her umbrella.

I earned a lot of dirty looks from many of my fellow performers that day. I could almost feel them thinking: "All right, so you're owner of this show. But does that give you the right to do *this* to us?" A few of them got into the spirit of the thing and saw its funny side but most of them were annoyed with me.

Needless to say, the arena was so waterlogged I did not

attempt to put on my full act or anything approaching it. One of my recollections of that day is the look of disgust on the faces of the lions as the rain matted down their hair and parted their manes in the middle. But once they realized I had no intention of calling upon them for any work that would cause them to skid around in the mud, they looked at me less reproachfully. The less expressive tigers were not pleased either as they picked their way daintily through the slippery footing. But neither the lions nor the tigers gave me any trouble. This was more of a "walk-through" than a performance, the kind of workout the animals don't mind too much, regardless of the conditions. I could attempt only the simplest formations that enabled me to get their attention without the use of my whip, which in a few seconds was too wet to pop.

Both lions and tigers like water, but they prefer an honest-to-goodness swim to sloshing around in mud. As I have mentioned elsewhere, the big cats enjoy the hosing we give them in warm weather, and once they adjusted to the rain they seemed to regard it as a new version of that ritual as they held up their heads and let the water drip down their faces.

The elephants, as was to be expected, enjoyed themselves the most. They love to slip around on a muddy surface and get down on their sides and backs and wallow in as much watery muck as they can find. But their trainer viewed things differently. After they had had their fun he would have to run a hose over them until all that mud was washed off. As he worked the elephants, he made loud heckling comments such as, "I hope *you* are enjoying this, *I* am not"—but if the old lady heard any of his caustic remarks she didn't let on as she sat huddled under her umbrella watching the show.

A clown is sometimes at his funniest—unconsciously, that is —when he blows his top. Kinko, one of our best clowns, told me in the bluntest kind of language, as the make-up streaked down his rain-drenched face, what he thought of my authorizing this "crazy performance," which I suppose it was. But Kinko and I were good friends and he subsequently forgave me for what he termed, for added emphasis, my "crackpot decision" to mollify that resolute character, the lady from Indianapolis.

When the show was over—that is, the condensed version we put on—our lone spectator thanked me but said she had been led to believe that there "was more to my act than *that*."

A frequent visitor to my dressing room in my Madison Square Garden days was Robert Stanley Dollar, president of the Dollar Steamship Line, who had achieved a high place in the business community. His own field was a fascinating one, but I never had much success getting him to talk about it. He was infatuated with the world of lions and tigers and animal training and that was his one and only topic when he called on me. He had a deep interest in the methods I used in teaching the big cats to perform and asked me countless questions—many of them shrewd, searching ones that revealed a wide knowledge of wild animals.

One day Mr. Dollar confessed that one of his hobbies was animal mimicry, and that he thought his best impersonation was of a lion roaring. Did I want to hear it? Of course!

Whereupon he emitted a bellow that went echoing down the halls of the Garden's office area. My dressing room was the office and anteroom of a Garden executive who had graciously made the space available to me for the duration of the circus's spring engagement. With the door open Mr. Dollar's roaring was especially audible to nearby personnel of the Madison Square Corporation and several of them came dashing in.

I explained that Mr. Dollar had been imitating a lion roaring. Winking at me, one of our impromptu callers said he had once heard something like that in a dentist's office.

Mr. Dollar decided that his imitation was not an unqualified success and that he would have to do some more practicing. The next time he dropped in he would roar for me again and he was sure I would notice the improvement.

When he returned a few days later to give a second performance, I got up, closed the door and told him to go ahead.
With the door shut my ears took more of a beating than they
did the first time. "What do you think?" he asked.

I told him I didn't think he would put the M-G-M lion out
of business, but that he was improving. Mr. Dollar had a lively
sense of humor and expected me to understand that the little
act he was putting on was designed to show his interest in my
work. I invited him to do another roar and to follow it up with
a few snarls to show he meant business. Either he was a rough,
tough lion or he wasn't. To make things more realistic, I picked
up a chair and pointed the legs at him and suggested that he
lunge at me as he emitted his next outcry.

While this clowning was going on, Mr. Dollar, achieving
his loudest roar, startled the wits out of an office boy who had
entered to tell me that some newspapermen were waiting to
see me.

Now and then spectators want to know why they were
turned back when trying to move to better seats that happened
to be unoccupied. The ushers have a way of looking in some
other direction when such a situation arises, especially when
children are the principal gainers, except when it happens
at a particular time and a switch cannot be permitted for
reasons that have to be explained.

Early in May 1963 I was about to start a matinee performance and the animals were being run through the tunnel into
the arena. At that particular moment a woman decided to
move her three children to better seats, which she sought to
reach by means of a short cut that would take her past the
center ring where I perform. She and her youngsters, as they
neared the arena, attracted the attention of the big cats. Some
of the animals, instead of mounting their pedestals, turned
around to see what was going on. Sudden movement outside
the big cage always attracts their attention, causes them to
try to figure out what's making those sounds so close to them,

and takes their minds off what I am trying to get them to do.

An usher, acting under instructions covering such a situation, dashed out and turned back the woman and her children. She didn't understand the situation and made quite a fuss. After I had completed my act she was permitted to take the unoccupied seats she had spotted.

Despite the precautions we take, a boy or a girl will sometimes manage to get into the big top with a dog, sometimes concealed. One of the responsibilities of the ushers and other attendants is to watch for dogs that get loose and wander into the performing area, where they can get into trouble.

When I was performing in Atlantic City a few years ago a little dog got away from his youthful master and started heading for my arena. An alert usher who was stationed near the center ring rushed over and grabbed him. He was tiny—one of those very small breeds—and could easily have gotten through the bars of the big cage. Had he done so the cats would have made short work of him.

Even if that dog had been a little bigger and had strayed close to the bars he would have been dragged through them by a lion or a tiger. We once had an accident of this kind and we don't ever want to have another.

Of the letters I receive from spectators the most entertaining usually come from children.

Among the thousands I have received from youngsters over the years, this one remains my particular favorite:

"Clyde Beatty is a trainer. He trains animals. He trains them by shooting them and hitting them on the head with a whip. Sometimes he hits them with a chair. He makes them jump around a lot and do many tricks. He has more lions and tigers than in the zoo. He has about a hundred lions and about a hundred tigers. And they all do tricks. When they do not obey, he hits them on the head or shoots them and then they obey. The lions and the tigers roar. They roar and roar. But he does not mind. Sometimes they try to scratch him with a paw. But he does not mind. He just keeps on making them do tricks. He was making a lion jump over a fence. The lion did not want to jump over the fence. The lion tried to knock him down. So he hit him on the head with a chair and shot him. So the lion obeyed and jumped over the fence."

The author of the foregoing had been asked by his teacher to write a composition describing something he had witnessed. He decided to describe my act, and sent me a copy of what he had submitted. I never did learn what his teacher thought of it.

I got a particular kick out of that letter because not long before I received it a woman tried to have me arrested in Madison Square Garden for "beating" my animals. Every time she heard my whip crack, she maintained, she "shuddered for the poor animals that were taking such a beating." She didn't back down until it was explained—and did she take a lot of convincing!—that the cracking sound she heard was made by a cotton popper at the end of the whip. The sound was designed to get the attention of the animals. There would be none of those "awful cracking sounds" if the whip actually struck one of the big cats.

I've appeared in a number of motion pictures, beginning many years ago, so it is understandable that circus fans should ask me, as they have many times, how I like Hollywood.

I've had happy and unhappy experiences there, which I suppose is typical. Hollywood converted one of my pictures, *The Big Cage*, into something entirely different from the story that was originally sold to the studio's New York office—one that stuck reasonably close to the facts and flavor of my career. It developed later that at the time there was a feud on between the Hollywood and New York offices, and that what the latter liked was considered expendable on the West Coast.

There is nothing new, to be sure, about a motion-picture company changing its mind about what it buys. In this particular case the New York office was emphatic about wanting the picture to retain "a circus wholesomeness," a quality, they argued, that was a decisive factor in so many parents' view that the circus was ideal entertainment for children. One of the big moments of the picture was a scene in which a cage boy was presented with a silver dung scraper by admirers from back home. A Hollywood gag-writer came up with that idea and the producer and his staff thought it was simply wonderful.

A well-organized national women's group, which then made up so-called "recommended lists," attacked the picture for its bad taste in introducing the theme of dung, disapproved it for viewing by children, and misguidedly decided that *I* was the person at fault. Actually, to make room for that dubious scene the masterminds had to throw out one in which I appeared with my lions and tigers!

An otherwise intelligent director expressed surprise when I hesitated to adopt some of his suggestions in connection with the same motion picture. One of them called for my re-enacting the scene in which Nero, the lion that had attacked me a few years before, dragged me around the arena and almost killed me, as described earlier in this chapter.

The director expressed his frank astonishment when I told him that would be a foolish thing for me to attempt. He had heard that "the great Beatty" could get a lion or a tiger to do *anything*, and now—poor man!—he was disillusioned.

Before I realized what I was doing I agreed to re-enact the Nero attack. I subsequently came to my senses and insisted on modifications of what the production staff wanted me to do—changes based on my knowledge of how far you can go with wild animals. If I hadn't, I probably would have gotten myself killed. As it was, I was lucky to escape serious injury.

On and off, over the years, there have been in Hollywood a few freakish animals that could be called upon to do "unbelievable" things before the cameras and this may have played a part in confusing the group responsible for the production of *The Big Cage*. If Hollywood stunt men could perform all sorts of "daring" feats with these "wild" animals available to anyone who chose to rent them, why was the "death-defying" (see any one of a hundred circus posters) Clyde Beatty holding back?

I'll try to answer this question by telling a story.

Having been an enthusiastic movie-serial fan as a kid, with a love for most of the continued-next-week melodramas of the day, when in the 1930s I was offered an opportunity to star in serials, I jumped at the opportunity. (I was subsequently cured of this kind of stardom, but that is another story.)

By one of those strange coincidences, animal-trainer Louis Roth, my mentor in the days when I was a bear trainer, owned Bobby, "the wrestling tiger," one of Hollywood's most accomplished stunt animals. Bobby had been reared in captivity by Louis as a pet for his son, whom he had decided to launch as a Hollywood stunt man.

This looked like a good move to a man who was trying to find a career for his son, as there weren't many people in the animal branch of the stunt game. Roth, who knew the big cats as well as he knew bears, trained the young man to do close-contact work with Bobby suggestive of fierce struggles to get out of the clutches of this "demon," this "descendant from a long line of man-eaters." And the tiger, an intelligent animal, responded.

All big cats are dangerous, even those reared in captivity as pets by an expert like Louis Roth. But Louis had minimized the danger by making a one-man tiger of Bobby—that is, it was unlikely that the animal would make any trouble for young Roth, to whom he had become accustomed.

When I found myself in the serial field, a situation developed that necessitated the use of a wrestling tiger, and Bobby was offered to me, although originally the elder Roth had planned to make only "package deals" involving the services of both his son and the wrestling tiger.

I didn't like the idea of working with Bobby because he had never worked with anyone except Roth's son, and I made the point that the animal, like a one-man dog, would want no part of anyone except his master. It was an ironic situation. Young Roth, who knew nothing about animal training and whose whole experience in the big-cat field was confined to doing stunts with one freakish animal, was better qualified to work with this tiger than I.

But I was the star of this epic, and although the assignment I was given by Reeves ("Breezy") Eason, one of the most successful of the old-time serial directors, didn't appeal to me, I agreed to undertake it. My experience with tigers told me that when Bobby found himself playing opposite me instead of his master, he would be hard to handle. And having just completed a pretty rugged circus season, I was not in the mood for needless problems.

The script for this serial involved a mythical jungle invented by a Hollywood screen writer who had devised his own particular version of the ancient formula in which you throw together wild animals, superstitious natives with weird tribal customs, a white man who gets into trouble and has to extricate himself, etc., etc.—and then hope for the best.

One of the big moments of the story called for my capturing a tiger in a camouflaged pit. It developed that in this particular jungle if a white man captured a tiger this meant bad luck for the natives. To placate the tiger the natives in turn captured me and tossed me into the pit with the animal— Bobby—as a sort of offering. If the animal had me for lunch this would pacify him and he would forgive the natives for their carelessness in letting me capture him, etc., etc. It was a very involved story and perhaps I'd better spare you the rest of it.

To foil the natives and save myself from the "murderous beast" that was bent on "devouring" me, I was supposed first to wrestle him into submission, then put him in a trance with the magic of my hypnotic eye.

I hadn't wrestled with Bobby very long when it became apparent that my original hunch was correct and that I was going to have trouble with him. Louis Roth, perceptive animal trainer that he was, had decided to stand by for possible emergencies; he could see that things were not going well and called to the animal from above in order to get the obviously tense and nervous creature to relax.

Bobby, in unfamiliar surroundings and with a new wrestling mate for the first time, became overexcited and to show how he felt about things bit me in the shoulder. He could have removed my whole shoulder if he had been in a better position to get set and give his jaws full play. In fact, he might have killed me. Anything can happen when a so-called "tame" animal panics. He had me against a wall of the pit and was struggling to maneuver himself into a position for a fuller and more authoritative bite when I hauled off and clouted him behind the ear with everything I had.

Bobby, who was accustomed to being petted, not socked, was shaken up by my wallop. It was a new experience for him. Before he could decide what to do about it, the excited animal looked up and caught Louis Roth's eye. Louis saw the bloodstain spreading over my shirt and beckoned the tiger out of there. Bobby complied. Roth had trained him from the beginning, and Bobby recognized him as the final word, just as he accepted Roth's son as his sparring partner.

Breezy Eason, the director, acting as if nothing had happened, cupped his hands and yelled down to me after Roth had gotten Bobby out of the pit, "In a few minutes we'll do it again. That was pretty good—almost the way I want it."

I yelled back, "You come down and do it yourself."

My wound, it developed, was not serious, but it was a pretty bad rip that required medical attention to prevent infection.

I decided that whatever wrestling took place after that experience would have to be done by Roth's son. No one had ever doubled for me before—in fact, I had doubled for others

—but it was senseless to take any further chances with this one-man animal.

So henceforth in that serial I worked exclusively with my own animals—any one of which could have made mincemeat of Bobby, but whose characteristics I knew. They had been trained by me and were used to me. There is plenty of risk in handling *any* big cats, but if they are animals you have worked with before, you at least know what to expect and how to handle the problems that arise.

One thing that never ceased to amuse me—if I may digress to make a zoological point—is that in these Hollywood-made jungles, which are a combination of studio-manufactured trees, underbrush and other greenery, and the real thing, not once did any of my animals try to sharpen his claws on a phony tree. They knew what was genuine and what was fabricated. I recall quite vividly that one of my young lions was about to go to work on a realistic-looking Hollywood-made tree, then sniffed it and backed away. A few seconds later he was sharpening his claws on what *really* was a tree.

I am grateful to members of the audiences—the people who are interested enough to want to know *why*—for the questions they have thrown at me. They remind me of so many things I had forgotten until—by letter or verbally—they bring them back to mind.

2. When the Big Cats Break Loose

The Lion That Escaped without Meaning To – Gracie,
the Wily Tigress Who Thought Her Way Out of a
Cage – Three Tigers Loose in a Packed House – A
Tiger Loose on a Wharf – The Biggest Nuisance: A
Big-Cat Escape on a Train – Big Ross, the Tiger That
Pulled the Cleverest Job of Them All

M ARION, Indiana, was the last place in the world where
one of my animals should have been permitted to escape.
Mayor M. Jack Edwards, an old friend, had made the coming
of my circus to his town a big event by inviting and personally escorting a large group of children—some of them from
an orphanage, some from an institution for the handicapped—
and the mayor and his party of youngsters were seated next
to the band.

This location gave them an excellent view of the tunnel
through which the big cats pass on their way to the arena. The
sides of the tunnel are built like the front of a cage, and
through the bars those who are seated nearby get a good close-
up of this interesting procession.

I always try to put on a good show, but that day I made a
special effort, getting as much action out of my animals as I
possibly could. The closer I can draw the animals to me the
more exciting the show is, and during that particular performance I kept them practically on top of me in an effort to give
those kids a few extra thrills.

But the biggest thrill came unexpectedly after the conclusion of my act. The ringmaster, "Count" Nicholas, as dapper a figure as ever wore the bright red coat that symbolizes his office, was announcing the next act. His spiel over, the Count was about to withdraw to a nearby aisle where he would wait until it was time to face the mike again and make his next announcement. He had not moved more than a step or two when startled cries from the audience caused him to look around. There, a few yards behind him, stood Pharaoh, one of the biggest lions I have ever trained—magnificently proportioned and weighing almost seven hundred pounds—but fortunately not the killer type.

Any wild animal loose in an audience is a serious threat, but the problem would have been much worse if the escaped animal had been one of those that attack without provocation. Just as there are killers among humans, there are killers among the big cats. Pharaoh would not attack unless accidentally bumped by panicky spectators rushing for the exits. If anything like that happened, this powerful lion would be capable of putting his claws and fangs to terrible use, thinking he was being attacked, and he would be as dangerous as *any* lion. Fortunately, though we were playing to a capacity crowd, the spectators managed to give Pharaoh a wide berth.

All of this was going on while I was in the bathroom section of my trailer preparing to take a shower. I had finished my act, had removed my perspiration-soaked uniform and was about to step under the water when there was a pounding on the door. Half-hiding behind it in my naked state, I unlocked and opened it as a frightened, excited animal hand sputtered out the information that Pharaoh had escaped.

I grabbed a bathrobe, quickly slipped it on and dashed outside and into the big top in time to see Count Nicholas, coattails flying, sprinting down the hippodrome track to put as much distance as possible between himself and the fugitive.

Pharaoh, it developed, had made no effort to escape. When, after the act, he had trotted from the tunnel into his cage, a

careless attendant had forgotten to drop the slide door, and
since that left his cage frontless, he figured he might as well
wander back and see what was going on. He arrived as Eddie
Dullem, our chief clown, was about to unburden himself of a
commercial describing a wild-animal coloring book for children that the circus offered for "only twenty-five cents, the
fourth part of a dollar." Eddie, standing on a platform, was on
the point of delivering his spiel when something prompted him
to turn around and look down.

There was Pharaoh, a few feet below, looking up at him.
Eddie left in a rush, and as he did there was laughter from
those who thought this was a clown gag.

"I was pretty sure he didn't want to buy a coloring book,"
Eddie told me later.

It should be pointed out that in a situation of this kind
bewilderment is the predictable reaction of an animal like
Pharaoh. He was as puzzled and startled to find himself out
of his cage as was the audience. His expression and the look
in his eyes clearly indicated that he didn't know what this
was all about. He looked at the chair in my hand as I approached, and seemed to be wondering if I expected him to
perform out there on the hippodrome track.

Those who realized this was *not* a clown gag began hustling
their children out of the big top, and their excited cries were
clearly having a befuddling effect on the involuntary fugitive.
As I moved toward him he edged back a little, stood stock-
still, backed away again as the bedlam around him increased,
then made a sudden decision to trot off to an opening under
the general-admission seats, whose occupants, many of them
hemmed in, were moving forward toward the exits as fast as
possible for a capacity house. Now that Pharaoh was racing
around under the seats some of the people who had started
vacating those seats weren't sure what to do. Some thought
they would be safer where they were, others disagreed and
pushed as best they could past the lingerers, who slowed

them down and in some cases practically halted their forward progress. It was a chaotic situation. You couldn't expect many people to remain calm. Some did. But many were frightened, and these reminded one another excitedly that that big lion was racing around under the seats and might decide to dash out from under the stand and come leaping at them. They had seen him jump some fairly high hurdles and realized it would be a cinch for him to catapult himself up among them if that was what he felt like doing.

The band, which had started to leave—and you couldn't blamed them, as they were uncomfortably close to Pharaoh when he made his startling appearance on the hippodrome track—was rallied by William R. ("Boom Boom") Browning, Jr., the conductor and a great trouper. As soon as they resumed playing you could feel some of the tension go out of the crowd.

While all this was going on I was under the stand trying to coax Pharaoh out. I had given instructions that an extra sidewall be added to the regular sidewall of the big top, which would give me an enclosure into which I could drive the loose animal. The next step, getting him back into his cage, should not be too difficult, I figured. Pharaoh had not tried to escape. He was on the loose because of the carelessness of a cage boy.

My first and toughest job would be to get this big husky lion to stop racing around nervously under that stand. Once I got his undivided attention I felt reasonably sure I could arrest his puzzlement and communicate to him that I was there to help him. Pharaoh and I had always hit it off. I've always thought of him as the most businesslike animal I have ever trained, and one of the most cooperative; and again I found myself giving thanks that it was he and not one of the others I was dealing with in this ticklish situation.

One of my difficulties was that I had to do some stalling in my pursuit of Pharaoh until that extra sidewall was up. There was no point in driving him out until I was certain that the canvas pen in which I sought to enclose him as a prelude to maneuvering him back into his cage was in readiness, with assistants posted outside to protect the crowd in case my plan misfired.

Once I got the signal that the sidewall was up, I could stop stalling and make my bid for Pharaoh's complete attention; and when I had it I would be able to start communicating with him. My main problem was the noise overhead—the scuffling of feet and the shouts.

When it got around that I was walling in the escaped animal, the excitement began to subside, but my associates later informed me that the crowd was still apprehensive and fearful, with many people yelling questions at the circus personnel who were trying to restore order. What most of them wanted to know was whether "he" (the lion) could claw and bite his way up through the seats. A few times Pharaoh had lunged upward and banged a heavy paw against the general-admission planking.

This overhead noise and confusion made it difficult for me to deal with Pharaoh properly. To get him to do what the situation called for, it was essential that he concentrate on me and what I sought to convey. No matter how manageable an animal normally is, in a situation of this kind he is inclined to be fretful, fearful, angry. The benign expression so characteristic of Pharaoh had vanished. There was an unfriendly look in his eyes. His teeth showed when he curled his lower lip down and his ears had flattened themselves against his head, unmistakable signs that what had started out to be mere annoyance had now hardened into hostility.

To an assistant who was posted at the entrance to the opening under the stand, I shouted instructions to have the seats overhead cleared of spectators. Once this was done the overhead scuffling ceased and Pharaoh became more manageable.

I got him to stop his nervous pacing, and as I drew him toward me I could see him relaxing. His expression changed, the vexed bewilderment now supplanted by a look of understanding. I soon drove him into the enclosed area formed by the extra sidewall, which ran parallel with the animal cages. Pharaoh seemed relieved as I steered him toward his cage. He offered no resistance as I cued him into it.

I learned afterward that the only reason there had not been a full-fledged panic when Pharaoh started wandering around on the hippodrome track was that the audience's first reaction, mentioned earlier, that this was a clown routine, had relaxed a sizable percentage of the crowd. A group of clowns had made their appearance at precisely the same time Pharaoh found himself free to roam about, and when they scattered and ran this was interpreted, as loud bursts of laughter attested, to be a bit of slapstick featuring a comedy lion (one of those freaks which, born in captivity and raised as pets, can sometimes be trained to play a role of this kind).

The audience didn't know the true situation until an announcement was made over the loudspeaker telling them what had happened. We didn't want to scare anyone but we simply had to warn these people that a dangerous animal was loose in the big top. At least we could get them to observe a few precautions, such as the admonition not to run. Experienced wild-animal men know that a big cat roaming free is tempted to pursue man or beast in full flight, and usually does. A few spectators foolishly ignored our warning and broke into a run, but fortunately they were not in Pharaoh's field of vision.

Whatever panic followed the announcement over the loudspeaker was minor by comparison with what might have happened if the crowd had realized, as soon as Pharaoh made his appearance on the hippodrome track, what the hazards were.

Sometime I'd like to sit down with an experienced animal psychologist and try to figure out what went on in Pharaoh's head that day. I've often wondered whether it was the "ham" in him, one of his most endearing qualities. He'd won a lot of applause that day and as he headed back in the direction of the arena, now partly dismantled, he could have had thoughts of jumping a few more hurdles, or whatever it was he felt like doing, and earning additional plaudits.

In the past year Pharaoh has won new laurels as a ham. As the act nears its conclusion, the last thing I do before leaving the arena is to drop the kitchen chair that has served me so well as a shield these many years. Every now and then Pharaoh, the only animal left in the arena after my departure, wraps his powerful jaws around the back of that chair, and, head held high, parades around the arena with the chair in his mouth as the crowd laughs and applauds. From the safety cage I recently caught Pharaoh's eye as he executed this maneuver, and his expression seemed to say, "Just a little added touch I thought up all by myself, Boss. How do you like it?"

I like it a lot. In fact, I wish I could get Pharaoh to do it after every performance. Like many another creative artist he is unpredictable, and he gives this little encore only when the spirit moves him.

Perhaps the spookiest of my experiences with escaped animals took place some years ago in the Shrine Temple in Detroit. I was to give a private show there for a convention of automobile salesmen, and had quartered my cats comfortably in the basement. One large room was filled with supplies, including a truckload of sawdust, a battery of water buckets, and a lot of extra pedestals and other equipment. This room was also used as a "pantry," where my men cut up the meat for the lions and tigers. Beyond, in dimly lighted corridors, the cages were ranged along the concrete walls.

The building above was only partly finished at the time. The upper floors that were completed were cut up into hotel rooms, about half of them occupied. As I remember it, about one hundred guests were sleeping there that night.

A little before midnight I made the rounds of my pets, and gave a few words of advice to the watchman, an experienced man I had brought with me. For some reason I felt uneasy, but I laid this to the fact that the cellar was still somewhat damp, probably because the concrete was not yet perfectly dry. I went over all the cages again and inspected the bars and fastenings carefully. One of my lions had a slight infection from a scratch on the foot. I treated this foot before leaving and instructed the watchman to telephone me at my hotel if the animal didn't quiet down.

I was somehow reluctant to leave. I tried out the telephone, which connected with a switchboard on the main floor of the building. Learning that the board was manned all night, I gave the operator the number of my hotel. While I was talking to him over the phone, I noticed a stairway leading upward from the basement, and idly speculated on where it went. Evidently it was just a flight of service stairs leading to the hotel floors above, and to the big swimming pool, still uncompleted, which was to be an important feature of the building. I envied the hotel guests snoring comfortably in their rooms above.

Bidding my watchman a hasty goodnight, I hurried over to my nearby hotel to crowd in as much sleep as I could.

From a dream about the old days in the Chillicothe High School, I was suddenly awakened by a ring that had something peremptory about it, like a fire alarm. My watch, lying on the table beside the telephone, registered three o'clock as I switched on the light.

It was the night clerk downstairs. His voice was shrill and excited.

"Hell's broke loose at the Shrine!" he shouted, almost wrecking a perfectly good eardrum. "Your watchman's here at the desk. . . . Says your tigers are out. . . . What's that? . . . All of them, I guess."

It's odd how a fellow can be amused even when an

emergency like this suddenly arises. I recall a curious desire to laugh as I quickly pulled on my trousers. There was no more likelihood of my tigers *all* being loose than of the Shrine Temple disappearing into a hole in the ground. Probably just one, I reflected, and not much danger of that one getting any farther than the pantry, where the smell of meat would probably hold him bewitched for a while. But this was a contingency I couldn't count on. It was too pat—the kind of wishful thinking a guy does when he's still half asleep.

My watchman was waiting for me down at the desk. He was pale, his voice had taken on a nervous stammer and there was a frightened look in his eyes. He was too panicky to be very coherent, but I gathered from a few hasty questions, as I nudged him toward the door that led to the street, that he had been sitting in his corner of the basement when suddenly Gracie, my largest tigress, bounded past him and rushed off up the service stairs.

The watchman was still so shattered by fear that I left him behind me and raced down the street to the Shrine Temple. I dashed through the entrance and down the cellar stairs, into the corridor where the cages were lined up. I took a hasty look at Gracie's cage. It was one of my ordinary "shifting dens," consisting of a stout timber frame, with iron bars set firmly into the wood. Gracie had worked one of the bars loose, and then had bent the adjoining ones enough so that she could wriggle through.

Oh, for a flashlight! I remembered, ironically, an old resolve to keep one handy at all times. . . .

Quickly satisfying myself that the tigress had not stopped in the pantry, I grabbed the watchman's chair. It was a folding camp chair and would not be much good in a battle with Gracie, but I couldn't find anything better. Gracie had been upstairs for at least ten minutes, and I shuddered to think what might have happened in one of those guest rooms.

I dashed up the service stairs three steps at a time. Two

flights up a hall door was open, and I saw flickering light at the other end of the long corridor.

"Who's there?" I called.

"Night watchman!" came the answer. It was one of the hotel patrols. I called out again to him, asking him if he had seen anything of a stray tiger. (What a question to spring on a man suddenly in the middle of the night!) He gave me some befuddled reply. Not waiting to explain further, I hurried back and up another flight of stairs. On each floor I stopped and explored a little way down the corridor, calling Gracie by name. I have never yet seen an escaped animal that would not respond to its name—usually by turning and attacking. But there was no response from Gracie, not even a snarl.

I came to the top floor, the fifth. Here the door from the staircase was ajar. I pushed it wide open, holding my chair in front of me. The light from the electric bulb on the landing showed dimly a huge room, cluttered with a mass of timbers, scaffolding, bags of mortar and piles of building material. Only gradually did I begin to figure out that this was the uncompleted swimming pool, with half-finished partitions and cubicles that eventually would be towel rooms, shower baths, locker rooms and so on. Altogether it was a man-made jungle that offered as many treacherous hiding places for a tiger as any tangled forest or swamp that nature ever provided in India or Sumatra.

Although my calls to Gracie brought no response, I was fairly sure that the tigress was in this room. If that was the case, sooner or later she would respond when I called out her name. I closed the door and bolted it temporarily with a piece of timber across the doorknob, then went back downstairs and closed every door, so that when I found Gracie I could drive her down to the cellar without danger to the sleeping guests.

As I raced back up the stairs to the bolted door of the fifth floor, I had a feeling of relief. Things were not as bad as they might have been. It was unlikely that the tigress had taken any human victims, unless she had dragged some sleeper to the shelter of the unfinished swimming pool; and I couldn't convince myself that she could have done this without leaving quickly recognizable signs of her passing.

I opened the door to the swimming pool. Within, it was so dark that the little pinpoint of light on the landing merely accented the blackness. I'd have felt a bit safer if I could have known exactly what that room looked like, and what was going to be underfoot at my next step forward. If Gracie was here, near the door, she had probably taken refuge under some of that scaffolding on the right. Holding my chair in front of me, I peered into that corner, seeking two little spots of green reflected light, which would be her eyes.

Very slowly I moved forward. Suddenly my ears caught a soft sound just behind me, where I remembered a pile of mortar bags. I wheeled toward the sound. "Gracie!" I called, sharply. She leaped at me with a snarl, almost before I was really sure she was there. Intuitively I stepped aside as I felt, rather than saw, her coming. She lashed out at the legs of my camp chair as she swept by, and disappeared beneath a mass of scaffolding.

For several minutes I pushed cautiously around the room, trying to locate her again. I tipped over a keg of nails that went clattering down a slanting pile of floor boards with a din that must have frightened the tigress a good deal more than it did me. I nearly lost my footing in a mess of wet paint. Finally I came to a swinging door that apparently led to a dressing room or office. Through the glass of the door I could see Gracie's eyes. The tigress had plunged through the door and couldn't get back, because a piece of two-by-four timber had slipped down and prevented it from moving outward.

I picked up the two-by-four and let the door swing free as I again called Gracie's name, tauntingly. She came out on the run, full of fight. I fended her off toward the hallway, first with the two-by-four and then with my chair. She turned on me halfway across the floor, but as she turned she touched a great mound of spilled nails and loosened a few hundred, which made strange noises as her feet scattered them about. She hesitated and I gave her a shove with the timber, toward the door.

In the doorway she made a stand. I was in an awkward position, with a treacherous footing of littered tiles and mortar. As she came for me I realized that this was a time when I would have to suspend my philosophy that kindness to animals—the affectionate approach, in other words—is the one and only way to deal with them. What a rude reminder that there is an exception to every rule as I swung my two-by-four, with all my strength, down on Gracie's head. For after all, this was a matter of survival. Gracie reeled backward through the doorway, and immediately I began to force her down the stairs.

Two flights down she halted on a landing and showed her teeth. As she swung around, her weight against the door burst it open, and she disappeared into the corridor. This was a dangerous development, and I was after her with all possible speed. I was only a few feet behind as she turned into the open door of a bedroom. If there was anyone sleeping in there, he was going to have a few exciting moments.

But it happened that the room was unoccupied. I turned on the light with a button by the door, while Gracie retired, snarling and angry-eyed, into a corner near the bed. Retreating into the hall, I closed the door behind me. I needed a moment to plan my next move. I could get Gracie out of the room, but how was I going to prevent her bouncing back up to her hide-out on the fifth floor.

She was safely tucked away in that room for a while, so I began the task of lugging down from the swimming-pool floor a miscellaneous assortment of mortar bags, nail kegs, sawhorses, and timbers, to form a barricade across the stairs. Fortunately I found several broad strips of painters' canvas up there, and these I nailed across the hall, forming a frail cloth wall about ten feet high, blocking the way upward.

Now I must try again to drive Gracie down to the basement. As I entered the lighted bedroom, it was apparent that she had been enjoying a refreshing rest during my absence. She was ready to play in earnest now. For several minutes she charged me all over that room. My camp chair was smashed to splinters, and I replaced it with a red-plush chair that had been standing sedately before a small writing desk. The tigress quickly finished this new shield of mine and I armed myself next with the telephone table. All the time I was watching carefully for another chance to use my two-by-four. Finally Gracie gave me an opening and I swung for the top of her head, where I could stun her without inflicting any serious damage. She reacted by backing out into the corridor.

On the landing I approached her with my two-by-four up-lifted. She glowered and prepared to spring, but I rushed her before she could develop any momentum. To avoid my im-provised club she rose on her hind legs and swung at me with both forepaws. Her aim was so accurate that she knocked the two-by-four from my right hand and the remnants of the telephone table from my left. I was completely disarmed and at her mercy, if she had but known it. But, not realizing her victory, she whirled off down the stairs to the cellar, leaping into her cage through the widened opening that had been hopefully prepared for her homecoming, and retiring to its farthest corner.

One of the Temple watchmen helped me nail some timbers across the cage opening. Later, when Gracie quieted down, we transferred her to another cage. We always carry a spare.

That night's encounter with Gracie was as tough a battle as I've ever fought with an animal. It was well after four o'clock when the watchman and I sat down with his dinner pail; the duel had lasted over an hour and I was exhausted.

Certain aspects of Gracie's behavior interested me more than the escape itself—her cunning, for instance.

From the time he started his rounds, the night watchman—

the experienced animal man I had brought with me, not to be confused with the Shrine Temple's watchmen—had listened carefully for any unusual activity or sounds emanating from that part of the basement where my animals were stored. What we found later revealed that Gracie had been working away steadily at the heavy, stone-hard slab of oak into which the iron bars of her cage were sunk, hollowing out the wood with her razor-sharp claws at a point where one of the iron bars was imbedded in it. The rasping noise this makes would be noticeable at once to the animal-wise watchman, who checked the basement several times that night and reported no sound except the slumbrous breathing of the big cats and a few snores.

Apparently as soon as Gracie heard the watchman's footsteps she suspended operations, resuming when he departed. She kept this up until she had scooped out enough wood to loosen the bar and pull it out. This done, it was easy for so powerful an animal to grip the bars to the right and the left of the one she had removed and pull them outward until she had an opening wide enough to permit her to wriggle through. The ingenuity of the big cats is a never-ending source of amazement to me. It shouldn't be, when I think it over, because after all I have succeeded in teaching them some rather involved tricks that called for intense concentration on their part and keen perception.

But Gracie's trick that night went beyond anything she had ever done as a performer. This cleverly executed escape called for the ability to fool people completely. She knew she would be detected if overheard by the watchman. She also knew that he would regularly make his rounds and that perfect timing was essential if she was to avoid detection. So she scraped away at that floor board with her ears cocked for the inevitable approaching footsteps of the watchman. And she must have stopped her digging and scraping the very second she heard him coming. Complete alertness and clever planning enabled her to pull off one of the neatest animal escapes I can recall.

Today's all-metal cages would frustrate Gracie and make such an escape impossible. We still use a floor board, but the bars of the cage are imbedded in the metal base underneath.

The motivation of wild animals has always fascinated me. Why did Gracie work away at the bars of her cage until she was able to escape? Was she primarily interested in escape or was this a kind of occupational therapy to which she assigned herself as a means of filling in the time on a night when she found it difficult to sleep? Why her sudden capitulation at a time when she had the upper hand? (As I have suggested, perhaps she didn't know she had the upper hand, but who really knows?)

Several times my advice has been sought—twice over the long-distance telephone—on how to recapture escaped animals. Invariably I have predicted that they would be found near the place of escape and recommended that the search be confined to a rather small area.

Wild animals that live in captivity, especially the big cats, develop a practical point of view. They never lose sight of the food problem. The place from which they have escaped may have its disadvantages, but it also happens to be the place where they can depend upon the amount of meat they need to sustain them, and water to drink when the meal is over. And a safe place to take a nap when a full belly induces sleep.

Normally you can't generalize about wild animals. But in the area under discussion you can come pretty close to doing so. For almost half a century most runaway wild animals have been found reasonably close to the zoos, circuses, carnivals or dealers' warehouses from which they have fled.

The higher mammals are thinking creatures. As such, once they have had the thrill of roaming free they begin to think of food, which prevents them from straying too far from what they know to be a dependable source.

I recall, not too happily, another escape that ranks with Gracie's nocturnal adventure. It took place in Cleveland during a post-season engagement with that city's Grotto Circus, so ably managed by my friend Bill Schmidt; and it came so close to tragedy that I never think of it without a drop or two of reminiscent perspiration materializing on my forehead.

We were doing good business at the Cleveland Auditorium that week, and on this particular evening the crowd was all that any showman could desire. The arena boxes were filled, and my act was getting a fine response. The spirited work of the animals reflected the lively exercise run they had had, and I myself was in better condition than I had been in weeks, having gotten past a series of difficulties that involved overtime work which interfered with my sleep. My equipment had just undergone a thorough refurbishing. Everything had been painted and looked brand-new. And the twelve armed men who stood outside the arena in military-looking uniforms and brightly polished steel helmets looked smart and soldierly. Their presence gave our ringmaster a chance for one of his more florid spiels, this gem of reassurance that reached the audience through the loudspeaker system: "The guards are there for your protection, the trainer will take care of himself."

I completed the final flourish of my act, and the band blared forth an overwhelming chord in G, which the animals instantly recognized as the signal for them to leave the arena and return to the cages. Sixteen tigers rushed for the gate which led through the long wooden chute to the big room back of the arena boxes, where their wagons were waiting to receive them.

There was not the slightest premonition of any impending disaster. Three, four, five tigers poured into the chute. Then there was an odd pause, just for a moment, which flashed a sudden alarm to my brain. I looked down along the lengthy chute to the series of safety partitions, arranged to swing like doors so they would close against any animals that might try to turn back toward the arena.

The trouble, I quickly saw, was with one of these door-like partitions. My tigers continued to pile into the chute, but it was like jamming into a New York subway train during the rush hour.

"The door swings the wrong way!" shouted a perspiring attendant who was standing alongside the chute. "It's jammed tight shut!"

I dashed out of the arena to the chute. Sixteen tigers were trying to force themselves into six feet of space, and the wooden chute was rocking like a small boat in a heavy sea. I grabbed a pole and, working it through the arena bars, tried to prod the animals back into the arena. Two or three attendants followed my example, but we accomplished nothing.

There was a sudden cracking of timber, and the top of the chute rose straight into the air, exactly like the lid of a big box. Through the opening three angry tigers leaped to freedom.

Alan Hauser, the equestrian director, came to my aid. He was an all-around circus man who instinctively knew what to do in any emergency. Realizing that I was going to have my hands full with the escaping animals, Hauser leaped to the top of the chute and jammed the broken top down in an effort to keep the others from getting out. The breaking of the timbers had loosened the door so that it fell open, enabling the rest of the tigers to push on to their proper destination.

Meanwhile I was using my whip and gun to keep the three escaped animals intent upon me, rather than upon the audience. At the same time, out of the corner of my eye, I mapped out the path by which I hoped to drive them back to the annex, where their cages awaited them. Between them and the annex was an arena box, in which six women in evening gowns sat huddled together, a study in terror. I stood guard until somebody hustled them out of the box, and meanwhile I called to some animal men in the rear to clear the giraffe enclosure, which I could see in the background, so that the tigers could be rounded up in it.

It was only a few seconds before I saw that the giraffes had been driven into their wagon, so that the big wire enclosure where they had been standing was empty. Motioning to the animal men to open it on the inside toward me, I cued my three angry cats backward suddenly, so that they would be driven straight into the opening.

Two of the tigers responded as planned. They made a grand leap straight over the arena box where the six ladies had been sitting, and were promptly corraled in the giraffes' wire barricade, where it would be a comparatively simple matter to transfer them to their cages.

But my third trouble-maker declined to be so easily captured. This was Snip, and Snip was a big handful at any time. Suddenly she turned on me, but I deflected her first charge with a blank cartridge fired just above her head. She fell back and made a quick circle of the sawdust ring. I kept calling her name and trying to get her to charge me again. The greatest danger now was that the pandemonium which had broken out in the audience would divert her mind from me.

I started using my whip, cracking it in short, sharp snaps which penetrated even the tumult of the panic-stricken audience. Snip accepted my challenge, preparing herself for a heavy spring. Here was an opportunity such as she had never had before, for inside the comparatively narrow confines of the steel arena she had only a diameter of forty feet in which to maneuver, and this was cut down somewhat by the big pedestals that circled the arena. And frequently in the center of the ring there was equipment that amounted to an obstruction. Now she had a freedom of movement more like what would have been possible in her native jungle. She could get a running start at me; and when she leaped there would be a momentum behind her that I never had had to cope with before.

I had accomplished one thing, however. Snip was so intent on getting me that she had forgotten all about the milling audience. Even the nearby circus personnel, who had taken refuge in the overhead ropes and were swinging there like monkeys, failed to divert her attention. Out of the corner of my eye, I had seen my stalwart audience-protectors, the twelve tin-hatted "soldiers," throw down their prop rifles and rush pell-mell to safety. I stumbled over one of their tin hats as I shifted quickly to the right to deflect Snip's oncoming rush.

I took the charge, dodging quickly, and gave her two more blank cartridges as she catapulted past me. She landed, wheeled, and was after me again. Now I felt more confident. The danger to the audience was past, provided I could keep her anger focused on me. The only possible mischance, I felt, would be for someone to blunder into the area where the tigress and I were dueling and come between us. Every move I made now was designed to pull Snip over, step by charging step, toward the cages. Already my quick-witted assistants were bringing a canvas wall into a position where it would act as a tunnel out of the ring. Two or three more of those wheeling charges and I would have Snip at the mouth of the tunnel.

Carefully I forced the battling tigress backward toward that canvas improvisation. Two more charges and she was almost there. I moved four or five steps to the right, to draw her over exactly in front of the opening. As soon as she was where I wanted her, I moved forward, thrusting my kitchen chair toward her and making her retreat. I had her, now, exactly in line. Safety was in sight.

Then, suddenly, I saw something. Just beyond Snip, in line with the tunnel's mouth, an old circus hand—Dad Mitchell—was standing. Somehow he had been trapped there, unable to join his companions in their flight to the ropes overhead. Almost at the instant I saw him, Snip wheeled so that old Dad was directly in her path. His first instinct, of course, was to flee. I saw him jerk, as if about to run.

"Don't move, Dad!" I shouted. "Don't move a muscle; she'll chop you down if you run!"

It took all the will power he had to obey me, even though he knew as well as I did that a big cat will go for anything that flees. Dad stood motionless while I won back Snip's attention and forced her to attack me again. This time I gave ground to her, lots of it, drawing her far enough to enable old Dad to edge over to the canvas wall and step out of sight. Then I began the backing-up process again, and in a few minutes turned her down the tunnel and into the cage runways.

Not until the next day, when I felt somewhat relaxed, did I pay any attention to the reports from the auditorium. The newspapers carried comprehensive accounts. Some of the circus ushers added an assortment of details. A woman in the audience who had fainted was carried out by two men and dumped into a telephone booth, where she was left to recover consciousness as best she could, while her escorts disappeared. A dozen circus hands ran out of the auditorium and down the street, one of them dressed in a clown's outfit to imitate a giant nursing bottle. Five small boys climbed a pillar to the overhead beams, and then were too frightened to climb down again, so that attendants had to fetch long ladders to extricate them.

The occupants of the arena boxes had left in a hurry, and a large collection of men's overcoats and hats and ladies' evening wraps was left behind. Most of the articles were not claimed by their owners until the next day. One woman left her purse, containing thousands of dollars' worth of jewelry, on her chair, and forgot all about it until two days later.

The loudest protests came from those who claimed it was nerve-racking to be sitting in a box near the center ring and suddenly find a tiger go sailing over your head. A few people actually had had this experience. The Hagenbeck-Wallace legal department agreed it could not have been much fun and worked out settlements. But hysteria and exaggeration go hand in hand, and by the time we had pieced all the stories together it seemed that one of those tigers must have been jumping back and forth over people's heads just for the exercise. It developed that one of those who claimed a nervous breakdown as a result of what happened to him that night had not even attended the performance.

This Cleveland mishap led to the development of a type of tunnel that makes a recurrence of this kind of accident impossible.

The psychology of an animal that suddenly finds itself roaming free like Snip is different from that of one that plans its escape, as Gracie had in Detroit. Animals like people are creatures of habit. Snip, a tough customer to deal with under any circumstances, had been made more so by the upsetting of her routine. Countless times after the act Snip had trotted through the tunnel back to her cage without mishap. The most alert of tigers, she had never wasted a second's time in picking up the cue that signaled the end of the act. She would then head for the exit as matter-of-factly as she customarily picked up the signal at the beginning of the performance to enter the arena and mount her pedestal. Then all of a sudden in Cleveland the chute came apart at the top and Snip, being one of those closest to the opening, found herself in the clear. What flashes through an animal's mind in a situation like this is anybody's guess. Any one of a number of thoughts might have occurred to her. For the higher mammals have minds that react swiftly to new developments.

As she stood there free to roam wherever she pleased, Snip might well have had some doubts about the actuality of her freedom. She could, for instance, have had some vague feeling that she was about to be attacked. Tigers are notoriously suspicious. And if anyone had accidentally bumped into her as she poised herself to leap in any direction at a fancied foe, she would have given the bumbler a bad time. That is an understatement. She probably would have killed him. A tiger is always dangerous, but never quite so dangerous as when some befuddling new development fully awakens its primitive savagery and leads the animal to believe it will have to fight for its life.

As I went about the business of recapturing Snip, I didn't permit myself to forget that this tigress must not be made to feel she was being punished for anything. The ferocity of her resistance was to be expected. Something disturbing had happened to her—she had been catapulted out of her groove into a situation she did not understand and it was quite possible she had lost confidence in me. If that was so, I would have to re-win it after I had maneuvered her back into her cage.

Perhaps it sounds contradictory to say that tigers are naturally suspicious and then talk about winning their confidence. There comes a time when a tiger, however suspicious, is willing to accept that at a certain time and under certain circumstances its trainer can be depended upon to do thus and so. Many a tiger, in the early stages of training, gives the impression that it does not believe the trainer can be trusted, that the pedestal he is persuading it to mount will rear up and attack at the first opportunity. Gradually these suspicions disappear and the animal begins to realize that the trainer is friendly; but the experienced trainer, though he will find himself developing an affection for the tiger when this turning point is reached, never trusts the animal fully. This is a form of insurance and is not to be related to any lurking dislike of wild animals or to be contrasted by the cynical with my expressed love of them. The real point is that racing through the blood stream of what under certain circumstances may seem the most compliant of wild animals, are atavistic instincts that some sudden, unpredictable occurrence—perhaps an accident such as the one in Cleveland—may bring to the surface.

In my act today I have the friendliest tiger I have ever trained, Rajah, a big, handsome, perfectly marked, magnificently proportioned four-year-old. Rajah and I have become the best of friends. As I said earlier, he frequently purrs when I stand before his cage. If he doesn't and I want to get him started I can do so by making sounds suggestive of purring.

I'm not the best mimic in the world but I can do this imitation well enough to get Rajah started. Try to visualize a five-hundred-pound purring house cat and you have the idea. Pursuing the house-cat idea further, Rajah also reminds me of one when, as I suddenly appear before his cage just after he has picked up my scent, I snap my fingers, which sometimes is the signal for him to roll over on his back and purr upside down like a playful kitten.

During my 1963 engagement in Philadelphia my collaborator on this book remarked:

"Through most of the matinee today you were your usual serious self, but when it came time to work with Rajah and you faced him, you began to laugh. As you did, you said something to him that I couldn't catch even though I was standing right outside the arena."

I explained that as I started cuing Rajah, he began purring and I said, "Stop behaving like a house cat and act like a tiger."

Yet, though I love that animal, I would never be foolish enough to lower my guard completely with him. Even the most tractable big cats sometimes "go bad," as Frank Bostock has pointed out. But I doubt whether Rajah could ever become the potential menace Snip was during the Cleveland episode.

A less thrilling escape than the ones in Detroit and Cleveland, but one that was rather exceptional because of the surroundings in which it occurred, took place one day in the late 1920s on the San Francisco docks, where I had gone to assume charge of three tigers just arriving from abroad. There was a big cargo of animals on board the incoming steamer, consigned to various zoos, circuses and dealers. When I arrived, the unloading had already begun, and the dock was crowded with packing cases containing all sorts of live cargo.

The biggest noise came from forty or fifty cases of small Indian rhesus monkeys, which are incessant chatterers. They were shipped twenty-five in a case, with the top of each case slatted to allow them sufficient air. Inside their cases they were scrambling about in great excitement.

Several animals had already been unloaded, and I looked them over with professional interest. For instance, there was a black leopard, as large and fine a specimen as I have ever seen. It was consigned to a dealer who was on the dock. He had a stick in his hand, with which he pushed back the leopard's lips to be sure the teeth were in prime condition. The leopard resented this, snapping the heavy stick in two as if it had been a dry twig. There were also four or five fine tigers, and two tapirs that looked seasick.

Owing to the nature of the cargo, the public was barred from the dock. A burly policeman, whose favorite line was "I'm on'y doin' me duty," had let me by only after I had explained in some detail who I was and why I was there.

At the end of the pier there was a small booth in which an elderly clerk was checking the cargo as it came over the ship's edge under the guidance of a half-naked Lascar who operated the hoisting apparatus. I approached the clerk's booth and inquired whether my tigers had been taken off yet. He looked over the list and shook his head. "There's three more coming over now," he said, pointing up at the ship's deck. "Prob'bly them's yours."

I watched a big crate being lifted and lowered. I didn't think much of the way that Lascar winchman handled his job. He was pretty careless, I thought. He let the cable run through the winch regardless of whether the crate hit the ship's side or bumped on the dock. An animal cage should be handled as delicately as Bohemian glassware, for it doesn't do animals or cages any good to be banged about.

However, the crate landed all right, and two longshoremen gingerly wheeled it over to one side. I looked at the label. The crate was mine, and the animal inside was a fine one, so far as I could judge in the darkness behind the slats.

Another crate came over. Something was wrong with the

sling, and the cage nearly fell out in mid-air. I shouted angrily at the Lascar, who paid no attention. I shouted again, using strong language. This time he seemed to understand, for he shook his fist at me.

Well, here was the third and last of my tigers. The winchman was glaring at me as he handled this one, as if to say, "You'll try to tell me my business, will you?" He hoisted it off the deck with a jerk that would annoy the best-behaved animal in the world. It certainly made the occupant of the cage angry, for the tiger let out a series of ear-splitting howls that scared even the winchman. In his fright he let the big crate descend much too rapidly, actually allowing it to drop the last few feet. It struck the dock with a splintering crash, and a second later the tiger burst out, scattering fragments of wood all over the place.

"Tiger loose!" somebody yelled, and there was a general scattering of longshoremen and self-invited spectators who had heard that animals were being unloaded and had managed to work their way past the not overattentive policeman. Probably there were no more than thirty people on the dock, but in the wild disorder that ensued, they seemed more like a thousand.

The tiger made a short rush diagonally across the dock, then stopped and turned, dashing in another direction. He was confused by the excited outcries.

When he broke loose, I had been standing close to the checking clerk's booth. There was a tall four-legged stool inside, and I reached in and took it in my left hand. In my right I held a fragment of crate wood, about the size of a shingle. I struck the wood sharply against the stool, over and over again, to get the tiger's attention.

The animal had finally stopped in the middle of an open space bounded on one side by the high black side of the steamer, and on the other by a pile of bales. Several stevedores were perched on top of the bales, and the tiger was apparently considering the desirability of going up after them.

The tiger accepted my challenge. He charged straight into the chair, and I drew him over toward the checker's booth. Balked in his first charge, he tried again, and this time I drew him almost opposite the booth. I looked over my shoulder and was surprised to find that the clerk had somehow crawled back into the booth.

"Clear out!" I yelled. "I'm going to put this tiger in there!"

He scrambled out, an understandably frightened expression on his face, while I kept the tiger engaged, drawing upon what I had learned in the big steel arena about keeping an animal's mind occupied. The big cat whirled quickly as the disappearing clerk caught his eye, but I was on top of him before he could start in pursuit. I drove him back a few feet, then let him advance on me until he was exactly opposite the door of the booth. I kept the four-legged stool close to his face, and he backed precipitately into the booth. I had the door slammed shut before he knew what was happening.

Although there was a tremendous commotion inside the booth, and an occasional paw was thrust through the window, I signaled the stevedores and spectators down from their perches, and armed them all with stout poles from a pile of timber at the far end of the wharf.

While the pole brigade encircled the checker's booth, I got hold of the ship's carpenter and had him repair the smashed crate. We wrapped a lot of stout rope around it for good measure, and then I was ready to transfer the tiger from the booth to the crate. Stevedores carried the crate up to the door of the booth, and I placed the open end close against the door. As I was about to open the door and work the tiger through it, the checker came running up.

"Say," he demanded blusteringly, pointing to his booth, "who said you could put that tiger in there?"

"Who said he couldn't?" one of the stevedores asked him, with one of those winks you can see a mile off.

Not many minutes later my three crates were on a truck,

speeding out to the railroad yards, where a freight-car was waiting to take them to the winter quarters in Indiana.

The foregoing provides the student of big-cat psychology with several possibilities worth pondering. You can't make an exact science of such things but perhaps they merit a bit of speculation.

The tiger that got loose on the docks due to the callousness of a surly winchman had had a bad time. First he was hoisted off the deck with a jerk that was disturbing enough to draw loud and angry protests from the animal. Then he was stunned when the crate fell and cracked open on the pier. Less upsetting experiences have been known to bring out the killer instinct in a normally manageable cat.

As I mentioned earlier—the point bears repetition because it is so basic—the big cats are never so dangerous as when they think they are being attacked. That tiger might easily have thought he was being attacked when the crate containing him landed with a bang on the dock. When I found myself face to face with him, the first thing I noticed was the heightening of an already angry expression by the narrowing of his eyes, usually an indication of evil intent. And he went all-out in the matter of flattening his ears against his head; indeed, he did the ears-close-to-the-head routine as thoroughly as I've ever seen it done. His was so finished a version you had to look twice to be sure he was equipped with ears.

If that booth had not been there, anything might have happened; for this was an aroused animal. The danger was greatest when he was shaken up by the fall—that is, before his head had had a chance to clear, which must have taken a few minutes.

Although the booth was most welcome, it also prevented me from learning a lot of things I would have liked to know about how that animal's mind worked and what he was capable of doing.

Perhaps it is just as well. Animal behavior is a fascinating subject, but I'd just as soon not acquire greater proficiency in it at the expense of an arm or a leg.

When I think of the countless miles I've traveled by railroad up and down the country with my animals—(our show is now completely motorized, but that's a comparatively recent development)—it seems remarkable that I have had to deal with only two escapes on railroad trains. One of these took place on a journey across Ohio and Michigan for a series of post-season engagements with part of my act.

The animals were in a baggage car with two attendants. Eight other circus employees, including myself, were traveling in a Pullman just behind the baggage car. I was sitting in a front section having a friendly chat with the conductor, when the train suddenly stopped with a jerk that almost threw me out of my seat. Some of my fellow passengers fared worse than I did. Two of them landed in a heap in the aisle, and the conductor, an old-timer who should have been an accomplished equilibrist by then, joined them on the floor. I ran to the vestibule, opened the door, and stuck my head out to see what was the matter. My two cage boys had just leaped out of the baggage-car door and were running up the track toward me.

"Pep is loose!" one of them shouted. "I pulled the safety valve and—"

I didn't wait to hear any more. I jumped to the track and hurried to the open door of the baggage car. The conductor, who had come up behind me as I stood in the vestibule, followed some distance behind.

As I reached the baggage-car door, expecting to see a tiger come bounding out, I was almost bowled over by a stream of ragged-looking men that poured forth from the car exactly as similar characters did in the old-time slapstick motion-picture comedies depicting hobo life. They hit the roadbed as though pursued by an army of demons, and some of them had to pick themselves up before running on.

Where on earth they all came from was a mystery, both to me and the conductor, because we had supposed there was nobody in that car but my two cage boys. Of course, I didn't spend much time trying to figure it out. I had something else to think about.

I swung up the side of the car, entered and looked around. The two cage boys followed me. The conductor kept well clear of the car door, and waved back imperiously a group of passengers who had started to walk down the track to investigate. He had one eye on the car door and the other on his watch, which he was holding nervously in his hand.

The tiger, having got out of his cage, had not availed himself of the opportunity to escape into the open, although perhaps this is not as strange as it seems. An animal in brand-new surroundings is always at a disadvantage, and my escaped tiger, crouched in a corner, had every reason in the world to be bewildered by the meaningless picture that greeted him as he landed, free, in the aisle between the row of cages and the opposite wall of the car. This was entirely foreign territory to him, territory that meant nothing and might be full of unseen dangers; therefore it wasn't a bad idea to hang back and await developments.

A glance at the open cage assured me the tiger was really Pep, one of my toughest customers.

The first move was to close the door of the baggage car, so that Pep would not take it into his head to make a sudden leap for the open after having overlooked the opportunity for two or three precious minutes.

Apparently the conductor considered the closing of the door a signal to go ahead, for the next moment I felt the car moving. This didn't suit me at all. I prefer an absolutely sure footing when I am dealing with a big cat at close range. So I shouted to one of the cage boys to pull the valve again, thereby stopping the train after it had moved no more than thirty feet.

Then I opened the car door a narrow crack and yelled to

the conductor, explaining that I wanted the train held a few minutes longer, until I got my fugitive caged.

"Be quick about it," he yelled back.

Closing the door again, I turned my attention to Pep, still hiding in the semi-darkness at the forward end of the car. I directed the two cage boys to gather up a lot of props that were stored at the other end of the car, and use them to build an enclosure that would take in Pep's cage and the space beyond, where he was skulking. I stood on guard while they worked, armed with a chair and a short pole. Pep glared and growled as he watched the boys, but made no move against them.

Next I ordered one of the boys to climb on top of the banked-up cages and slowly move along until he was crouched on Pep's cage. I passed up to him the "front" of the cage—a solid wooden slab that slips into grooves outside the cage bars and is used to cover them at night, so the animals will not be disturbed by moving lights and shadows. It also serves to keep the cage warmer in winter. Ample allowance is made for air to enter around the edges of the cover.

The other boy, meanwhile, had removed the loosened bars through which Pep had escaped, leaving a sufficient opening for him to get back in. My plan was to drive the animal into the opening and have the boy above quickly slide the front into its grooves, thus effectually closing up the cage again.

There was some danger to the boy in this maneuver, for Pep might take it into his head to leap clear to the top of the cages instead of doing my bidding. So I warned the boy to hold the front so that it would act as a shield in case the tiger elected to lunge at him.

But Pep had no such plans. When I poked him out of his corner, he had no eyes for anyone but me. He came straight at me, in a single swift leap through the air. I stopped him with my chair, and then prodded him back into his corner. Twice more he came at me, repeating his maneuver in exactly the same manner, as if his chief interest lay in finding out whether I could be made to give ground.

After the third time he gave up and let me drive him toward the cage opening. He started to leap in, then thought better of it and whirled back in a snarling, claws-out circling movement which I promptly broke up with the chair and pole. With a last stab at me with one of his powerful forepaws, which broke two legs off my chair, he decided to submit, and a few seconds later he was back behind the closed front.

I opened the car door and signaled the conductor to go ahead. Then I examined the iron bars that had been removed from Pep's cage. He had done a remarkable job, and one that I should not have believed possible, for this was a new cage, specially constructed, with iron bars sunk deeply into the hardwood framework and reinforced all along the edges. It was evident that Pep had been working at these bars ever since we started out the night before. He had worked three of them out by the roots, and had bent two others about four inches out of true.

Pep was known for his peculiar habits—peculiar even for a tiger. He had long made a practice of keeping his paws going constantly along the bars, and each time he pressed forward against them he put his full weight behind the push. For that reason I made it my business to renew his cages frequently, to inspect the bars regularly, and to use the sturdiest metalwork I could find for added insurance.

My cage boys insisted that they had not deserted their watch and yet had not heard Pep as the tiger labored to free himself. At first I was puzzled. Then I stood in the baggage car for a moment and realized that the racket this ancient car made as it clattered along on an inadequate roadbed could easily have drowned out the noise made by Pep as he worked away at the bars.

At the first stop I left the baggage car and went back to placate the conductor, who I felt would be very much annoyed at the delay I had caused. He was worried, all right, and even angry, but not about the delay. The thing that had aroused his ire, I found, was the line of nondescripts that had spouted forth from my animal car and disappeared in the woods. He was convinced that they were friends of mine, whom I was trying to transport without cost.

"And if it hadn't been for that tiger getting loose," he insisted acidly, "you'd have got away with it. As it is, you'll have to pay their fare for the distance they traveled."

I had made some inquiries of my cage boys, and had learned that the hidden passengers were unemployed circus hands who had stolen a ride northward in hopes of finding some employment at the other end of our journey. They had been distributed along the tops of the cages by my boys, whose sympathies were naturally with these old friends.

I assured the conductor that his hidden passengers were no friends of mine, and that they had secreted themselves in the car without my knowledge.

"You'll have to pay for them, all the same," he repeated doggedly.

"But how can I pay," I asked, "if we don't know how many there were?"

That stumped the conductor for a moment. "I think there were about twenty of them," he said, probingly.

"Nonsense!" I replied, my serious manner belying my secret enjoyment of the situation. "You must have been excited. There couldn't have been more than five. Or maybe only four." Actually, I think there were nine or ten.

"There were twenty," he persisted, weakly.

"No matter how many there were," I said, trying a new tack, "I won't pay for them. Your railroad has no right to permit a lot of tramps to get aboard my car. Probably they freed that tiger, just out of meanness."

This irritated the conductor. "Say," he blustered, "what kind of a game is this you're working?" Then he stomped off, mumbling, "And me thinking all the time you were okay!" I suppose he was referring to the pleasant conversation we had

had before Pep's escapade changed everything. And now he had found me out!

Presently he came back and renewed his attack. He was really more trouble than Pep. He showed me my ticket. "This allows you to ride only two men in that animal car," he said, "and eight in this Pullman. You'll have to pay for those others, I tell you!"

"Have you decided officially how many there were?" I inquired politely. (The struggle to keep from laughing was getting to be a bit of a strain.)

"It's up to you to find out, not me," he replied. "They were in your car."

"But on your train," I suggested. "Maybe it *is* up to you."

I finally succeeded in convincing him that I wasn't going to pay for my uninvited guests. He could take it up with the circus management if he wanted to, but it was none of my business.

After a while I went back to the baggage car and told off the two cage boys, just to ease my conscience. Of course they had no right to take on a lot of extra passengers, but their motives were good. Circus people stick together in pretty clannish fashion, and I liked my boys for trying to help out these members of the army of the unemployed.

Scotty Kramer was one of the best of my animal caretakers when I was with the Hagenbeck-Wallace Circus, which at the time was owned and operated by Jerry Mugavin, a veteran of the big top.

Jerry and I got along famously until one of my tigers killed his favorite animal in the show, a performing donkey known as Dora Donk; and then I was almost fired. Dora was a remarkable animal, known for her ability to perform with the skill and grace of a well-trained high-school horse. She was popular with audiences and I could understand Mugavin's fondness for her as a pet and an attraction. He was so demonstrative in his love for his donkey that people around the show used to say that he thought more of the animal than he did of his wife.

We were in the railroad yards at West Baden, Indiana, preparing to leave for the West. I had about twenty lions and tigers loaded, not in a regular baggage car, but in one of those long, commodious circus stock cars. In addition to the cats, this car accommodated three camels, the performing donkey, and a good deal of miscellaneous equipment.

Monarch was the tiger that broke loose on this occasion. Monarch had a strong aversion to donkeys in general, and to Dora Donk in particular.

Dora Donk, for this trip, had unfortunately been tied up at a place in the car where Monarch could see her, and the mere sight of her annoyed him exceedingly. However, his snarls and roars did nobody any harm, and Scotty, in charge of the car, was no more than mildly interested, and perhaps a little amused that a mighty tiger should let a mere donkey agitate him so.

Monarch's mind was set, however, on doing something about the matter. Unknown to anybody, he worked steadily away at the bars of his cage until, after what must have been several hours of scraping at the hardwood in which the metal bars rested, and after much tugging at the bars, he contrived an opening large enough to squeeze through.

Scotty, a tall, lanky man, used to sleep on top of one of the cages, standard practice for animal watchmen. His height created a problem. But Scotty, a veteran of circus business, was adaptable and made a practice of retiring with his feet dangling over the sidewall of the cage on which he happened to be sleeping.

Scotty was weary after helping arrange the animals in the stock car and decided to take a nap on top of a cage—the "one that looked softest," as he used to put it.

No circus is complete without its practical jokers; so it was natural for Scotty to think that someone connected with the show was playing a prank when, shortly after he had removed his shoes and fallen asleep, he felt something tickling the soles of his feet. The first time it happened he said nothing, but when it was repeated a minute later my elongated caretaker thought it was time to declare himself, so he shouted, "Cut that out, whoever's doing it, or I'll knock your block off."

When it happened a third time Scotty thought the time had come for action, not words. He liked a joke as well as anyone but, as he put it, you had to draw the line somewhere; and tomfoolery at the expense of a hard-working man's nap was something only idiots practiced. And he vowed that if it was his last act on earth he would teach the guilty party a lesson. So, determined to carry out his threat to knock that party's block off, he was about to scramble down from the cage top when his eye lit on the scene below.

What he saw, as he later explained, was such a shock that he almost blacked out. It was, of course, a close-up of Monarch nervously pacing up and down in the aisle below. It was the fur of the tiger's tall back, and perhaps also his lashing tail, that had been brushing against Scotty's feet!

This is as good a time as any to add that Monarch was a Siberian tiger. The reader may or may not know that of the three breeds of tigers used as performers, the Sumatrans are the smallest, the Royal Bengals from India are somewhat larger (weighing from 350 to 500 pounds), while the Siberians are by far the largest, not infrequently running well over 600 pounds and measuring between thirteen and fourteen feet from the tip of the nose to the tip of the tail.

One thing is certain. If Scotty had been Monarch's objective, it would have been a simple matter to grab him by his overhanging feet and yank him down.

But Monarch had other plans. He had his eye on Dora Donk. If this had not been so he would have made a dash for Scotty as the frightened caretaker descended from his perch and rushed out of the car, closing the heavy swinging door behind him as he fled. Monarch was so preoccupied with the thought of getting at the donkey it is quite possible he did not even notice Scotty's exit.

It would have been foolish for me to enter the car and try to capture the fugitive as I had recovered Pep. As Scotty, out of breath and half-scared to death, told me what had happened, I realized that this emergency would have to be met differently. We were carrying so much stuff in the animal car on this occasion that I would have had very little room for effective footwork. The physical layout of the car necessitated an entirely different approach to a big cat on the loose.

Through a window at one end of the car I could see Monarch tearing at the mule's throat. It was too late to do anything for poor Dora Donk. Down went the donkey in a heap, while nearby the terrified camels strained at their fastenings and made a pitiful commotion.

It was unmistakable that Monarch had deliberately selected Dora for his victim, because he had to pass the camels to reach her.

But the three camels were by no means safe. For Monarch was on a rampage and even when surfeited—(I have seen such things happen)—he might decide to turn on the harmless trio just for the sake of killing. As the tiger gorged himself on the donkey, the terrified wailing of the camels seemed to annoy him, and he turned around a few times to eye them angrily. At least I would be able to save *them* if I worked fast.

I looked the car over carefully and felt it would be impossible to get Monarch back in his cage by any ordinary means, without almost certainly sacrificing the camels. So I decided to cut a hole in the side of the car. I summoned two circus carpenters who were on hand to do different chores and put them to work with chisels and saws, indicating the area where I wanted a section between three and a half and four feet square removed.

They are fast workers, these circus carpenters, and they had their job nearly done by the time I had gathered a squad of animal men to bring a shifting-den. We placed it on jacks, elevating it to the height of the square opening, and braced it securely in position. The den was now flush against the side of the car, exactly covering the opening. It was held in place by seven or eight huskies.

Now it was up to me to enter the car by the end door and drive Monarch into the heavy box. I armed myself with a short-handled pitchfork, for I realized that I could not manipulate a chair effectively at such close quarters.

The plaintive cries of the camels, panicky wails that are hard to describe, increased in volume as I opened the door and let myself into the car. The sight I witnessed was a bloody one and I will spare the reader a description of the mangled remains of Dora Donk.

Monarch looked up from his feast as I appeared on the scene. Wild animals, especially after a kill, are savagely resentful of anything that looks like interference or intrusion when they are gorging themselves. He turned his attention from his gruesome meal to me. From halfway down the car he came lunging at me. I kept the three-pointed pitchfork in front of me as I side-stepped his charge. He swung around for another try at me, but I had him at a disadvantage now, in an awkward corner, and I pressed him hard. In any walled enclosure of comparatively small dimensions a tiger as big as this king-size Siberian has difficulty in maneuvering. Monarch slipped and skidded into the side of the car as he was forced to turn.

A few prods of the pitchfork, with just enough force behind them to communicate that those pointed prongs could prove a serious menace, persuaded the big tiger to turn in the direction of the square opening which the carpenters had made. He was almost in it before he saw through my ruse, but now he veered away from the car wall with a vicious snarl. He wheeled at me as if he had been standing on a turntable. But I expected this move and gave him another dose of pitchfork. He somersaulted backward, and rolled like a great furry ball into the shifting-den, hitting the farther end so hard that it took all the strength of the men who were holding it to keep it from careening off the jacks.

Five minutes later Monarch was back in his own cage. Circus hands removed what was left of Dora Donk and sprinkled the floor with sawdust.

The camels, still trembling from fright, were removed to another car, where they could get a good night's rest. Monarch stretched out in his cage and slept off his banquet, which is characteristic of big cats that have gorged themselves. Scotty returned to his habitual resting place atop a cage and soon was sleeping too.

The death of Dora Donk affected everyone in the circus. Her unfailing good nature, dependability as a performer and reputation for harmless pranks had made her a general favorite.

Our chief animal caretaker swore that that donkey had a sense of humor. He had quite a fund of stories about how she loved to scare people, never, however, harming anyone. He claimed that she often feigned kicks that she never delivered and that when he fed her a lump of sugar or some other tidbit she would occasionally catch his fingers between her teeth, press gently and then let go.

Under the circumstances it was a miracle that Mr. Mugavin, boss of that circus, didn't discharge me. He had made a special point of asking me to look after his donkey—and now the animal was dead.

The cages we used in those days were nothing like the escape-proof all-metal type we use today. The cage from which Monarch had escaped was one of the outmoded variety in which the bars are set in a wooden frame. As thick and hard as the baseboards of those cages were, a clever, patient and determined lion or tiger could loosen the boards by working away at them steadily with its sharp claws (as in the case of Gracie in the Shrine Temple escape in Detroit).

Monarch had managed to loosen the bars of his cage unnoticed by Scotty or any of the cage boys. But the ultimate responsibility was mine, not Scotty's, and although I could not have prevented the escape, the standard practice in a situation of this kind is to fire the person in charge.

Mugavin had a violent temper. He was as irascible as they come—(he knew every cussword in the language and he used them all on me)—but he never carried out his threat to fire me. Knowing how much he loved that donkey, I considered him a good sport for letting me keep my job.

The most shrewdly calculated escape that I can recall was carried out by Big Ross, the brainiest tiger I have ever handled. What this animal succeeded in doing called for a careful study of the prospects, the decision that it was possible to break loose and the cleverest kind of planning of each and every step involved. For Big Ross was in surroundings ninety-nine animals out of a hundred would have accepted as escape-proof. He detected something that gave him an idea—something that only his kind of intelligence would have recognized as an opportunity—and he decided to give it a whirl. His analysis of the situation is one of the finest examples I can cite of the soundness of Sir Julian Huxley's statement: "Higher vertebrates, and especially the higher mammals, have brains and behaviors similar to ours in many essential ways."

For some time I had been organizing a zoo and circus in Fort Lauderdale, Florida, which I planned to open to the public on December 2, 1939. It was an elaborate undertaking, much more than a simple plan to exhibit animals in cages and to put on shows. Wherever possible I wanted the different species to roam free—lions, tigers, elephants, giraffes, etc., each species, of course, separated from the others—so that those who patronized my zoo would get a better idea of what these creatures were like than if they were displayed in small enclosures behind bars.

Everything was in readiness and we had announced one of those "grand openings." But Big Ross had other ideas.

A number of open sunken grottoes had been built for the accommodation of the lions, tigers and other animals just men-

tioned. I had the benefit of the advice of Dr. Theodore Schroeder, distinguished curator of the Detroit Zoo, on how to make
these grottoes escape-proof and how to design them so that
the public would get at least a superficial idea of the back-
grounds against which a variety of wild animals lived in their
native habitats.

In the grotto to which I had assigned Big Ross and three
other tigers there was a moat that would discourage—or so I
thought—even the most determined tiger with escape in mind.
There were eight feet of water in the moat, this depth being
necessary to prevent the animals from touching bottom solidly
enough to get set for a spring.

Ross could not possibly leap from the water's edge over the
wall itself, an almost straight-up jump of twenty feet. Rest-
lessly pacing back and forth in the enclosure, the animal kept
studying the encircling wall until he noticed something that
gave him an idea—a midway bulge in the cement. This de-
viation from the straight surface the specifications called for
was due to the carelessness of the workmen who built this
particular unit.

Time and again I had seen Ross do his pacing act while the
other cats in the grotto went about their business in a state of
relaxation. The agitated movements of the nervous cat did not
worry me or arouse my suspicion. There are as many kinds
of animals as there are kinds of people, and I could recall
countless times when a restlessness comparable to Ross's had
no special significance.

Looking down at the grotto from above, it was not possible
to see the bulge that the big tiger had noticed. It didn't jut
out much and looking at it casually it seemed as straight as
the rest of the wall.

Even if I had spotted the bulge, I doubt whether I would
have given it much thought unless I had happened to see Ross
staring at it fixedly for some length of time, which he must
have done before he worked out his plan. There is something
about a twenty-foot wall that gives you a feeling of security

even where a wily member of the big-cat family is concerned. I had never heard of a tiger scaling a barrier that high from what was practically a standing start.

Big Ross was smart enough to know that under normal circumstances he could not possibly leap from the water's edge over a wall that high. But . . . what about that place where the wall was not true, where it bellied out a little? Suppose. . . . He must have thought and thought about that, becoming more and more excited as he eyed the imperfection in the cement work that might prove the road to freedom. . . .

He finally was ready to put everything behind a desperate effort to carry out his plan.

I can't very well attempt to describe Big Ross's escape in actual detail, but he could have accomplished it in only one way. No one witnessed it, but he left enough evidence to indicate how he had accomplished the seemingly impossible. Appraising the problem with almost unbelievable brilliance, he had figured out that he could scale that wall by means of a leap that called for his aiming for the outjutting cement and using the bulge as a means of getting the leverage he needed to hurl himself upward the rest of the way, making a sort of two-stage rocket of himself.

It was an astonishing feat and Big Ross had figured it out perfectly. The claw-marks I afterward found on that small area of cement bulge made it unmistakable how that clever animal had executed his scheme. And on top of the wall itself I found little patches of tiger fur attesting to his having just managed to reach the top and then having just barely slid and scraped his way over on his belly.

The ingenious Ross made his escape toward nightfall the day before my grand opening was to take place, and it began to look as if that opening, if it took place at all, would not be so "grand."

Outside the main walls of my zoo—which Ross might be able to hurdle from a running start, having jumped over the not much lower grotto wall from a standing start—lay U.S. Route 1, with its gas stations, roadside eating places, strolling pedestrians. And near the entrance were some of my workmen doing last-minute jobs; they would be helpless against the big cat if he decided to go that way.

I remembered that the day we installed Big Ross in his grotto we passed the lake where Augie the hippopotamus was disporting himself. The tiger, picking up the hippo's scent, had thrashed about wildly in his cage and snarled out his innermost feelings about Augie and his kind. I decided to bet that my fugitive, instead of trying to make a clean break, was heading for Augie's retreat. It was beginning to turn dark and I would have to move fast if I hoped to have even fading daylight to help me locate Big Ross and get him back in his grotto.

A narrow embankment, barely five feet wide, rising to a height of fifteen feet alongside a little lake, was the course I took, and as I approached this precarious passage I suddenly pivoted, sprinted back and streaked away in a great circle. Big Ross had loomed up ahead of me, his glittering eyes plainly visible in the gathering darkness.

There was now not the slightest doubt that the big tiger was heading for the hippo and that he was aware that I was there to head him off. Crouching, hissing and snarling, he stood waiting for me to come on.

I don't want to overdramatize the situation. But there was a good deal at stake. If Ross, resenting my interference and frustrated in his efforts to get at Augie, went berserk, he was capable of killing anyone in his path. He had a violent temper. Not many weeks before, he had killed a tigress, and I still have visions of him dragging her limp body around. The combination of a clever mind and so cruel a nature was full of troublesome possibilities.

I let the escaped animal force the issue and gave ground as I tried to figure out a course of action.

There were two arenas on the premises—the one that had been set up as a permanent enclosure in which I would put on between-seasons shows at my Fort Lauderdale zoo and circus, the other the stacked-up sections of the one I used on tour during the regular circus season.

The cage boys and some of my other personnel at Fort Lauderdale had sought the safety of the permanent arena. They had locked themselves in it, and I could hardly blame them. They didn't want to be at the mercy of a tiger on the loose, especially one as ferocious and chronically ill-tempered as Big Ross.

It soon became known that I had located Ross and was dueling with him. This news proved reassuring, for now there was no danger of the animal suddenly jumping out of a hiding place and ambushing some convenient victim.

I was able to summon help from the barricaded group in the permanent arena, which fortunately was not far from where the escaped tiger and I were trying to outwit each other. I gave instructions that the road arena be set up, minus a few sections. It was my hope to be able to use it as a trap, driving the big cat into the open end, then blocking him off.

By now there was no daylight left, and while it was not the blackest of nights, visibility was inadequate for the job I had to do.

While the zoo hands started the somewhat involved job of erecting the arena, I grabbed a shovel handle that was lying around and went after Ross with it, deciding it was time to take the initiative. He had evidently picked up Augie's scent again, a good whiff this time, and his nervous pacing and flailing tail proclaimed his excitement. Once he momentarily stopped in his tracks, alternately glaring at me and casting angry looks in the direction of the hippo's lake.

Suddenly there was a puffing and panting behind me and something seemed to be blowing down my neck. Is there *another* animal loose? I wondered, and looked fearfully around. But it was only my guest and good friend, Frank Walters, the Houston oilman and operator of the one-day-a-year Underprivileged Children's Circus.

A big man like Walters—he weighed about three hundred pounds and was slow-moving—would be at a serious disadvantage if Ross decided to head for him; but there was nothing wrong with Walters' courage.

Augie's scent proved a fortunate distraction. Ross's interest in it prevented him from giving us his undivided attention. With a hippo's scent to tantalize him he was not, as far as I was concerned, as deadly an adversary as he might have been. But, by the same token, since I could not get him to concentrate sufficiently on me, it was difficult to maneuver him as deftly as would have been possible under different circumstances.

Creeping closer to my fugitive, I jumped up and gave a great shout. Ross turned, laid back his ears, and wheeled around. In this position he was directly between me and the arena, and with luck I hoped to drive him into it.

I kept yelling at the tiger in an effort to get and keep his attention, for he was a discipline-minded performer and though I didn't expect him to take cues seriously in a situation of this kind, I felt that I would be able to communicate with him to some extent by letting him know what I wanted him to do.

I kept forcing him back toward the open door of the arena— and then in the darkness I failed to see a plank that had been dropped by a careless workman.

I lost my balance and fell to the ground, the shovel handle flying from my grasp. Big Ross, seeing his advantage, came lunging at me. He missed my head with a tremendous swing of a paw heavy enough to knock me out if he had connected. That miss threw him into an awkward position and I was able to recover the spade handle with a quick grab and scramble to my feet.

I have never enjoyed striking an animal, but when it's a question of survival I sometimes have to. As Ross moved up to attack, I banged him over the head with that shovel handle hard enough to stun him but, as it developed, not with suffi-

cient force to injure that unusual brain of his that was capable
of such brilliant analysis.

As I flailed away with my improvised weapon, Frank Walters, whom I had ordered to drop back, ignored my concern
for his safety and came lumbering up to join me.

Twice Ross started for us, and twice I drove him off. He
went into a crouch, as if preparing to leap, then changed his
mind and raised his head and emitted a deafening roar. Having registered this protest, he backed off and turned around,
his head now facing the arena.

This was the kind of opportunity I had hoped for. I rushed
him again, forcing him straight ahead into the arena. He was
still a menace there, for it was only twelve feet high and had
no protective net over the top. There had not been enough time
to put one in place—the men had just barely had time to put
up the arena sides and clamp them together.

Twelve feet is an easy jump for a tiger. Big Ross raced
around and around, then backed off and stood still as if trying
to figure out the best spot from which to take a flying start.
But before he could carry out his evident design, my crew put
a shifting cage in place. I maneuvered Ross into it and subsequently we installed him in a more permanent cage where he
would be less likely to cause trouble.

I couldn't take a chance with him again in his grotto. He
had demonstrated that he could think his way out of that enclosure, which my experienced staff and I considered escape-
proof, and which *was* except for the Big Rosses, those one-in-a-
million types.

I have always regretted that I didn't have the time or the
facilities to study and record the most important facts about
Big Ross's mental processes and behavioral pattern. Although
he had killed another tiger, it was hard to think of him as an
authentic killer. I would have given anything to be able to
find out whether he was indeed a vicious brute that slew for
the sake of slaying or whether he was the victim of some kind

of mental aberration when he murdered that tigress. And, if the latter was the case, what had caused it?

Darwin and others have convinced me that such things can be established once you collect all the evidence and devote enough time and study to its proper evaluation.

I have made a few appearances with my act on Ed Sullivan's television program. It's a show on which I like to appear because of Ed's warm, friendly interest in my work and for the additional reason that it is one of the nation's great show windows. It has a vast audience and has enabled me to make many new friends.

The least I could do to show my appreciation was to keep my big cats from getting out of the arena into Sullivan's Sunday-night studio audience.

But I'm getting ahead of my story.

The right kind of footing is important in my work—both to me and the animals. We have to be able to "grip" the surface on which we are working.

Having previously found the animals and myself at a disadvantage because of the nature of television studio floors, when Sullivan last asked me to appear I suggested that the cameras pick me up in a parking lot outside the studio where the animals and I would have a footing more nearly like the kind of surface on which we perform under the big top. On the dirt surface of that parking area I would be able to perform with greater confidence and precision.

Ed Sullivan is a reasonable man and perhaps if I had insisted he would have approved such an arrangement. Second-guessing myself, I imagine I should have pressed my point more vigorously.

Ed takes his studio audience seriously and puts a lot of emphasis on their seeing as good a show as possible. Had my act originated from the parking lot, they would have missed seeing firsthand something Ed was eager to have them see in the studio.

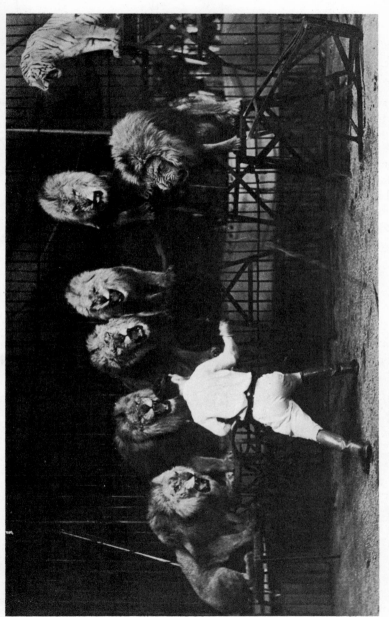

[1]   Although I don't seem to be paying any attention to the lion on the extreme left, he is my main concern. I am watching him out of the corner of my eye, ready to wheel around and block him if he decides to spring down, which he has done before and may be preparing to do now.

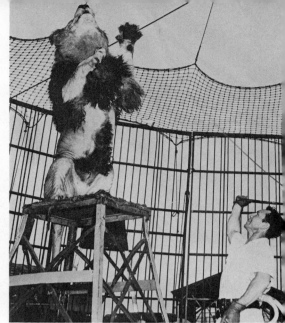

[2-3]   First picture shows a lion doing the sit-up, a stunt which has given me many insights into the big cats. In the second picture the lion doing the sit-up is nonchalantly performing while nearly surrounded by tigers. I would be unable to achieve a similar result with a tiger almost encircled by lions.

from the collection of Robert D. Good

[4]   The tiger shown here is new to the sit-up and has not yet learned to do it without support. After a few more rehearsals he will be able to do the sit-up without the aid of that iron bar on which he is leaning.

[5]   Here I am playing with a four-month-old cub. I'm having a little fun and also trying to find out how good a balancer this baby tiger is by getting it to reach for the pole in my hand. While this is going on, the bored mother is yawning.

[6]   Caesar II, a formidable lion. Wielding that upraised paw in clublike fashion, this animal in his native Africa could snap a zebra's neck
with one well-aimed blow. . . . Only once did Caesar injure me, and that
was my own fault. I got too close to him, so close he was able to reach
over my chair and claw my right arm. The injury was not serious.

[7-8] The first picture shows Sultan, one of my favorite animals, who is discussed in Chapter Four. This type of lion, with the big round head, makes a better and safer performer than the kind with a long narrow head and eyes close together. The lion in the other picture is about to swing his left forepaw at me, and I am moving out of range.

Mary Kennedy Photo

[9-10]   LEFT: Here I am rehearsing Rajah, the unusual tiger mentioned in Chapter Nine, to do the rollover. First, I give him the cue that starts him off his pedestal.

RIGHT: I am maneuvering him to the place in the arena where I want him to lie down. Next . . .

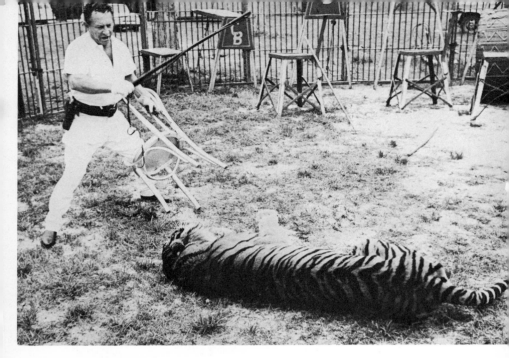

[11-12] I signal him to get over on his side (TOP PICTURE). Then I get him to rotate on his side in a series of rolls.

Under the big top my arena is a circular affair, forty feet in diameter. For the purposes of the Ed Sullivan show this had to be changed to a long narrow enclosure in which the pedestals were stationed in a manner slightly unfamiliar to the animals, as is always the case when the proportions of the performing area have to be altered.

Returning to the original problem, had we been able to sprinkle a heavy layer of dirt on the stage we would have had the footing we needed, but for a variety of reasons this was not feasible.

My act was almost over when Singapore, one of the best of my performers and normally a dependable tiger, had a bad moment as he leaped up on a pedestal that slipped and skittered on the smooth hard surface of the television stage. To Singapore a pedestal was something that was firmly planted and did not yield, and it was obvious from his startled expression and nervous movements that he wasn't quite sure what to do.

To steady himself, the bewildered tiger made a reach for the bars of the arena, and once he had a firm grip on them he started climbing. If he reached the top it would not be difficult to rip the safety net aside and jump down into the section where the spectators sat.

There was much excitement backstage among the cameramen, technicians and stagehands, but nobody panicked. Cage hands who had been stationed around the arena to handle just such an emergency got busy with their poles and started prodding Singapore down. One of them recklessly reached through the bars and grabbed the tiger's tail and tugged at it in an effort to yank him down. As often as not, spectators witnessing a development of this kind think it is part of the show.

At a signal from Sullivan the cameras flashed to the studio audience. Many a television viewer was puzzled that night as to why my act had ended so abruptly.

Sullivan moved down into the studio audience, chatting affably with his fans. It was a shrewd move because if any of them realized that something had gone wrong they must have been reassured by the calm presence of the man who ran the show.

3. Little Big-Cat Friends

Leo, the Cross-eyed Lion Cub – A Lioness Has Quintuplets – A Seaman in Love with a Baby Tiger – Dogs
as Replacements for Lion and Tiger Mothers

Ever since I entered the animals-training field I have been
asked questions about lions and tigers, many of them having
to do with cubs. Where can I buy a lion cub? How much
would it cost? How long can I safely keep it as a pet? These
and many other questions are regularly put to me, and have
been for years.

In recent years there has been a marked increase in such
inquiries, as reflected both in the mail I regularly receive from
the public and in the questions asked me by circus-goers who
call on me in the house-trailer I use as a dressing room. I in
turn ask questions, and the answers I get convince me that Joy
Adamson's remarkable books about the lioness Elsa and her
cubs have stimulated interest in the kittens of the big-cat
world.

Among the people I have heard from are several who have
acquired cubs on trips to Africa but who can't understand—
as one correspondent recently put it—"why my baby lion
didn't turn out better. He was so cute when I first got him
and now he's beginning to play rough. I've heard about lion
cubs that are always playful and never scratch or claw. What
do you advise?"

I couldn't help wondering how this woman had gained the impression that a lion cub, however blessed with charm, playfulness and a benign expression, could be counted upon to check its primitive instincts at the entrance to her home. I also found myself wondering what mistakes she might have made that could have brought the animal's latent wildness to the surface sooner than would have happened if the cub had been more expertly handled.

In another somewhat similar circumstance there was a clue to what had been done wrong. A family had brought a two-month-old lion cub back from an African jaunt. They genuinely loved animals and their interest in their baby lion was real. Not many weeks after they had arrived home with their pet they began to have a disillusioning experience. The cub, which they had selected because of its gentle and playful disposition and its sweet expression, had "turned mean." It snarled at those who came near it and lashed out with its paws, claws showing. A member of the family wrote the local newspaper explaining the problem and seeking advice. Would the paper publish an article on the cub-owner's predicament stating that he was desirous of selling the animal to a zoo or circus?

The clipping was called to my attention. Was I interested in buying the animal? That I was unable to do. I had a full complement of lions for my act and several understudies. Animals reared in captivity seldom make good performers, and while this cub when full grown might prove the exception to the rule, I saw no point in investing money in anything so speculative at a time when I was amply stocked. I was then asked whether I would accept the animal free. I could not risk this either until I had had a firsthand report on the animal by someone experienced in the ways of lions. I was too busy to make the trip myself.

There was a clue in the news story that intrigued me. It had to do with a wide, heavy leather collar the owner had placed around the animal's neck. I had a hunch that as the animal developed—lion cubs grow at a faster rate than the uninitiated realize—that collar might have started digging into its neck. Whether I took possession of the animal or not, I decided to play my hunch. In the event that I was right, I would at least be able to relieve the young lion's discomfort— and, possibly, pain. I asked my assistant, Red Hartman, to notify the family that he would call on them and see what he could do to help.

Shortly after his arrival Red telephoned me to say that I had guessed right. Ironically enough, the owner of the cub, a person who really loves animals, had placed a collar around the neck of this family pet that allowed no room for growth. It must have been a snug fit originally, and as the cub gained weight the heavy collar and its big buckle started cutting into the animal's neck. It is one of those things I so often see: the unwitting maltreatment of animals by people who, however well meaning, are not qualified to look after them.

Far be it from me to teach the African animal dealers their business, but I really believe they make a mistake every time they sell a lion cub—or any other animal new to the average person—to a man or woman who has had no experience in such matters. Either people know how to take care of wild pets or they don't. Enthusiasm engendered by reading Joy Adamson or one of the other talented chroniclers of wildlife is not enough.

I agreed to take the cub with the sore neck as much out of compassion, if I may give myself a minor pat on the back, as for any other reason. I have doctored countless animals and consider myself a pretty good amateur veterinarian. I have taken stitches in lions and tigers that got themselves chewed up in fights, and I have gotten up in the middle of the night to perform an extraction when the diseased look of a big cat's fang made it clear that the tooth could not be saved. I was curious to see if I couldn't do something to cure that young lion's sore neck and improve his disposition.

At this writing, several months after I acquired the animal, the last vestiges of the damage done by that collar are disappearing. The cub's neck is no longer sensitive to the touch, his ruff looks practically normal and his disposition is good; and, best sign of all, he now has his playful moments. He and I have become friends and when he picks up my scent as I approach his cage I usually find him presenting an ear against the bars with a look that unmistakably means "Please scratch." For lions—including the big ferocious ones that would just as soon knock you down as not—have their tender moments when they want to be scratched behind the ear like the most affectionate of dogs.

My advice to you, if you are thinking of acquiring a lion or tiger cub as a pet, and you have had no experience in handling such animals, is: don't! In offering this advice I have your best interests and those of the community of big cats in mind. You will save yourself and the animal you are misguidedly planning to adopt a lot of grief.

Lion and tiger cubs grow rapidly. It takes experience to recognize the change from one phase to another. For instance, the transition from what might be called the days of puppy-dog sportiveness to a really rough kind of playing is usually a sudden one. I recall a situation in which a young woman was painfully scratched by a lion cub. A gentle youngster up to this point, it had been seized by a sudden whim to use its claws, which at that early stage in its career were more like the points of needles than honest-to-goodness lion claws, yet destructive enough. One never can be sure, but it was my belief that this baby lion had no intention of inflicting any damage. It was beginning to grow up and in bringing its claws into play it may merely have been governed by instinct. The young woman was not seriously injured but wound up with some fairly deep scratches on her face and arms.

When Jack Paar was running his daily *Tonight* show I appeared on it several times. Jack and I became well acquainted, and more than once I was impressed with his knowledge of wild animals. You can't discuss the big cats with Jack for any length of time without realizing that he knows a great deal about them and that his feeling for lion and tiger cubs is pure, unadulterated love. His is the belief that *all* babies, human and animal, are cute—not a new or original concept, to be sure, but one that few will be disposed to dispute with him.

A few years ago, after appearing on his show, I happened to mention to Jack that one of my circus's tigresses had had a litter of three of the most charming cubs I'd ever seen. As I recall it, they were about three months old when I made this offhand remark.

Jack went into action immediately. "Three tiger cubs? And you so casual about it, Clyde! For heaven's sake, get 'em here so I can use them on the show!"

"When?" I asked.

"How about tomorrow night?"

This was a little more pressure than I was prepared for. We made a date for a week later.

Jack said I would go on a little after midnight and asked me to show up with the cubs at eleven-thirty. To play it safe I arrived with my striped trio at eleven. A friend accompanied me, and since we had some time to kill, we headed for a nearby restaurant for a sandwich and a glass of beer, leaving the cubs in a room adjoining Jack's studio. As a precaution, I left a message with a member of Jack's staff stating where I could be reached.

Not many minutes after I arrived at the restaurant a messenger came dashing in to tell me, breathlessly, that Mr. Paar wanted to see me immediately.

Back in the studio I found Hugh Downs, Paar's right-hand man, nervously pacing up and down. Hugh, normally calm and collected, was in a state of great excitement. "Jack's waiting!" he shouted. "He's furious!"

I told Downs that I was not to go on until after midnight. Jack had so informed me and it was clearly understood. Downs, still excited, sputtered out that he knew that. Things had changed, however. When Jack had seen how cute the cubs were, he decided to put them on immediately and he was upset when he couldn't find me.

This was typical Jack Paar procedure. Even his friends—and I consider myself one—find it necessary to jolt him out of such sudden emotional unreasonableness, which as often as not is based on some new enthusiasm. I told Downs I was sorry that Jack was hot and bothered but that I wasn't a mind reader and had no way of knowing Jack would want to change his timetable so abruptly.

When Jack appeared he gave me one of his patented hurt looks and announced that I would appear on the program at eleven-forty instead of after midnight.

Always a showman, Jack had made ingenious preparations for the appearance of the three little tigers. The studio carpenters had been instructed to build a miniature replica of the big steel cage in which I perform, with three tiny pedestals to match, copies of the ones I use in my act, as seats for the tiger-cub trio. After they were seated on their perches Jack picked them up so that the audience could get a good close-up of them. He took my advice and wore the long fleece-lined leather gloves I provided. Even a three-months-old tiger, if it decides to extend its tiny claws and bring them into play, can make considerable trouble. As undeveloped as they are, these claws can cut fairly deeply into a person's skin. Imagine a series of sharp tacks digging about a quarter of an inch into your arm and being drawn across it, and you have the idea.

Under normal circumstances these very young cubs, all three of good disposition, could be counted upon to be gentle and easily handled. But I cautioned Jack that if the bustle backstage and the strong lights upset the animals, any one of them might lash out at his face, and that unless he held the cubs as instructed he ran the risk of getting those tack-point claws in his eyes. Jack insisted on handling the cubs, and since he carefully followed instructions he put on a good show, sprinkled with appropriate patter, and the three little tigers gave him no trouble.

I wasn't too enthusiastic when Jack asked his daughter Randy to step onto the stage from the studio audience and hold one of the cubs. But luck was on our side. The little tiger behaved and all went well.

I tell this story because it illustrates how people can be carried away by the charm of big-cat kittens. One look at those tiger cubs and Jack Paar was so hypnotized by them that he issued peremptory orders that upset the carefully planned programming of his act.

I have seen people so overcome by the cuteness of their big-cat kittens that they momentarily forgot that their little pets were lions and tigers and took needless risks.

Oftener than not, nothing disturbing happened, but when a big-cat cub, perhaps in a moment of excitement, used its claws or its teeth, the aggrieved owner would decide that his little charmer had "turned bad," instead of realizing that the animal was merely giving vent to a wholly natural primitive urge to protect himself.

What with my correspondents and callers putting so much emphasis these days on the younger generation of the big-cat family, I find myself thinking of the many cubs I have raised as pets and the fun I have had with them.

The most lovable of the lot was Leo, a cross-eyed baby lion. His right eye was normal; his left was askew, squinting off crazily in some unfollowable direction. To understand him and to communicate with him, you had to look Leo squarely in the good eye, which usually sent forth the message, "Don't just stand there, boss!—let's have a bit of a romp." Usually he confirmed this message with a playful slap at my leg or thigh with a claws-retracted forepaw and a doglike wagging of the tail.

By the time Leo was about six months old his idea of a good time was to wrestle with me on the lawn of my home in Rochester, Indiana, where I once lived between seasons. Leo then weighed about one hundred pounds, was muscular and full of fun, and gave me quite a workout every time we wrestled. I would let him tangle with me to his heart's content, sometimes doubling up in mock distress and emitting a few silly moans as he wrapped himself around me.

I have never seen a lion actually laugh. Leo came the closest to it with the tickled expression that came over him, highlighted by a merry gleam in his good eye, as we played this game over and over again.

For some time past I have read everything I could get hold of on the subject of animal psychology, beginning with the grandpappy of all such books and still the best, Charles Darwin's *The Expression of the Emotions in Man and Animals*. I have long tried to figure out what was going on in the minds of the animals I trained to perform and those I raised as pets, and this interest has been heightened by what I have read and by the observations—many of them tallying with my own— of the curators of zoos and members of their staffs with whom I have discussed this absorbing subject.

As often as not, it is difficult to figure out with any degree of certainty what a member of the big-cat family is thinking about. In the case of Leo it was a cinch. It was seldom that his good eye did not send forth the message "Let's play!" When I had had a tough day at winter quarters where I trained and rehearsed lions and tigers for the following season and found myself too tired to give Leo a good workout, his reproachful look plainly said, "You'll have to do better than that." So sure was I of his meaning that I would not wrestle with him again until I felt equal to giving him a vigorous tussle.

After I had Leo housebroken, I set up his headquarters in the basement. There I placed his box, a rather large one whose base was liberally sprinkled with sawdust topped off with a layer of cut-up newspaper, and it was understood that this was his comfort station. Not once did that intelligent and cooperative cub violate this understanding. In my time I have had many dogs as pets, raising them from puppyhood, and have trained them all to observe the Law of the Box, but no dog I have ever owned was a better pupil in this respect or lived up to the code more scrupulously. A few of those dogs, I might add, did not do as well as Leo in observing the rules of sanitation.

I also trained Leo not to wander off the premises. There were no fences to confine him. My task was to communicate to him what the boundaries were. At first he made a few mistakes, which were my fault more than his—(I was crowded for time and wasn't as patient and deliberate a teacher as I normally am)—but as I found more time, he picked up the idea and once he did I could count on him not to leave the grounds, an area of about an acre and a half.

The fact that Leo was now housebroken and that I had succeeded in teaching him not to leave the premises does not mean that he did not present further problems. One day he discovered the stored-up lawn furniture in the basement and proceeded to do a thorough job of sharpening his claws on it. This, to put it mildly, did the furniture no particular good. When Leo got through, some pieces had to be repaired and a few were beyond repair, including a favorite wicker chair that was on the collapsible side by the time my energetic cross-eyed cub had finished with it. It is a bit contradictory— but quite normal—to see a gentle animal like Leo, who almost never used his claws, spending so much time putting them in fighting trim.

No matter how much you love an animal you have raised as a mascot or companion, there comes a time when he has to be disciplined, although I am a sissy in such matters and use nothing more formidable than a folded newspaper (as when housebreaking a dog). You needn't use stern measures to get compliance from a pet, be he dog or lion. If the animal is basically intelligent and friendly, all you need do is make your point. The gentler you are with the Leos of the pet world the more cooperation you get.

It was not long after I got it into Leo's head that he was to leave the lawn furniture alone that he discovered the baby grand piano in the living room. One day after a long training session I returned home to find that Leo had decided that the baby grand was as satisfactory for claw sharpening as lawn furniture. He gouged deeply into the mahogany legs and had time left over to do a matching job on the legs of the oblong stool that went with it. Needless to say, Leo and I had a heart-to-heart talk, in the course of which I sought to communicate to him—with the aid of the same old device, a folded news-paper—that piano legs were out of bounds. The swats I dealt him bruised his ego more than his backside, and from that day on the cub showed no further interest in piano legs or the destruction thereof. In fact, in my presence he now made a practice of looking away from that piano, as if to say, "Look, I'm not even tempted!"

Leo was something of a practical joker. When he was in the basement and heard someone descending the cellar steps, his idea of fun was to hide and remain perfectly still. I recall hearing him scurry off to a hiding place a number of times as I started down those stairs; and when he leaped at me with the enthusiasm of a child playing hide-and-seek and I responded with mock cries of alarm and did all I could to seem frightened to death, Leo's appealing little lion face would take on that expression I have described earlier as the closest thing to a laugh I have ever seen in all my experience with members of the big-cat family.

A new house was being built for me that would have its electric meter on the outside. But in the old one in which I lived meanwhile the meter was located in the basement, and the man who came from the local power company had to go down below to make his reading.

One day when I was busy in the garage a man called to read the meter. Less than a minute after he had made his descent an agonized shriek came from below and up the stairs bounded the meter reader, Leo in hot pursuit. I heard the outcry and came dashing into the house.

"He tried to kill me!" the meter man moaned between gasps. When he had caught his breath he looked at me sternly and said he would have to report the matter. He had no intention of ever returning to the home of an "irresponsible person" who kept "ferocious brutes" on the premises nor did he intend to have any of his fellow inspectors subjected to a similar "outrageous attack."

In the excitement of the moment the meter reader had scuffed his hand against the rough wall of the cellar, and he thought he had been clawed or bitten or both. When he calmed down, I was able to convince him that this was not so.

"Just the same it's no fun having an animal spring at you like that!" the meter man moaned. With this I was compelled to agree. It's a bit nerve-racking to have 125 pounds of lion—Leo was growing rapidly—jump at you out of the semi-darkness.

When the power company wrote me about the incident I apologized, and, echoing their phraseology, promised to remove from my cellar "all savage brutes that made a practice of attacking human beings." The story got around and for several months thereafter when a man from the power company called to read my meter he would first inquire whether there were any "wild animals" in the cellar.

Leo and I celebrated the departure of the meter man he had "attacked" by having one of our best wrestling matches on the lawn. These games usually started with Leo jumping at me and bumping me, and my pretending he had knocked me over. Now I no longer needed to pretend. His 125 pounds, plus the force of his forward motion, would be enough to bowl me over, and I began to teach him not to rush me so hard. After he realized I was trying to sell him the idea of restraint his disappointment registered in the form of an expression that seemed to say, "What's the matter, Clyde? Are you turning chicken?"

Sometimes Leo would pout to make it plain that he disapproved of something I had done—as, for instance, when I put a lock on the door leading from the cellar to the ground floor. The cub had the run of the house and it was a joy to have him around. That is, *I* thought so. Occasionally someone disagreed.

Leo loved people, and when he was down below and heard voices up above, it was quite natural for him to want to join the group and give everyone a friendly paw-pat, his way of saying hello. Sometimes the suddenness and heartiness of his greeting and the sheer weight and size of his paw would startle the uninitiated.

Even when he was not invited up he would sometimes join the group himself and occasionally succeeded in scaring some person who was inclined to be apprehensive in the presence of animals. Entering the upstairs part of the house was a simple matter for Leo, who had figured out how to open the door atop the cellar steps and let himself in. This involved raising himself on his hind legs and manipulating the knob with his forepaws. Standing up, he kept turning the knob until it opened. When I decided to place a latch on the other side of the door and Leo no longer could let himself in, he was a most bewildered cub. But he resigned himself to this new development when he discovered that, in the main, he still had the run of the house. I never barred him except when I sensed that some guest might be uncomfortable in his presence.

Sometimes I had the feeling that Leo wanted to come upstairs just to see what was going on. Having satisfied himself on that score, and having had his ears rubbed and his back patted, he would retire to the lawn, where he would sit on his haunches and observe the passing scene by the hour.

Martin Johnson and other firsthand observers have written about the insatiable curiosity of lions and I can vouch for the accuracy of their observations. I recall Leo watching the movements of a sparrow for what must have been a half hour or longer. He showed not the slightest interest in reaching for it, and didn't even stir when it came fairly close to him; his role was strictly that of a bird watcher. If it is possible to see curiosity in an animal's expression—and I believe it is—Leo was full of it that day as he cocked his head from side to side as if to say, "How do you manage that flying business? I'm trying to figure out what keeps you from falling when you take to the air." For it seemed to me that that cub's curiosity was at its peak when the sparrow, after hopping about on the grass following a brief flight, was swiftly airborne again, and came down for a quick landing to gobble some morsel he'd spied.

From time to time I have told friends about lions and tigers "talking" to me, and occasionally their reactions have suggested they thought I was indulging in a bit of fantasy. Actually, the big cats do try to "talk" to me. Their lips move and they give forth indescribable little mutterings that can only be called big-cat talk. What I see in their eyes, in their demeanor and general expression clearly indicates that they are trying to tell me something.

Rajah, as striking and powerful a member of the big-cat family as I can recall, "talks" to me constantly. I can't quite make up my mind what Rajah is trying to tell me. But I have a pretty strong hunch that he is asking me to move him to another seat in the arena. He occasionally jumps off his present one before he is cued to come down, and I will make it my business to find out why he would rather be placed elsewhere in the act, assuming I have guessed right about what he is trying to get me to do. My best present guess is that Rajah doesn't want to be too close to another tiger—one he doesn't seem to trust—that is in a position to slash at him from the rear. Once I confirm this I will move Rajah to a pedestal on the other side of the arena.

At this time I am also trying to figure out what a big black-maned lion in my act is trying to communicate to me. Uncued, he sometimes starts whirling around in the manner of Frisco, my spinning tiger, and I am being forced to the conclusion that he is trying to show me that a lion can do the same trick.

Even if I had not read it in Darwin and in the works of other authorities in the field of animal psychology, I would know from experience that the higher mammals are sometimes motivated by jealousy, and it is quite possible that the lion that does those gratuitous whirls likes applause sufficiently—many performing animals seem to love it, as I have pointed out—to make a point of showing me that anything Frisco can do he can do better, or at least as well. Frisco always gets a big hand when he finishes his spinning act, and perhaps there will be no living with that lion until he is permitted to do the same trick and earn the same kind of applause.

The trainer can learn a lot from the animal that is trying to "talk" to him. My act today has a much improved finish because I succeeded in grasping what Pharaoh, who is featured near the end of my act, had been trying to tell me for some time. Occasionally an animal as intelligent as Pharaoh winds up by training the trainer.

I do my best to pick up the "message," but I would hardly claim that I always succeed in doing so on these occasions when I am convinced that the big cats are talking to me.

My mother was incredulous—and on thinking it over I can hardly blame her—when I told her that in some "conversations" I had had with Leo I became convinced that my favorite of all the cubs I have ever raised was trying to get me to teach him how to get a drink of water by himself. Mother was visiting me—(she lives in Bainbridge, Ohio, where I was born) —and at the time of her visit she had been out of touch with my work for several years. Which reminds me—perhaps irrelevantly—that she has seen me perform only a few times and I have a hunch she would have liked to see me enter some other field. Being a good sport, she has never made an issue of it.

Mother thought I was having fun with her when I told her I was so sure I had "read" Leo correctly that he fairly leaped for joy as I showed him how to turn on the cold-water spigot in the kitchen. She requested a demonstration and I gave her one. First I showed her how I had taught the cub, leaning over the sink and cuing Leo to climb up my back until he could reach forward and turn on the tap with a slap of the paw. Then I stepped away from the sink and cued Leo to get a drink all by himself.

The demonstration amused Mother, but not enough to change her previously expressed view that the cub should not have the run of the house. Her first meeting with Leo was not quite a success and because of that I understood how she felt. This was before I discovered that Leo sometimes scared people and before I had installed the latch that prevented him from letting himself into the house from his headquarters below whenever the spirit moved him. Mother had just arrived when Leo, deciding he ought to be on the reception committee, rushed at her from behind and dealt her one of his most affectionate and vigorous greetings, a slap on the thigh with what became known as his "hello paw."

I felt as happy about teaching Leo the difference between the hot and cold water taps as if I had taught him to do cartwheels or to perform on the flying trapeze. Not once did he turn on the wrong faucet or forget what I showed him about how to tilt his head so that the cold-water tap became a sort of drinking fountain. To the layman this will seem unimportant; to the animal trainer seeking confirmation that he has found the key to the mental processes of a certain animal it is one of those little satisfactions that I find hard to explain.

On those days when he had the run of the house, which was most of the time, I found Leo more and more reluctant to retire to his sleeping quarters in the basement when it came time to go to bed. I tried the experiment of arranging sleeping quarters for him on the ground floor. Very much like a child who is loath to go to bed, he indulged in stalling tactics. One night not long after I had fallen asleep I was awakened by the sound of water running in the kitchen. Whether Leo started out by taking a drink of water and then letting the tap run until it attracted my attention I don't know. At any rate, he succeeded in getting me out of bed, and he continued this little game for several nights in a row. I thought I could break him of the habit but discovered I wasn't that good an animal trainer. So I had to return Leo to his sleeping quarters in the basement, always leaving a pan of water for him so that he would have no complaint on that score.

A friend once asked, "Why do you let that pestiferous cub run you ragged?" The answer of course was that Leo, far from being "pestiferous," was a lovable little guy; and, viewing the matter from the practical standpoint, I learned a great deal about lion cubs by observing him. My one regret is that I was unable to find a way of spending several weeks with him exclusively, with a view to keeping a complete record of his activities and his developing personality. I believe a fairly worthwhile contribution to the rapidly growing science of animal behavior might have resulted.

One day I decided to take Leo for a ride in my convertible, with the top down. My decision stemmed from the fact that once as he sat on the lawn on a gusty day I noticed how much he enjoyed sticking his face into the breeze and letting the wind play about at will on his brow, his neck, his ears and seemingly all the rest of him. In an open car, if I had guessed right, he would be able to enjoy himself even more.

That first ride proved that Leo was even more of a breeze-lover than I had thought. I placed him on the seat behind me and he lost no time re-establishing his affectionate nature. We hadn't been in the car more than a few minutes when he placed his paws over my shoulders in a sort of semi-embrace. It was a smart move, enabling him to use me as a means of bracing himself; for thus he was shaken up less and got a more solid ride. When it was safe to do so, I stole an occasional quick glance at him, and I'll never forget the pleased expression on his face as he became more and more wind-blown. He did everything but purr, "talking" to me with animation to indicate his pleasure.

Leo and I began to attract attention. Some people recognized him as a young lion, while others wanted to know what kind of dog he was.

Leo, to show his appreciation, locked his paws together in a tight embrace, necessitating my pulling over to the side of the road before the overdemonstrative cub could interfere with my driving. He was growing rapidly, had great strength in his paws, and one of his more strenuous hugs almost cut off my wind.

I have had a lifetime of experience in communicating with young animals on matters of behavior, and there at the roadside I delivered a little sermon on the folly of choking the driver, illustrating my talk with gestures—a kind of sign language I had developed for Leo's benefit and which he seemed to understand.

Leo got the message. He continued to use my shoulders as supports but discontinued that hugging business.

When you deprive an animal like Leo of one way of showing his affection, he substitutes another; and the first thing I knew he was licking the back of my neck with his rough tongue and irritating the skin. Again I had to pull over for a conference with my riding companion. What I tried to get across to him, by word and gesture, was this:

"Look, Leo, you've got to remember that even a young lion like you has a file-like surface on his tongue. It's good you didn't lick my neck any harder or you might have scuffed off patches of skin. That tongue of yours is quite a contraption; when you are older it will be so powerful you will be able to use it to peel big slabs of meat right off the bone. And since it's raw meat we are talking about, that's quite a stunt. Keep that in mind, will you, lad, the next time you are tempted to give my neck another massaging. It's the only neck I've got."

I've had my successes and failures in making myself un-

derstood by members of the big-cat family, and I was hopeful
that this was going to be one of my triumphs. The responsive gleam in Leo's good eye seemed to say, "Relax, my friend.
I get your point."

During the next few rides Leo remembered my lecture; but
subsequently there was another neck-massaging incident. The
day was windy to begin with, and the minor hurricane I
stirred up as we sped along left Leo so ecstatic that before he
realized what he was doing he was once again stroking the
back of my neck with his tongue, this time with greater vigor,
as he put the full measure of his happiness behind it.

There was a burning sensation all over my nape as once
again I pulled over to the side of the road, and when I ran my
fingers over the area affected I discovered that my loving cub
friend had managed to roll back the skin in several places.
So thereafter when I took Leo for a ride in my open car I
arranged to have someone from the circus's winter quarters
accompany us as protection against the young lion's overdemonstrative nature.

One day my old friend Walter Fuller of the Detroit *News*
visited me to see how I was faring with some new lions and
tigers whose early training I had just begun. Walter is a circus
fan in general and a wild-animal fan in particular, and he
has written some of the most perceptive stories that have appeared about my work. He was pleased to learn that for dinner that night my cook was preparing a roast turkey, to be
stuffed with a dressing Walter particularly likes.

A conversation Walter and I were carrying on in the living
room was interrupted by strange scuffling sounds from the
kitchen. I decided to investigate and left for the kitchen,
Walter right behind me.

We arrived as Leo was pushing the now wingless, neckless
and drumstickless fowl around on the kitchen floor and
skidding after it on the linoleum. It developed that the bird
had been ready for the oven when the cook stepped out of the

room to answer the doorbell. In her absence—(the poor woman, it seems, was stuck with a long-winded door-to-door canvasser)—Leo had walked in, noticed the turkey and made a dash for it. Actually he was merely playing with it, and the game consisted of trying to get it to wrestle with him. When there was no response, he decided this must be something inanimate and began pulling it apart. Drumsticks, wings and neck were scattered about on the linoleum, along with a chunk of the breast. But you could tell at a glance that he hadn't eaten any of the bird he had had so much fun dismembering.

We dismissed Leo and picked up the pieces of turkey. A few minutes later when my astonished cook returned and recovered from the shock of what had happened, she thoroughly scrubbed each and every part of the dismembered fowl, put the pieces together until they fitted neatly (which required a little stitching here and there), swept the floor clean of the stuffing Leo had scattered all over the place, made a fresh batch of same, restuffed the bird and put it in the oven.

Walter and I decided later that night that we had never tasted better turkey, and we have since wondered whether the mauling Leo gave the fowl had not tenderized it and perhaps also subtly added to the flavor.

From Walter Fuller's standpoint the evening had only one unhappy aspect. After dinner Leo ripped Walter's trousers. It was the first time this friendliest of all the cubs I've reared had done anything like this—although even then he had extended his claws almost imperceptibly. Leo had merely been trying to get Walter to play with him, albeit too enthusiastically and too strenuously. But fortunately it proved to be one of those bloodless pants-rips, the skin having been nowhere punctured or scratched. The incident had a certain value as a conversation piece, giving Walter a chance to tell about the time he was attacked by a lion.

The damage to his trousers did not affect Fuller's fondness for Leo, and he made me promise that on my next trip to Detroit I would bring the cub to the *News* office. I kept this promise not long afterward and Leo behaved beautifully—in fact, much too well, Walter thought. *This* was the time and place for that cub to do violence to someone's pants, coat or other wearing apparel. Walter had decided to write something about Leo's visit to the Detroit *News'* editorial rooms, and quite understandably he had hoped that the frisky young lion would do something newsworthy, stipulating only that I not allow Leo to wander into the sanctum sanctorum and scare hell out of the editor-in-chief.

But Leo, as unpredictable as ever, decided to be a little gentleman that day. "He's given me hardly anything to write about," moaned Walter. "Why couldn't he have knocked over the water cooler or at least upset a few wastebaskets? What's more, the photographer assigned to the story won't speak to me. He'd hoped for some good action shots."

Fred Ringler, who for years has operated a drugstore, is another Detroit friend of mine who grew fond of Leo. A few days after the cub had paid his respects to Walter Fuller and his associates at the Detroit *News,* Leo and I called on Fred. It was a Sunday, a day when it is not unusual in certain parts of the city for a pharmacist to place an "out for dinner" sign on his door. Fred had a bit of a romp with Leo and then we departed for dinner, leaving the cub in the back room of the store. (I forgot to tell Fred that Leo knew how to manipulate knobs and open doors!)

When we returned there was a big crowd in front of the Ringler Pharmacy. Leo was in the show window playing with the window display, which by this time he had completely dismantled. At the time of our arrival he was toying with a large dummy bottle of simulated pills which was lying on its side. Anything that rolled had a fascination for Leo. With a slap of the paw he pushed the bottle away from him, and when it came to a halt he put himself into a stalking posture, tried without much success to look ferocious, and suddenly pounced, while his audience howled with delight.

Fred and I pushed our way through the crowd to the store's entrance, and when we were inside he said, "The people are enjoying this so much it's a shame to break it up, but I'd better before I get arrested for blocking traffic."

I have always been interested in the effect of applause on wild animals. Some respond to it, others do not. As I stood and watched Leo before I removed him from that window, what struck me most was his seeming enjoyment of his audience's enthusiasm. Every time he picked up something in the window and threw or pushed or slapped it—and once when he knocked over a cardboard sign—there was a burst of handclapping mingled with cheers.

I wouldn't think of attempting a scientific explanation of just what it was the applause touched off in Leo's brain, but I got the impression that he loved it and was trying to earn more and more, as when, running out of ideas for wrecking the Ringler Pharmacy's window display, he dealt that big pill bottle still another whack and sent it spinning, to the accompaniment of new bursts of handclaps and raucous laughter.

Leo had as sensitive an ear as any big-cat cub I have ever owned. He could tell the sound of one automobile from another. If a stranger drove up my driveway and Leo was on the grounds, he would investigate or not, according to his mood. But the second he heard my car drive in he would come bounding toward it, and as I stepped out he would come charging at me, the gleam in his good eye communicating "How about rolling around on the grass with me, pal?" Leo would quickly get the game going, and since I wasn't always dressed for this kind of roughhouse, it proved a good thing for the local dry-cleaning establishment I patronized.

Leo was now growing so rapidly that before long when he leaped at me, the combination of his weight—now about 150 pounds—and the impact of his charge was enough to throw me heavily, especially when he came at me before I could brace myself.

The time came when I had to install Leo in a cage, which I did reluctantly. Whenever I approached his cage he would pick up my scent and make such a commotion that I would make an occasional exception to my own rule and release him from confinement for one of those wrestling matches he loved so much. But only when I had work clothes on, because Leo, even though he always kept his claws retracted during these workouts, played hard, and in my effort to respond, buttons would pop and seams rip.

Finally the day came when I knew that I could no longer keep Leo. If I continued to keep him in a cage and ignored his pleas for release, which my better judgment told me was the thing to do, he would be unhappy. Years of experience told me it would be unwise to let him roam free any longer. I was reasonably sure I could keep him under control myself, though this would become increasingly difficult. One can't overemphasize the fact that, where wild animals are concerned, anything can happen; and I had to think of the possibility of an unexpected incident, brought on by unpredictable developments, that might endanger the lives of others.

One phase of the trainer's job is to outbluff his charges. It is hard to bluff an animal born in captivity. It's quite a job to convince such an animal that man is very formidable; he is more likely to consider man a softy.

Animals fresh from the jungle can be fooled. Man is something they know nothing about and is therefore something to be studied, and, if he is forceful enough to take command, to be treated with the same kind of respect an unknown quantity is accorded in the wilds.

Of course, Leo was an extreme case. I had made more of a pet of him than any dog I have ever owned. If I had decided to keep him as a performer, I would have had to wait until he was three or four years old.

And then I would have run the risk of trying to make a performer of a pet. This would have been hazardous for both Leo and me. If while my act was in progress he had been seized with a sudden whim to wrestle me, the second he had me down other lions would pile on—for this would look like a fight, and lions are gang fighters. What would have happened to Leo and me is anybody's guess.

I decided that a good zoo would be the best place for Leo, and gave him to Chicago's Lincoln Park Zoo, one of the best in the country.

When the following year I found myself in Chicago, I was tempted to visit Leo—I loved that cub and missed him—but I came to my senses and decided against it.

For once you say good-by to an animal, it's best to leave things that way. I had heard that Leo had adjusted nicely to his new surroundings and was enjoying life to the fullest.

On May 28, 1934, the famous Dionne quintuplets were born —five baby girls, who were christened Annette, Cécile, Emilie, Marie and Yvonne. Not many months afterward one of the lionesses in the Clyde Beatty-Cole Brothers Circus got into the spirit of the thing and gave birth to a litter of five cubs—all females (or so we thought).

Naturally this gave our publicity department a great opportunity. And, as is well known, circus press agents live for such moments.

A litter of five is not uncommon in the African veld and other haunts of the lion. In fact, in the wilds a lion mother, like the ordinary house cat, produces two to six kittens. But the birth of five lion babies in captivity was unusual. And of course it was a perfect tie-up with the miracle that Mother Dionne had wrought in Canada.

There was an immediate demand that we put the lion quints on display, but anyone who knows anything about wild animals realizes what a mistake it would have been to do this before these delicate little creatures—each of which weighed less than two pounds at birth—were permitted to grow and gain strength.

These lion quints were born shortly before the close of the

circus season, and I sent them to my home in Rochester, Indiana, with an experienced animal man to look after them. The plan was to put them on exhibit in a cage with a glass front when I started the first of my post-season engagements in Detroit.

Once the season was over I would be able to look after them myself and satisfy myself that they were strong enough to travel before putting them on display. What agony it was for our press agents, who seldom had a story as good as this, to wait for me to give the signal that would permit them to pour forth the superlatives that would proclaim this as "the ninth wonder of the world." (They conveniently designated the Dionne quintuplets as the eighth, while our lion counterparts of Annette, Cécile, Emilie, Marie and Yvonne were to be announced as next in line.)

Needless to say, my home in Indiana was quickly dominated by those five little balls of fluff. It became a nursery for baby lions.

Everyone in the house—my wife, the cook, the handy man and even our Gordon setter, Lucky—was affected. But Lucky most of all.

I've owned a number of dogs over the years and developed an affection for all of them; but I never had one I liked better than Lucky, easily the gentlest dog I have ever known.

The lion quintet soon made a playmate of Lucky—or tried to. When they saw him lying down, they would crawl all over him. Not once did Lucky so much as growl at them; and as for nipping them or dealing them an occasional slap of the paw, that was unthinkable. Lucky suffered in silence.

Time and again my quints decided that Lucky was their mother, and they would crawl under him and probe for a place to nurse. Lucky, too gentle to push them aside, would try to edge away from them, but this he found difficult to do. They refused to be dismissed and kept pace with his withdrawal. Half-defeated, Lucky would now and then halt in his tracks and let them continue to run their little snouts under his belly in quest of teats; then, with a look of annoyance that seemed to say, "How long does a manly he-dog have to put up with this?" he would take to his heels, the cubs in pursuit. He would seek out a hiding place where he felt reasonably safe from these furry little intruders.

I witnessed this performance several times and marveled at Lucky's patience and understanding. But for all his forbearance, he knew when he had had enough—and more than once he gave me what seemed a reproachful look, as if to say:

"Really, boss, you should not have let me in for this."

Lucky and I were good pals, and usually when I was around the house he liked to be near me; but even my presence was not enough of an attraction to keep him in the house when the quints overdid their determination to adopt him as a steady companion and playmate. More than once they drove the dog to the lonely grandeur of his kennel on the lawn.

Inevitably the cubs discovered this hideout. One day when Lucky was having a mid-afternoon nap they invaded the kennel and crawled all over him until they had wakened him, their manner seeming to say, "That's enough of dozing, Sleepyhead. How about a bit of a romp?"

Lucky quickly took in the situation, gently extricated himself from the clutches of the playful five and escaped to a neighbor's back yard.

That poor distracted Gordon setter, after much experimentation, decided that his safest retreat was the upper floor of the house; and even though he was sometimes in the way as he lay stretched out in the area at the top of the stairs, I understood his problem and let him stay there. Subsequently I taught him to leave enough space to permit access to the stairway.

The closest I've come to seeing a dog gloat was the day Lucky stood atop that stairway watching the ineffectual attempts of the miniature five to get up those steps and pay him a visit. First one, then another of the cubs would hook its tiny claws into the carpeted rise of the first step in an effort to scramble up, presumably as a prelude to negotiating step number two; but none of them could make it. Lucky's expression was something to behold as each of the quintet made a stab at it and finally tumbled back exhausted.

A few weeks later there was an alarmed look on Lucky's face as the quints negotiated the first few steps. He relaxed and seemed to breathe a sigh of relief when, too tired to sustain this newest effort, they gave up.

Lucky, of course, was due inevitably to suffer another invasion of privacy. Not long afterward the resolute five managed to climb and tumble their way up those stairs, and Lucky's expression eloquently reflected his consternation. As he retreated he seemed to be asking, "Isn't there any place where a dog can be alone with his thoughts?"

But Lucky was a philosophic dog and he knew how to adjust to circumstances. In the spirit of "if you can't fight 'em, join 'em," he decided that they might as well all be friends, especially as the cubs were now of a size where it was becoming fun to play with them—though of course as lions they were still tiny.

Now that they had the know-how and the strength to climb, they found it easy to scramble up the side of a sofa where I occasionally stretched out to read. The reading stopped as soon as they discovered me. Up they came, one at a time, to be petted. They seemed to know that if they flopped around on me long enough I would finally surrender and get up and take them outside and play with them on the grass.

My five little lions made their first public appearance in a display case with a glass front at a post-season engagement in Detroit. Charming enough to make a hit on their own, they had the added advantage that the Dionne quintuplets were constantly in the news in those days. To some circus-goers, lion quints seemed as remarkable as the human variety, although, as I have pointed out, they were not.

One day I made the discovery that two of our "world-renowned five little lion sisters" were boys. Only the most minute examination would have established early in the life of these cubs whether they were male or female, and that would have meant more handling than would have been good for them at that particular time.

To this day I am not sure how it was originally decided that our lion quints were girls; but I had read it in the newspapers and I suppose our publicity department, giving us the benefit of the doubt, had decided that these baby lions were females, thus giving themselves a continuing tie-up with the Dionne story.

The discovery that two of the girls were boys gave me an excuse to withdraw them as a circus attraction. They drew great crowds, but if we took them on an extensive tour, which would involve many one-night stands, they would be subjected to too many changes of temperature—also they would take too much jouncing and shaking up in the process of being moved daily from the circus grounds to the railroad cars, and back again. Some of the roadbeds we traveled were none too smooth and the rough ride they were sure to get over certain stretches of track would not be good for them. Babes of the big-cat family pick up infections quickly; and one reason why I have succeeded in raising so many of them is that I have always kept this possibility in mind. One of the best safeguards is to minimize travel.

I also feared that some humorless scientist might decide to brand me as a nature faker in a solemn statement pointing out that lion quintuplets are quite common in the lion's native haunts in Africa. I had mentioned this several times in newspaper interviews, although I did add that this was the first time I had heard of the birth of a litter of five in captivity.

The press quoted me accurately on the lion quints, although some reporters wrote tongue-in-cheek stories implying that these four-legged quints were as important as Mrs. Dionne's two-legged ones. I've had plenty of experience at seeing such kidding stories picked up by overly sober-minded eggheads and grimly dissected by them, so I was relieved when my five little lions ceased to be "that greatest of all menagerie attractions in the long history of circusdom, the Dionne Quintuplets of the Jungle World."

Things have a way of happening to me in Detroit. Another time when I was showing there I had three tiger cubs that were real charmers. They made a big hit with my friend Harvey Mack of that city. Harvey's wife was in the hospital and when I asked him to suggest something I could send her to cheer her up, he replied, "One of those cubs."

I laughed, thinking he was clowning, whereupon Harvey said, "I don't really mean 'send.' Let's take one over to her. She still thinks the most lovable creature she ever saw was the tiger cub you showed us a few years ago. These new ones are even cuter. What do you say?"

There was no mistaking Harvey's genuine belief that if we smuggled a tiger cub into his wife's room it would do more to give her a lift than anything else. She was not suffering from an infectious disease, so this would not involve exposing the cubs to trouble-making germs. I'd do anything, however foolish, for a friend, so I agreed to cooperate with Harvey Mack in his plan to sneak a tiger cub into his wife's room in the hospital. It was January and I was playing a post-season date in Detroit, a two weeks' engagement.

If it had not been overcoat time we would not have been able to pull off our coup.

The situation called for deception, since we were both reasonably sure that the hospital's rules governing visitors were not meant to include tigers. It was decided that Harvey would carry the cub, a little fellow about as big as a medium-size dog, under his overcoat.

We got past the desk in the main entrance, and from there into the elevator, without incident. Then, for some unaccountable reason, as Harvey stepped out of the elevator into the corridor he broke into a run as he headed for his wife's room. I followed suit, though it was not quite clear to me why my friend was running.

Excited and out of breath, Harvey opened his coat and dropped the tiger cub on Mrs. Mack's bed. All three of us—Harvey, the cub and I—made such a sudden appearance it's a wonder the patient didn't swoon. As a matter of fact, she almost did—from sheer delight.

The noise we made in clattering down the hardwood floor of the corridor attracted the attention of the floor supervisor, who made her appearance as Mrs. Mack, cuddling the tiger, exclaimed, "My baby!" The astonishment of the supervisor could not have been any greater if indeed Harvey's wife had just given birth to that tiger. Mrs. Mack continued to cuddle her "baby" as the supervisor, standing there in blank amazement, still found it hard to believe that what she saw on the patient's bed was a tiger cub.

Pulling herself together, the floor boss told us we'd better get that animal out of the room before the hospital's top management learned what was going on. Then, momentarily forgetting her official capacity, she smiled as her patient kept fondling the cub. And when Mrs. Mack exclaimed, "Isn't he cute!" the supervisor expressed her full agreement.

I'm not sure how it happened, but before many minutes had elapsed the room was full of nurses admiring Mrs. Mack's "baby." The news spread fast and some of the ambulatory patients joined the gathering, which overflowed into the hall.

The supervisor, realizing that something had to be done, disbanded the cub's impromptu audience. But, noting how much pleasure the patient was deriving from her unorthodox visitor, Madam Supervisor told us we could keep the cub in the room "a little longer," after which she expected us to exercise as much ingenuity in spiriting the tiger out of the hospital as we had in sneaking it in. I will always think of her as a good sport.

In the elevator, on the way out, the cub worked its way up under Harvey Mack's overcoat and poked its head out to see what was going on. Harvey quickly covered up the inquisitive animal. But not before a fellow elevator rider, an elderly man with a sense of fun, had caught a glimpse of the tiger and remarked, "I didn't know they treated animals here. Who's your veterinarian?"

The animal psychologists haven't yet gotten around to figuring out what thoughts a baby tiger has on being smuggled into a hospital. When they do, I don't want to hear the answer. Some of those cubs have a wise, perceptive look and I wouldn't be surprised to learn that they are capable of thinking caustic thoughts about the things people do.

During the winter of 1961 I was aboard a freighter with my lions and tigers bound for Honolulu, to begin there a tour of the Hawaiian Islands with my circus. In my big-cat entourage were Princess, a nursing tigress, and her three cubs.

There was a junior officer on the ship—let's call him Mr. Smith—who was as fond of animals as anyone I've ever known. It would be hard to describe adequately the delight that was written all over that man's face the first time he saw Princess and her babies. It was one of those cases of love at first sight, and from then on he spent so much of his time watching the tiger quartet that I began to fear he might be neglecting his duties.

He was captivated when I explained why I had brought the tigress and her brood with me. Princess was a beautiful animal and with her charming youngsters would make a first-rate display in our menagerie tent. She was a good mother, so I had not found it necessary to separate her from the cubs. This has to be done when a tiger mother is the nervous, excitable type that might accidentally roll over on her babies and crush them, which has been known to happen in the native habitats of these striped cats as well as in captivity. Occasionally, too, there is a cannibal mother who eats her young. From the beginning Princess had handled her brood so intelligently that it was obvious she could be trusted to take good care of them.

Smith haunted the quarters where I kept Princess and her children. Through the freighter's kitchen steward I had arranged to have the nursing mother receive an adequate daily supply of milk, which the enthusiastic junior officer would sometimes deliver himself. He just couldn't keep away from that tigress and her cubs.

I also fed Princess meat, and Smith seemed horrified to learn that it was horse meat. Even when I explained that it was the best government-inspected grade and that the big cats throve on it, he seemed to think I should do a little better for so noble a mother, and one day he turned up with a ten-pound roast. He actually indulged in baby talk, this rugged seaman, as he stood beside Princess's cage and explained that this was a special present for her which he hoped would give her extra strength to nurse her darling itty-bitty babies. Several times he also brought her thick juicy steaks.

Some people show their love for animals by overfeeding them, and though I recognized in Smith a reasonably knowledgeable animal fan, his excessive enthusiasm worried me a little and I instructed my cage boys to keep an eye on him to be sure he didn't give Princess too much to eat.

I don't know whether Smith was on leave when we opened in Honolulu or whether he had a lot of time between trips, but I do know that he was on hand daily during the two weeks we played there. The man had become tiger-smitten and wanted to buy one of the cubs and raise it as a pet. While he was one of those people you couldn't help liking, I wasn't enthusiastic about his proposal. His love of those tigers was touching, but how could I be sure he would be able to take proper care of such an animal? It takes knowledge and patience. So I told him—thinking this would prove an easy out—that I couldn't very well let him have a cub until they were about three and a half months old and ready for weaning. This meant a long wait and I thought that would discourage him.

But Smith was the type you couldn't discourage. He kept following me around until the cubs were weaned and again appealed to me to let him buy one of them. They were a frisky trio and frolicked and played much as puppies do in a dog-shop window. They were beginning to take on weight, and though I found myself weakening in the presence of such persistence, I was afraid that in another three or four months Smith would find his pet—assuming I let him have one—somewhat unmanageable.

Smith's persistence eventually wore me down. I finally agreed to let him have one of the cubs. If he wasn't the happiest man in Hawaii, he came pretty close. There are people who think they love wild animals and others who really do. Smith certainly behaved like an authentic member of the second group.

I gave him detailed instructions on the care and feeding of the cub. I also briefed him on things to watch for as the animal grew older. There would come a time when it would no longer be safe to let this young tiger roam free. I strongly recommended that when that time came he sell or give it to a good zoo, and I gave him the names of several I thought would be glad to acquire so fine a specimen.

I have often wondered where that tiger is. At this writing he would be full grown and, judging by the early signs, a handsome animal.

I have lost contact with Smith and don't know where he is. Should he hear about this book and read it I hope he will get in touch with me and let me know where that tiger is.

When I was with the Hagenbeck-Wallace show we had considerable success in breeding the big cats, and litters of lion and tiger cubs were quite common. Whenever I sensed that the mother of a brood could not be depended upon to look after them properly, I had the little ones removed from her cage. It was not a question of whether a particular lioness or tigress had the maternal instinct or not. I make this point because I am always asked questions along that line when I speak of separating a big-cat mother from her young, which should never be done unless it is clearly indicated as a necessary step.

In captivity the lioness is a better mother than the tigress. It is more a matter of temperament than anything else. The caged lioness is less nervous, less excitable, than the caged tigress.

I imagine that is why I have found the lioness a bit more far-sighted—more inclined, for instance, to see where her cubs are before she stretches out or rolls over on her side, alert to the possibility that she might make a sudden move that could crush the life out of one or more of them.

As the foregoing indicates, I have had to separate tigresses from their young oftener than I have had to remove a lioness's brood. But though the undependable lion mother happens less frequently, she does exist and she can be spotted as quickly as her tiger counterpart.

Once I had such a situation involving a new lion mother. I removed her and tried the experiment of a substitute mother in the form of a collie that was in the show's dog act, a good-natured animal that had just given birth and had a goodly supply of milk.

All went well the first few days. Then the tiny claws of the baby lions, which quickly develop a needle-like sharpness, made themselves felt as they probed for the big dog's teats. I well remember the look this collie gave me the first time this happened. Her expression practically said, "Wait a minute! What are you putting over on me?"

Thereafter we made a practice of holding the cubs in such a manner that they could nurse without pricking Mother Collie's tender underside. Subsequently I hit upon the idea of having booties made, which were slipped over the cubs' paws and tied in place. From that time on the tiny lions could do their probing without scratching one of our best performing dogs.

Circus people—both performers and general personnel—love dogs. The canine population of any show such as ours—pets, plus the inevitable dog act—is quite considerable. In those Hagenbeck-Wallace days it was not often that we didn't have a nursing dog of sufficient size—thoroughbred or mixed breed —that could be pressed into service as a lion or tiger mother.

Someday someone will write an article—or a small book— about the anecdote-laden dog population of circuses. It's a good subject. For instance, I can no more think of "Kilowatt" Fitzpatrick, chief electrician of the Clyde Beatty-Cole Bros. Circus, without a dog trailing after him than I can of a circus without clowns.

The reasons why more big-cat cubs were born in the Hagenbeck-Wallace Circus than in my present one is that in those days I had lionesses in my act. Frank Bostock, the renowned British animal trainer, urged me early in my career to remove the lionesses, insisting that they added new hazards to an already hazardous act without contributing much from the spectator standpoint. His point was that a female lion in heat excited the males to such an extent that sooner or later the disruption of the act would be inevitable, and I would be in serious danger when I tried to restore order and get the sex-disturbed animals to concentrate on performing. Eventually I took Bostock's advice and stopped using lionesses.

Oddly enough, I have never found it necessary to dispense with tigresses in my act for similar reasons. I use male and female tigers in the arena today as I did thirty years ago. The striped cats seem to have inhibitions that the less self-conscious lions do not have, and they reserve sex relations for the privacy of the cage.

Over the years the tigers in my act have produced a great many cubs. One of the most interesting of the more recent litters—a trio—arrived November 13, 1963. They were born to Princess, the same wonderful mother that gave birth to the baby tigers described earlier in this chapter.

I have many friends in Florida. The winter quarters of our circus is in Deland, and the Miami Tent of the Circus Saints and Sinners, named for me, is one of the biggest and most active in the country.

So when I was asked to head the annual New Year's Eve Orange Bowl Parade—the one that took place the night of December 31, 1963—I agreed. The committee in charge asked me to ride in a howdah on the back of one of my circus's biggest elephants, and in each hand hold one of Princess's offspring.

The more I thought about this proposal the more ambitious it seemed. It would be a simple matter to get the right elephant. I planned to use the most striking-looking and reliable one in our show, Big Sid, who starred in *Jumbo* and stole the picture. But I made a firm decision against using *two* tiger cubs.

To those unfamiliar with the trouble-making potential of a tiger that is only seven weeks old, it probably does not sound like much of an undertaking to hold one in each hand for the duration of a parade (a rather long one, in this case). After all, as one of the city fathers declared, "They're only babies!" It was thoughtfully pointed out that I could set one down on the floor of the howdah when holding both became too much of a burden; but at the risk of having the committee think I had turned chicken I voted against displaying more than one tiger cub, a fortunate decision, it later developed.

Well, the evening of December 31 rolled around, the parade was forming and there I was ascending the ladder to the howdah on Big Sid's back. Ronny, one of my cage boys, followed me up the rungs, carrying the little tiger I had selected for this outing. Before he could hand it to me, the cub, excited by the pre-parade uproar and the television cameras, the shouts of the crews and the bright lights, tried to wriggle out of Ronny's grasp and in so doing scratched and clawed the young man, inflicting superficial though painful injuries. The scrappy little cat—he was immediately named Spitfire by the press, a name that stuck—was lashing out in all directions with all four

paws out of sheer nervousness and bewilderment. The cub, up
to that time, had been easy to handle. All baby tigers are potential spitfires, but my particular one that night was more like
a frightened child.

Once I got the cub inside the howdah, I managed to calm
him down. His big amber eyes reflected his pleasure as I
rubbed first one ear, then the other. I tested him to see
whether I could hold him up with one hand for the benefit
of the cameramen and wave with the other, as one of the parade officials suggested when I chickened out on the two-cub
deal. But I realized as Spitfire squirmed and twisted and I felt
the ripple of his strong young muscles that it would not be possible to hold him that way for more than a few seconds at a
time, that it would require two hands to do the job with any
degree of safety.

Half the bands in America were in that parade and they
seemed to be tuning up simultaneously as my puzzled little
cub gave me a troubled look that appeared to say, "That racket
is terrible. Would you mind asking those musicians to pipe
down?"

At last the parade was under way and we were swinging
down Biscayne Boulevard. I guess I'll never outlive my love
of a parade and the tingling sensation that goes up and down
my spine as a good band strikes up and plays a stirring march.
There were many fine bands on hand that night and countless floats that showed imagination. Light seemed to be stream-
ing from everywhere. And the hubbub continued. Still and
movie cameramen and television crewmen were yelling, "Hold
him up, Clyde!" and as I held Spitfire as high as I could, one
of his slashing paws struck the band of my wrist watch,
snapped it and sent the watch crashing to the pavement below.
It was a good watch; the manufacturer proudly claimed a lot
for it, but not that it would survive a fall from a howdah on
an elephant's back. A helpful photographer picked up the
pieces and gave them to me later.

This development gave Gene Miller of the Miami *Herald*

an opportunity to refer to me as an animal trainer who "didn't know what time it was." I am always glad to provide an opportunity for the press.

As the parade swung past Bayfront Park with its towering royal palms, the combination of the roar of the crowd in the bleachers to the east and the crash of cymbals and the beat of drums was the signal for Spitfire to go into a new and more sustained paroxysm of excitement. He wriggled and squirmed and kept moving his forepaws up and down like a politician waving to a throng in which he didn't want to miss a single voter. He continued this until he almost slipped out of my fingers. (I made a point of not gripping him too hard, as I didn't want to hurt him.) To play it safe, I deposited him on the floor of the howdah. This would give us both a respite.

As the procession moved down Flagler Street through the canyon of light from the brilliantly illuminated stores and hotels on both sides of the thoroughfare, the cameramen started yelling: "Where's that cub?", "We want the tiger!" etc., etc.

So I reached down and produced Spitfire. Blinking as this new blaze of light hit him, and wriggling and writhing with renewed vigor, he made his most determined effort to shake loose.

As I tightened my hold on him the cub did a most undignified thing. Apparently unable to control his bowels and bladder, he let go. I will spare the reader a description of what my shirt and breeches—the all-white uniform I wear in the arena—looked like. Suffice it to say that I was a mess.

While this was going on, the cameramen were shouting for more shots. I put the cub back on the floor of the howdah and began wiping myself off. Some of the photographers were unaware of my predicament, perhaps momentarily blinded by the dazzle of lights—or if they were aware, they were pulling my leg. At any rate, they kept shouting, "We want Spitfire! Hold him up!" I was more than willing to comply, because by this time the cub had discovered my ankles and legs and was giving them a workout with his sharp little claws.

There were predictable jokes as I rode along on my favorite elephant holding the little tiger aloft. "Why didn't you diaper him?" someone yelled. As I caught the comments of those spectators who were close enough to see what had happened to me, I hit upon the idea of holding the baby tiger so that he shielded my once white shirt.

If the parade functionaries who tried to persuade me to hold and display *two* baby tigers should happen to read this book, I trust they will understand why I decided to bring only one.

When they were a little over four months old, Princess's youngsters had developed so much personality I decided to have them photographed for this book.

First I wanted some action shots of their mother, so I ran all four into the arena. I signaled the mother to a pedestal, then deposited the cubs some five yards off, hoping the ball I gave them to play with would keep them quiet.

As the photographer got his camera ready, I cued Princess off the pedestal and soon had her doing the rollover. The youngsters, thinking they had been separated from their mother long enough, came loping over to see what was going on. Two of them jumped on her stomach as she rolled over, and one of them started biting her tail.

This is considered good clean fun in the tiger world. But, like the true artist she is, Princess didn't want to be interrupted while pursuing her art, so she let out a yip that apparently meant "Scat!" At any rate, the playful trio went galloping off and allowed mama to do her stuff.

A few minutes later they were back, trying to get their mother to play with them. She was about to drive them off again when there was a clatter of hoofs outside the arena that had an unsettling effect on Princess, perhaps because of its suddenness. The tigress was on the floor of the arena at that particular moment executing a series of rollovers. She scrambled to her feet and hurled herself against the bars of the arena, where twenty feet away she could see one of the horses in the equestrian act go trotting by.

Princess hit the arena with such force it swayed. Although as usual the sections of that heavy metal enclosure were solidly clamped together, I thought for a moment that the section the tigress hit with the great forward thrust of her 450 pounds would shake loose or that perhaps the whole arena would come toppling down. At any rate, Princess wound up leaning against the side of the cage, her forefeet propping her up as she stood there full length glaring in the direction the horse went.

With characteristic imitativeness the cubs assumed similar positions, but as they looked out through the bars they were too happy to do any glaring. After holding the pose for perhaps nine or ten seconds, one of the trio decided to scamper over for another nip at her mother's tail. The other two trotted off after her and soon the three youngsters got their mother to join them in a romp, which seemed to take her mind off the horse that had angered her.

An interesting study in supply and demand is a big-cat mother whose cubs continue to suck at her teats after her milk has been drained. The odds are two to one that the youngsters have had enough, but they keep probing for more milk until mama is compelled to call a halt and shake them off. If they persist, she may have to shake them off again and again.

To the cubs, who do not require any more nourishment, this becomes a game; and how much disciplining they get— by which I mean the equivalent of a spanking—depends on the amount of patience the mother has.

I love to watch a lion mother pick up her young when they have finished nursing and "burp" them. One by one she grips them loosely in her mouth and gently shakes them.

Once after one of my lion mothers, a most conscientious one, had burped her four cubs, they started working at her underside again—either because they wanted more milk or felt like playing. They kept it up until the lioness's nipples were sore. She moved away from the overbusy quartet and stretched out to rest. When they followed her and started working away at her underside again, she dealt them each a whack. She hit one of them harder than she had intended and sent it sprawling.

Eventually I was forced to remove all four from their mother's cage. They were driving her crazy and I feared that sooner or later she would lose her temper completely and seriously injure one or all of her youngsters.

Although I have publicly expressed myself on the subject many times, people continue to ask me about the advisability of raising big-cat cubs as pets. As a supplement to the random remarks I have made in these pages, I submit some light-hearted verses on the theme written by an old friend of mine who says they are based more or less on things he has heard me say from time to time. I don't know how good a poet he is, but I commend him for getting so many accurate observations into a piece of humorous writing. Here is a sharply cut version of the original, presented, at the author's request, anonymously:

> I bought a tiny lion cub, he made a wondrous pet,
> But did he have an appetite! He et and et and et
> Until it looked as if he'd plunge his master deep in debt.
> His hunger was a constant thing, to me it was no joke,
> I conjured up a vision sad of someday going broke . . .
> At first I bottle-fed him, which the neighbors thought was cute,
> But later on for nippled milk he didn't give a hoot.
> He graduated to a plate, which naturally he busted,
> And from that day with crockery no longer was he trusted . . .
> I next employed a wooden bowl, but as that cub expanded
> His appetite for seas of milk a bigger dish demanded.

And so I bought a basin big of sparkling white enamel
From which he lapped the lactic fluid much like a thirsty camel.
He stepped into that basin, yes, and drank and splashed and drank,
And when he'd finished with his meal the nearby walls were dank . . .
When he was only three months old he lapped a gallon a day,
An item that began to dent my not excessive pay . . .
I also fed the little imp a midday meal of steak,
Chopped fine, so when he ate too fast there'd be no belly-ache.
He loved to leap, and leap he did all over everything—
One day he made the mantelpiece in one tremendous spring
And sent a lovely Chinese vase a-crashing to the floor,
A family heirloom (Ming, no less!) that's gone forevermore.
He also scratched the furniture and chewed up rugs and shoes
Till I was just about to sing *The Lion Puppy Blues.*
He pulled my draperies to the floor and ripped them into shreds,
Then fell asleep amidst the ruins, which made the best of beds . . .
Housebreaking him was quite a job. At times he would forget,
And then a sofa or a floor was suddenly soaking wet . . .
I never knew that cub to show a single vicious sign,
Yet when we'd play, his little claws, so needle-like and fine,
Would innocently tear my clothes and leave me full of scratches
Until my suits and diaphragm were appliquéd with patches . . .
I loved that cub but knew ere long I'd have to give him up,
For soon he'd be a full-grown lion, no longer just a pup.
I gave him to a public zoo and when I came to call
He greeted me so joyfully he nearly made me bawl . . .

These verses wind up by recommending that people in quest of pets dismiss from their minds the wild-animal category and content themselves with such old reliables as dogs and house cats.

This makes sense to me, although I'd like to add this thought: if you have decided that your pet *must* be a cat and you want something larger than the familiar pussycat, why not an ocelot, assuming you can afford one? These spotted leopardlike felines that range in length from about two-and-a-half to three feet are almost unfailingly handsome and make wonderful pets. I prefer the South American variety. There is a growing number of ocelot clubs in the United States and any one of them will be glad to supply information on the subject.

4. A Trainer's Mistakes Can Be Costly

Excitement in Honolulu – The Lion That Bossed Another – The Day the Boss and His Stooge Almost Got Me – Was Sultan Trying to Save Me?

I HAD A serious accident in Honolulu in February 1961. I came close to losing my right eye and might have lost my life.

This is what happened:

My lions were on their pedestals and I began bringing them down for the so-called "laydown," in which I range them in a straight line across the floor, each animal stretched out on its belly with forepaws extended. It is a position the animals find comfortable and relaxing once they decide to respond to the gestures by means of which I convey to them that the laydown is about to begin.

From the audience standpoint this seemingly simple formation can be exciting. It is one I am seldom able to get the lions to do without some "action" resulting.

Sometimes, for instance, a lion that has taken his place in the line gets restless, scrambles to his feet and starts wandering around. If he happens to be in the path of one of his co-performers who has just left his pedestal and is about to take his place in the forming tableau on the floor, they might collide or perhaps only graze each other. If they are friends, nothing will happen. If there is a grudge between them and they happen to be carrying on one of those inexplicable arena feuds, a fight usually results. Lions are temperamentally geared for combat. And once a scrap starts most of them choose up sides and get into it. It is as natural for a lion to fight as it is for him to eat. It is the trainer's responsibility to anticipate these incipient brawls and prevent them or break them up fast when this can be done.

That night in Honolulu all my lions had come off their pedestals for the laydown except Brutus. This puzzled me because I had trained him to come down just before Pharaoh and he had become letter-perfect in this maneuver.

But the big cats, like people, are sometimes absent-minded. Occasionally the roar of a big crowd will cause an animal's thoughts to wander, and we were playing to a packed house. It is not unusual, in a situation of this kind, for a lion or a tiger to forget that he is supposed to keep his eyes on what is going on in the arena so he'll know what to do next.

Curiosity is another factor. I agree completely with Martin Johnson that lions are constitutionally curious about practically everything that is going on around them. Several times during performances I had seen Brutus turn around on his pedestal to study the audience, and he may have been preoccupied with something along that line when he should have been concentrating on the laydown.

At any rate, there he was on his pedestal when supposedly the "last man on the totem pole," Pharaoh, was already stretched out on the floor in the "lion line." Pharaoh, tired of waiting for Brutus to descend, had made up his mind to wait no longer. He looked at me as if to say, "Sorry, Boss, but I thought it was the best thing to do under the circumstances."

Pharaoh is my most dependable lion. The biggest and most powerful beast in the act, he performs with spirit and never makes any trouble. More than any lion I have ever trained, he has curbed the fighting instinct. He gets into very few brawls, but he is a strict disciplinarian and when one of the other lions—perhaps a newcomer to the act—makes the mistake of advancing toward him with an angry growl and bared fangs, Pharaoh takes care of the situation by sending the offender spinning with a slap of one of his mighty paws. He has more natural dignity than any big cat I have ever handled. He comports himself with a kind of majesty that almost seems a reminder to the other animals that he expects them to be respectful in his presence.

Pharaoh is seldom challenged. Among his co-performers there are some pretty tough lions, but they don't seem to want to tangle with him. He is so sure of himself and so confident that his authority will be respected that, having sent the offender sprawling, he goes about his business, sometimes insultingly turning his back on the animal he has whacked. He seldom goes in for such disciplinary measures unless he is personally involved. If two other lions want to scrap, he leaves them to their own devices, depending on me to break it up.

Once I got Brutus's attention that night in Honolulu, I had no trouble getting him to respond. He looked around for Pharaoh, his expression suggesting puzzlement that Pharaoh's seat was unoccupied. A crack of the whip was all that was needed to bring his mind into focus and to start him loping down the stairway of pedestals. He came at me with a rush as if trying to make up for lost time.

I backed away, not wanting him to lunge at my chair so hard he might knock it out of my hand. Then I stood my ground and let him "bounce" me, as we animal trainers say. It is another way of saying I let him charge me. Audiences love it and so does a zestful performer like Brutus who enjoys a good workout.

I was set for him when he moved in fast and dealt the chair a hefty wallop that cracked one of the legs. But I was able to hang onto this shield of mine and that's what counts. I use about a hundred of these reinforced kitchen chairs per season, and if Brutus felt like putting a leg of this one out of commission, that was all right with me.

It was a game for both of us—one in which I could not relax my vigilance because in my curious field the unexpected has a way of happening. I never know what form it will take; and I'm beginning to believe after years of sudden surprises that I'll have to adjust to regarding the unexpected as something to expect, if that doesn't sound too contradictory.

I tried to move Brutus backward a few feet, but he wouldn't give ground, so I let him continue to "fight" me where we stood. He roared as he lashed out with his paws and the audience howled its approval.

To avoid overexciting him, I stood stock-still for a moment and managed to get him to follow suit, using my whip as a pacifier by stroking the top of his head with it. Then I tried again to get him to take his place in the line of lions stretched out on the floor.

But Brutus wanted more excitement. After a brief respite he resumed his forcing tactics and was so determined about it I was forced to give ground.

Just as a boxer must know at all times how near he is to the rope, an animal trainer working a "fighting" act makes it his business to remember how close he is to the bars of the arena. Even when you are fighting an animal that is not out to hurt you, it is not advisable to get too close to those bars. For the closer you are, the less room you have for maneuvering.

I know every square foot of my arena so well that I can tell, with almost mathematical accuracy, how far I am from the bars at almost any time. I figured I had four or five feet and decided that if Brutus kept rushing me I would take a few additional steps backward as a concession to his exuberance. He was fighting me with spectacular abandon, the audience was responding with almost uninterrupted applause and I would let this continue for a minute or so before edging the animal back to the center of the arena for the laydown.

I have never forgotten Ernest Hemingway's remark in my

S. H. Ringo Photo, The Virginian Pilot

[13-14]   The top picture shows an early stage of the formation known as the "laydown," in which I range ten recumbent lions in a row across the floor of the arena.

The bottom picture shows a section of the line straightening out.

Edward Lewis Kennedy Photo

[15-16] Both lions and tigers like to have their heads stroked. ABOVE: I have just thanked a lion I am breaking for the laydown for quickly picking up his cues by gently running the stock of my whip across the top of his head.

RIGHT: That tiger trainee will look less menacing when I have performed the same thank-you ritual with the pole in my hand in recognition of his having clambered up a pedestal for the first time.

[17]   In this scene there are two male lions and four females. I eventually stopped using lionesses. When one of them is in heat, the competition for her is keen and creates needless hazards. In addition, it has been reported to me that spectators frequently don't recognize lionesses and wonder what they are.

[18] Scientific interest in the interbreeding of lions and tigers has lessened since the 1930s. Here is Primba, one of the few tigresses ever bred to a lion. I raised her and Simba, her lion mate-to-be, from cubhood in the same cage, and they grew genuinely fond of each other. There was no issue.

[19-20] ABOVE: Having not yet succeeded in getting this tiger trainee to follow the chair, I have substituted a pole and am trying to get the animal to follow it. Next, I will coordinate the two, then de-emphasize the pole and get the big cat to keep its eye on the chair.

The photo below shows how I have accomplished this with a lion.

[21-22]   Ernest Hemingway was the first to point out that my chair at times serves as the equivalent of the matador's cape. In the top picture, the lion is following the chair as I want him to; in the one below, he is overdoing it. My face reflects the strain of coping with that much weight with one hand.

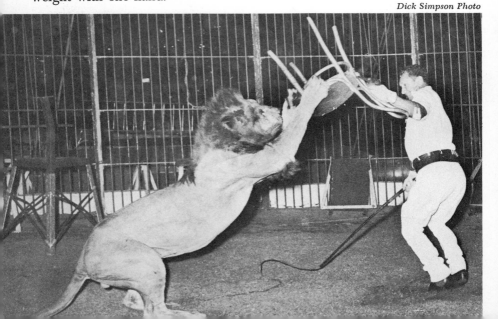

[23-24]   ABOVE: The tiger is following the chair perfectly. The animal that concentrates on it makes my job less hazardous.

BELOW: A lion charging hard, forefeet off the ground. I would be in trouble if his objective was to get under or over the chair, which, in this photo, has his undivided attention, enabling me to control him.

Edward Lewis Kennedy Photo

[25-26] In my right hand (TOP) I am holding Smiley, a merry lion cub whose expression often suggested laughter. In the other picture I am holding a pair of baby tigers that enjoyed each other's company. Occasionally a cub is a loner, the self-sufficient type that manages to have a good time by itself.

dressing room in Madison Square Garden to the effect that my act reaches a peak of excitement whenever I manage to keep a spirited animal coming toward me. As Brutus continued his pressing tactics I backed away a few additional feet—and found myself flush against the bars!

It was not until then that I recalled my decision, on the eve of my departure, to leave out a few sections of my arena as part of a plan to cut down the tonnage we had to lug across the Pacific. (Each of these sections is so heavy it takes two men to carry it.) So here I was pinned against the bars because I had forgotten I was working in an arena whose diameter had been cut down by several feet!

Brutus, puzzled and excited and not knowing what he was supposed to do next, raised himself on his hind legs until he was almost leaning against me. His expression had changed completely. He was no longer the study in eagerness he had been a moment before as we played our little game in which he fought me while we moved back and forth on the arena floor. Now he was angry, his expression conveying some such thought as: "What are you trying to put over? You never prepared me for anything like this."

Brutus bared his teeth and I was convinced that he was about to sink them into my face. As I ducked he dug a claw into my left shoulder, which I might have prevented if he hadn't knocked the chair out of my hand.

I simply had to recover that chair. Fortunately, when Brutus dealt it the clout that tore it from my grasp, it landed against the bars and traveled only a short distance from where I stood. To reach over and try to pick it up would be a risky move, but I was in danger regardless of what I did, so I had no choice. I stooped down quickly and grabbed the chair, emitting a piercing yell as I did so.

From long experience I have learned that sometimes the best defense in a close-range emergency of this kind is a deafening outcry that comes with such suddenness it startles the attacking animal and arrests his purpose for a few seconds. As my shriek hit his eardrums—I did my best to make it a blood-curdling one—Brutus jerked his head back and I was able to recover the chair with my left hand, the one in which I normally carry it. My right hand still clung to my whip.

With my chair I tried to push Brutus away from me. My left shoulder ached where he had dug in and I was unable to get enough leverage to budge him, but the chair offered a little protection and that was better than nothing.

Meanwhile I had reversed the whip in my hand and with the heavy butt-end tried to knock the animal away from me. As I aimed it at Brutus's face, which was uncomfortably close to mine, and tried to hit him with all the strength I could muster, the lash freakishly entwined itself in the bars and that solidly built stock recoiled and banged with tremendous force against my right eyeball and the bones directly above and below it.

I will never know how much time elapsed between Brutus's pinning me against the bars and that blow I sustained when the whipstock struck me on the rebound. I will spare the reader the details—they were pretty agonizing—because pain has a way of dulling the memory and I doubt whether I can do more than a hazy job of reconstruction. Perhaps it all took place in ten seconds, but they were surely interminable ones.

The audience was applauding wildly as I stood there trapped. They seemed to think this was part of the act.

Even Randy, my cage boy, didn't realize the extent to which I was in trouble until I called out to him that I couldn't see a thing. The blow from the whipstock had blinded both eyes. I instructed him to guide me from the outside with a pole as I worked my way to the safety cage. I inched along slowly and deliberately toward my goal. The safety cage was directly opposite the spot where I had been attacked. Fortunately I knew every square foot of that arena and approximately where to place my feet. This knowledge, plus Randy's guidance, enabled me to negotiate the distance of about thirty feet without stumbling into anything. In a sense it was the longest trip of my life. It is hard to avoid stock phrases in explaining a nerve-racking situation of this kind. It seemed like several eternities before I stepped into the safety cage.

The sudden realization on the part of some of the other animals that here was a chance to get back at Brutus, self-appointed arena boss, had distracted him sufficiently to give me a break. He was not overpopular with some of his fellow performers, with special reference to two new lions he had cuffed around by way of initiation, and it was not surprising that he found himself being nipped and clawed at.

Such a situation can lead to a free-for-all, a pitched battle in which none of the animals is quite sure who is fighting whom or why. The trainer is no longer in command and the primitive instinct to start a brawl asserts itself. Big cats that have been under control for a long period of time need no specific reason for squabbling. It's a kind of spontaneous declaration of independence. But of course a development of this kind has its specifics too—the opportunity to square old and new grudges.

From my standpoint the most fortunate circumstance was that the laydown comes a few minutes before my act is over, signifying to almost the entire group that they will soon leave the arena. I instructed Randy to signal the man at the door of the tunnel leading back to the cages to let the animals out of the arena immediately. They started to leave as he rattled the door, the time-honored attention-getter, but some of them took their time instead of bounding out with the *esprit* that usually characterizes their exit. These dawdlers were milling around on the arena floor as I edged my way to the safety cage.

I was rushed to Queen's Hospital, where the doctors quickly discovered that I had fractured the bone above the right eye and the one directly below it. The eye itself was just a bloody red blob. Dr. Pinkerton, one of those who so ably attended me, thought the retina was detached. My lack of vision in the other eye was attributed to shock.

Vision returned to my left eye in about an hour, but at the

hospital they kept both eyes bandaged during the three weeks I was a patient there. Oddly enough the right eye, which sustained the blow, is now as good as ever. But to this day I have trouble with the left, and the highly regarded ophthalmologist whom I consult from time to time has more than once hinted at the possibility of an operation. However, he doesn't think I need concern myself about this for several years.

In the days when Martin Johnson and I used to see each other, we agreed that there were lions that were instinctive man-killers and that there were also border-line types whose killer behavior was unnatural, a temporary mental aberration brought on by special circumstances. I gave the matter considerable thought during my hospitalization, and as I weighed the pros and cons I conducted a kind of debate with myself, one moment taking the position that Brutus was an honest-to-goodness killer and the next minute knocking down my own argument. All of this, of course, was by way of trying to figure out whether I should or should not keep Brutus in my act.

I found myself thinking of certain scenes in Johnson's remarkable contribution to big-cat lore, *Lion,* a book that has permanently fixed itself in my mind. There is an unforgettable description of a lion tearing a man to pieces on the Kapiti Plains. It contains one especially meaningful observation that has stayed with me over the years, a quick picture of what the lion looked like before he made his kill: "Its tail was slashing and its head dropped low."

Well, that describes Brutus perfectly just before he upraised himself and pinned me against the bars. And that is why it had flashed across my mind that this was no longer the Brutus I knew, that this was a Brutus bent on killing.

Yet as I looked him over in his cage when I recovered from my accident and was back on the job again, I decided that this was the *old* Brutus, my good friend. At any rate, his good side was showing. For once again he wanted his ear rubbed and as I performed this ritual his expression was as benign as that of the most harmless and docile of house cats.

But Brutus is one of those friends who likes to play rough, a kind of rowdy practical joker. And I watch him carefully as I scratch the back of his ear, for some sign that he is setting a trap for me with this affectionate approach and that what he really has in mind is to test my reflexes and see if I am quick enough at this little game to withdraw my hand before losing a finger. There are lions that behave this way and it is something the experienced trainer accepts as part of the game.

More than once I have confused people by referring to a lion or a tiger as a friend. Without having any illusions about their trouble-making potential, a trainer develops an affection for his animals. It is possible to love them without fully trusting them. There are little ways in which these big ferocious beasts convey that they have confidence in you and trust you—to a point.

You never quite forget the early days of their training. It is like thinking back to the school days of children. You remember, for instance, how touchingly eager Lion A was to perform as soon as you and he understood each other and he knew exactly what it was you wanted him to do. His seeming recalcitrance when you were teaching him his ABCs was not real opposition or resistance. It was bafflement based on his inability to understand what teacher was driving at. As soon as he grasped the point he responded, and to show that he understood he would repeat over and over again what you had asked him to do, looking up now and then for some sign of approbation. As the reader now knows, the trainer wishing to register appreciation can do so by running his whip gently over the top of the head of his big-cat pupil.

You get accustomed to the idea that wild animals never lose their primitiveness and that these are friends that have to be carefully watched. It doesn't alter your affection for them—to some extent, it must be admitted, because they help

you earn a living. But there is more to it than that—a bond
that is hard to describe without seeming to be somewhat
maudlin. It is a feeling that was summed up effectively by
Julian Huxley when he wrote that "the investigator [of wild
animals] will only obtain his most valuable results by sup-
plementing his scientific objectivity with an understanding
and even affectionate approach to the animals with which he
is working. This applies with special force to any attempts to
discover the extent of unrealized possibilities latent in his
animal subjects." Huxley then emphasizes that it is "important"—and his message could not be clearer—for "animal
trainers and zoo keepers and officials" to bear this in mind.
I don't find it hard to do this. Wild animals—with special
reference to the big cats, even the wildest and potentially most
dangerous of them—have a way of subtly getting under your
skin.

It was assumed by those who witnessed the Honolulu
accident, by those who read about it and by my associates
that I might remove Brutus from the act.

If I removed him he would wind up in the circus menagerie,
a sort of traveling zoo. He would be exercised daily like the
other animals, but I felt sure he would miss the excitement of
the arena. He was one of those audience-conscious creatures,
and though I am not enough of an animal psychologist to
prove my point, I regarded him fundamentally as a crowd-
pleaser. He had a bit of the show-off in him, liked applause
and would, I am convinced, have become morose and dis-
spirited as a menagerie exhibit.

Some of the big cats thrive on the menagerie life. Fifteen
pounds of horse meat daily, followed by a long nap when
they are surfeited, is enough to keep them happy. But Brutus
was not that type. He needed action, and when I succeeded
in convincing myself that it was not over-risky to confront him
again in the arena, I decided to retain him in the act.

There were still other factors in my decision to retain Brutus as a performer. The realistic trainer knows that if he discarded every animal that ever made trouble for him he simply wouldn't have an act; for sooner or later—and here I am dealing specifically with lions and tigers—every single animal will have done something of a disturbing nature. For these are wild animals and they never completely lose their wildness no matter how well-behaved they often seem.

In that running debate I conducted with myself on whether to retire Brutus to the menagerie I couldn't quite forget the killer expression I saw on his face—the mouth more twisted and the eyes angrier than I had ever seen them—nor could I forget, in rebuttal of myself, that if I had not had that lapse of memory I would not have gotten into all this trouble.

Then, recalling some of Brutus's antics, I would be unable to restrain a smile and I'd cheer up about the whole situation. There are times when the fiercest of big cats can be the most playful. Brutus is my top-mounter, the animal that has the highest perch in the arena. He is within reach of the overhead netting, and when the mood strikes him he plays with it. He likes to make it ripple with a stroke of the paw, and when children notice him playing this little game, it amuses them.

My collaborator, who has made many tours of audiences to get reactions, tells me that "Isn't he cute!" is one of the favorite comments of youngsters and adults as Brutus sets up undulations in the net.

This, of course, can be overdone. For instance, these antics sometimes have the attention of the audience at the very moment I am cuing a lion or a tiger into a major trick on the arena floor.

Brutus, when in that clowning mood, sometimes offers a variation of the prank just described. Now and then he runs his tail through the webbing of the overhead net, holding it straight up, as if to show all the world what a beautiful long appendage he has and how handsomely it is tufted at the very end. This is always good for a laugh, one that increases in volume if I happen to look up and catch Brutus in the act. His unfailing reaction is to withdraw his tail quickly, and immediately give me his undivided attention, much like a school child who has been caught doing something behind teacher's back.

I have seen Brutus display ferocity and charm within the compass of a few minutes. With a smash of one of his heavy paws he would send a lion or a tiger reeling, bringing horrified gasps from onlookers, and then ascending to his high perch, he would pull one of his laugh-provoking antics. There is nothing unusual about the dual-personality aspect of the big cats, although I have never seen it so markedly as in Brutus. In both the wilds and in captivity they are creatures of moods. The unpredictability of these moods is what gives them their never-ending fascination.

An animal like Brutus is so interesting, has so many colorful facets, that you feel you would be depriving the public of contact with a "character" if you dropped him from your list of performers.

Brutus has often been classified as an applause- and laugh-lover. Yet I sometimes think that his antics are designed for his own amusement—as when it was reported to me recently that he was seen doing his tail-through-the-net stunt while the spotlight played on a tiger that I was putting through the rollover on the arena floor far below. Only circus personnel who were standing close to the arena could see clearly what top-seated Brutus was doing, for the lights above had been dimmed to emphasize the tiger's solo feature—demonstrating that, with or without an audience, Brutus has his playful moments.

About six months after the Honolulu misadventure I noticed that Brutus had selected as his particular arena crony one of my mightiest and most striking-looking lions, a big fellow I call Sultan. Before long this friendship became very real. Whenever an animal took a swipe at Sultan, Brutus would come to his aid, and vice versa. These little spats are quite common, and except in unusual circumstances I don't have much trouble breaking them up.

The bond between Brutus and Sultan was now so clearly established that some of the animal hands thought they were brothers. They were not. They were in the same consignment when I bought them as youngsters from a wild-animal dealer not long after their arrival in the United States. They had gotten used to each other, although I didn't recall one coming to the aid of the other in arena spats until after the Honolulu incident.

When two animals "buddy up," as we say in the circus, the trainer realizes that if one of them decides to attack him the chances are that he will have to take on both. It was not quite possible for me to forget completely that murderous expression of Brutus's as he pinned me against the bars, and I couldn't help thinking how slight my chance of escape would have been if he had had any assistance from Sultan.

I began to wonder whether I shouldn't protect myself against possible trouble from the Brutus-Sultan axis. Both were in the laydown and several times I noticed Brutus, as he battled me before taking his place in the lion line, looking around at Sultan as if to say, "How about joining the fun?" Animals have a way of "speaking" to each other, and though the trainer is usually too occupied with the task of the moment to detect everything that is going on in the arena, when he happens to look in the right direction he senses the flashing of a message from one beast to another.

It was not difficult to discourage Sultan when Brutus, giving me a workout before joining the laydown group, tried to call his friend over by means of a come-hither look. Even so, it kept occurring to me that I should give serious thought to the trouble-making potential of this duo.

I'm not a procrastinator—not more so than the average person, at any rate—but the fact is that an animal trainer's work is never done. There are so many demands on his time that he has to establish priorities. If, for instance, Tiger A shows signs of a toothache, that will have to be checked promptly. Lion B has developed a slight limp, and I'll have to look into that quickly too. Perhaps he was nipped by one of his fellow performers as he made his way through the tunnel leading from the menagerie tent to the arena, and I must determine whether he has developed an infection. If he has, it will have to be treated immediately.

Then there is the never-ending job of training new animals as replacements. And so it goes, with the result that the trainer sometimes finds himself unable to do all the things that should be done.

It became apparent on May 9, 1963, at Elizabeth, New Jersey, that I had not given enough thought to the problem of Brutus's steadily growing domination of Sultan.

On that day, for some reason that eludes me, Brutus, his face distorted with rage, came lunging at me, teeth bared and claws ready for action. Sultan had joined him and the two animals converged on me. They collided. Brutus, annoyed with Sultan for bumping into him, stunned his partner with a tremendous paw-clout. This fortuitous spat gave me time to get behind a pedestal after one of the closest calls of my career.

Sultan, still a bit groggy from the wallop Brutus had dealt him, responded when I left my place of refuge and motioned him back to his pedestal. Brutus, the spell broken, did not resume the attack. He could see his pal deserting him and evidently did not want to go it alone that particular day.

I've done a lot of thinking about that Elizabeth incident. I never tire of problems involving animal motivation in general and the arena comportment of certain big cats under certain specific circumstances.

The "young science of ethology," as Julian Huxley calls it, has thrown considerable light on the behavior of wild animals, but there are many answers it does not provide. To some extent this field of animal psychology is a guessing game; but I believe that those who have handled wild animals for years have the best chance of guessing right—assuming, of course, that they are diligent observers and genuinely interested in the subject.

An experienced "cat man" will sometimes object to his analysis of the conduct of a lion or a tiger being labeled a guess, or even an "educated" guess. I am here referring to dealers and zoo officials who hold strong opinions on why animals do what they do. These strongly held opinions are justified in cases where animals develop fixed-pattern reactions under certain specifically defined circumstances.

A veteran animal man of my acquaintance—a man who has handled countless big cats—has boldly suggested that Sultan deliberately bumped into Brutus when the two converged on me in Elizabeth. Sultan, dominated by Brutus, was willing to join his crony in the escapade described earlier, but that's as far as he was willing to go. His theory is that Sultan was resigned to Brutus's bullying tactics but welcomed an opportunity to fall short of full cooperation.

This big-cat authority has even suggested that Sultan may have been trying to save me. I can cite emergencies in the arena in which I practically convinced myself after studying the facts that this or that animal was making an effort to get me out of a jam. But under somewhat different circumstances.

In the case of Sultan I just didn't know, although it had occurred to me independently that he might have been trying to help me. It would be wonderful to be able to establish such speculation as fact; for the reading public loves stories about animals that rescue their masters. The lion that saves his trainer is even a better story than the dog—usually a big handsome collie—who performs a similar service for his doting owner.

The Brutus-Sultan picture was a confused one and I found it hard to arrive at any firm conclusions regarding Sultan's behavior. I have never seen a kindlier expression on a lion's face.

It is more than a friendly look, it suggests complete trust-worthiness. When you look at a face like Sultan's you wish more than ever that the zoologists' dream of eventual full—or at least fuller—communication between man and beast could become a reality in a few years rather than a few centuries.

The scientists speak of centuries as though they were minutes, and I admire their casualness about the long view. But I also have a normal amount of impatience, and there is so much I would like to learn about the mental processes of an animal like Sultan. If you look at him long enough you find yourself about to dissolve in the warmth of his wonderful amber eyes. Then you pull yourself together and remember you are supposed to know something about primitive creatures. And your mind drifts back to the men who have contributed so much to our knowledge of them—Sir Alfred Pease, Martin Johnson and others. Johnson in particular. If I keep mentioning him it is because I believe his contribution is not sufficiently appreciated. Once I heard him called "too commercial." He made those motion pictures and still-photos of lions to make money! Think of that, now!

At any rate, Johnson's observations on the hundreds of lions he photographed have my complete respect. Here he is, for instance, describing a lion whose appearance appealed to him greatly:

"He was a beautiful beast; very dark tawny, with a mane that was almost black in places and gray in others. His face was wise and kind—or as kind as a lion's face can be. For no matter how benevolent a lion may seem, there is always a slight tinge of cruelty in his deep-set eyes."

So it was with Sultan. The benign—even gentle—look was there, but when you studied his expression long enough you could also see that "tinge of cruelty" Johnson spoke of. And not even the greatest animal psychologist in the world would be able to say with any degree of certainty whether this big cat was motivated more by his kind or his cruel side.

After the Elizabeth incident I found myself reviewing the thoughts I had had in Honolulu after the accident there in an effort to determine whether I should take Brutus out of the act. Before I made the move, however, I decided to try an experiment I had been considering ever since he had established domination over Sultan and taken him in as a junior partner.

Brutus's best opportunity to influence Sultan came during the formation of the lion line. It was those few minutes that were worrying me and I thought it would be interesting to see how Brutus would react if I dismissed his junior partner before the laydown.

Following Elizabeth we had a two-day engagement in Newark, and I would try my experiment there. Accordingly, I left instructions that just before the laydown Sultan was to be cued out of the arena.

It took Brutus some time to break himself of the habit of looking around for his buddy at the start of the laydown, but he finally got used to the idea that Sultan was no longer part of the formation that gave him his best opportunity for domination over his former junior partner and joint action against me.

Since I had long regarded Brutus and Sultan as an interesting—and possibly important—study in animal behavior, I began wondering if I could find some way of adding significantly to my information about them.

How, I often speculated, would Brutus react to my restoring Sultan to the laydown? To place Sultan in this formation near Brutus would, after what had happened at Elizabeth, be needlessly risky.

As this book was nearing completion I tried the experiment of restoring Sultan to the laydown in a spot where six lions separated him from his erstwhile self-appointed boss.

Would Brutus accept this or would he seek to restore his domination over the animal he once was determined to make his stooge? So far nothing has happened. This may mean that after the Elizabeth incident Brutus doesn't think he can count on Sultan to follow his lead. Or it may mean nothing.

After this book is published something could happen to give me entirely new ideas on what Brutus had in mind when he originally set out to make Sultan his man Friday. As well as different ideas of how Sultan really feels about Brutus.

In the meantime Brutus is behaving like a good trouper, performing on cue without any hitches. I might add that when the spirit moves him he still pulls his clown act, seemingly getting as much fun as ever out of erecting his tail through the webbing of the overhead safety net.

5. Henry, the Bob-Tailed Lion— and Other Stories

It's Hard to Look Kingly without a Tail – Muggsy, the Lion with a Novel Slant on Fighting – A Black Leopard Turns Peacemaker

SOME DAY there will be big-cat psychiatrists," said my friend Don Hayman, formerly an executive with my circus, who has returned to his first love, the newspaper business. "And when that time comes maybe there will be a scientific explanation of what happened to poor Henry."

"Poor Henry" was one of the lions in my act. He was not a star—that is, he did not perform any of the major tricks—but he was an able member of the supporting cast. Despite the fact that he was one of the smallest lions I have ever used in the act, weighing only 350 pounds, he made a place for himself by his dependability.

I used him in the huge "pyramid" of lions and tigers I build early in the act, and while he wasn't nearly as impressive-looking as my big lions, the ones that ranged in weight from 450 to 650 pounds, it was a comfort to look up and see him on a pedestal because I knew he was going to stay there until he got the cue that told him that this particular tableau was over and he could break the pose. Every once in a while one of the big lions decides to jump off his pedestal ahead of time—per-

haps to start a fight—and it is always reassuring to have a few
Henrys around that are all business.

Moreover, there was leonine strength and majesty in his appearance, and unless you happened to be standing right outside the big steel arena in which I put the big cats through
their paces—a courtesy accorded newspapermen and other
writers when they want to see me work at close range—you
were not more than casually conscious of the fact that Henry
was appreciably smaller than the other lions.

Early in Henry's career as a performer I noticed that whenever he found himself close to one of my brawnier, heftier
lions—for instance Jimmy, who weighed over five hundred
pounds and measured ten feet from his nose to the end of his
tail—he seemed eager to move away and stand beside an animal more nearly his own size. In training quarters he frequently pulled up beside Jenny, a tigress a little smaller than
he. Or, if not Jenny, one of the other cats that was not quite
as big as some of the real heavyweights in the act.

It is as natural for wild animals to fight as it is for them to
eat or breathe. If there is no real reason for a brawl, one of
the big cats, deciding that this peace business is overrated,
starts a ruckus just for the hell of it—more frequently a minor
spat than a violent scrap. During these fights, most of which
I have learned to break up before they get out of hand, it
seemed to me that the other lions were trying to protect Henry.
One way of doing this was to make a point of not encouraging
him to join the battle.

It would take a Charles Darwin or a Julian Huxley to determine whether the other lions were actually trying to protect Henry or didn't take him seriously enough to care what
he did. At times it looked to me as though the former was the
case.

The kind of fight lions like best is the free-for-all, and usually when one takes place and any of their kind hang back
and seem reluctant to join the brawl the ringleaders communi-

cate to the non-combatants that they want them to participate in the scrap, and if they are still reluctant they find themselves attacked and drawn in.

Henry was an exception to this rule. When a fight broke out in the arena, he would stay out of it and no effort would be made by the combatants to drag him in—for either of the reasons I have given, or perhaps a combination of both. There is so much variation in wild-animal character and behavior that there is lots of room for speculation here.

Occasionally I had still other thoughts on the subject. For instance, once or twice I wondered whether the other lions didn't regard Henry as a comedy cat somewhat in the tradition of the Cowardly Lion in *The Wizard of Oz*. I never thought of Henry as cowardly, even though some of my circus associates did. Certainly there were signs that could be interpreted that way. But I chose to think of Henry as either smart enough not to overmatch himself or as a freakish leonine pacifist. There is precedent for both. While there are pugnacious undersized members of the big-cat family that sometimes pick fights with larger and more powerful adversaries, there are also lions and tigers that are too practical-minded to tackle a larger and more powerful beast. Then there are the Henrys, the ones that don't like to fight at all.

On Martin Johnson's expedition to Africa that resulted in the best early motion pictures of leonine subjects—lions of every kind and description, both physically and behaviorally —he reported seeing a lion, one of a group of four or five, that had killed a zebra and insisted on gorging himself while his companions waited their turn. When one of the other lions tried to join the feast, the original diner sent him reeling with a smack of his heavy paw and a roar you could hear a mile away. Between them, the lion that was walloped and the others that were watching the feast could have torn the greedy monopolizer to pieces. They did not choose to do so. They waited for him to eat his fill, then shared what was left. According to Johnson, they were just not in the mood for a brawl. I felt that here there was possibly some kind of tie-up with Henry, though frankly I wasn't sure what it was.

But it doesn't necessarily follow that because you are a peace-loving member of the big-cat family you are going to lead a peaceful life. Henry found this out. I'd like to point out that Martin Johnson also reported a situation where the basic facts were similar to the ones in the incident just recounted but where the results were entirely different. This time the other lions did not choose to wait for the would-be monopolizer to finish. They jumped on him and took the dead zebra away from him. Johnson explained that his principal reason for recording these contrasting stories was to emphasize something he felt could not be repeated too often—namely, that you simply cannot generalize about wild animals.

One day a donnybrook broke out in the arena. Henry, finding himself in the midst of a milling mob of lions and tigers, made an effort to break away and find peace in a protected spot behind a pedestal. I could see him eying a pedestal, then starting to move toward it. But he never reached it. In picking his way toward his objective through a traffic jam of lions and tigers, his tail chanced to sweep across the face of Jenny, the tigress in whose presence he had always felt comfortable because she had never shown any animosity toward him. This happened as Jenny, teeth bared, was heading for the hindquarters of a lion that had once clawed her. Jenny became enraged when Henry's tail obscured her vision just long enough to let her target get beyond the range of a quick pounce. To make her feelings crystal clear, the angry tigress pounced on Henry instead and bit his tail off!

This was very much in line with the typically erratic behavior of a tiger (or tigress) in a free-for-all. The lion is always coldly calculating in a fight, seldom making a move without figuring it out. In a situation of this kind the tiger is inclined to lose his head, grabbing blindly for what is nearest, and ripping and tearing at it.

So there was poor Henry howling in pain as Jenny spat out his tail and joined the free-for-all, lashing out tiger-fashion at any target within reach. Assistants on the outside of the arena equipped with long poles helped me break up the battle, which had not yet gone beyond the point where the animals were sparring for position. Their roars and snarls gave the impression that all hell had broken loose when as a matter of fact Henry was the only animal that sustained an injury.

Poor Henry! He was quickly cued out of the arena and as soon as he was back in his cage a first-class veterinarian was summoned. It developed that Jenny had not done too neat a job of severing the luckless lion's tail, so Henry was anesthetized and a minor operation was performed. When this was done, there was nothing left of his tail except a few inches of stump, and from then on that unfortunate animal became known as "Henry, the bob-tailed lion."

I knew that Henry, his stump nicely healed, was himself again one day when I approached his cage. Well before he could see me, he picked up my scent and greeted me with what can only be described as cheerful lion chatter.

Lions are so often depicted—and accurately—as snarling, emitting throaty rumbles that are usually described as "guttural," or roaring their heads off, that some people think they are always that way. Except by such experts as Joy Adamson, the exclamations of pleasure are seldom recorded. To the untrained ear they don't sound much different from the more typical product of leonine vocal cords.

An honest-to-goodness snarl is a snarl, to be sure, but there are somewhat subdued roars (if that isn't too much of a contradiction) that the trained ear recognizes as friendly expressions. And that was the kind of greeting I got as I neared Henry's cage.

It practically said, "Here's my ear against the bars as of old, Chum. Please rub same." The tail-end soreness that had developed as a result of Henry's accident was now gone and he was in the mood once more for fraternizing.

My problem now was: should I keep Henry in the act or should I remove him? In the case of Henry, the only way to find out what was in the animal's best interests was to experiment. One or two performances would not suffice to supply the answer. Wild animals are mercurial and you can't get a clear picture unless you watch a situation of this kind until you are reasonably sure you have the answer, and that meant several weeks of watching Henry closely in the performing ring.

Henry, let me remind the reader, was small for a male lion. But he had a great ruff of hair around his neck, resulting, when you viewed him from certain angles, in your thinking he was bigger than he was. And there was a suggestion of power in his tawny yellow body that rippled with muscle as he lithely moved about the arena. His shyness, which some interpreted as fear of the bigger and more powerful animals, made Henry a baffling contradiction. Time and again I thought I had solved the riddle of his personality only to be floored by something Henry did that somehow failed to conform to what I had fixed in my mind as his normal behavioral pattern —and once again I would find myself stumped.

In addition to placing him in the pyramid, I had used Henry in the laydown. The first time I tried Henry in the laydown after his accident he was reluctant to come down from his seat to join the group. I coaxed him down and when he reached the arena floor he looked over to where, with three big lions as a starter, I had the laydown under way. Instead of trotting over and taking his place, he looked hesitantly over to where the recumbent trio were stretched out full length, gave me a look as if to say, "Sorry to do this to you, Boss," and heading straight for a floor-level pedestal, hid behind it. Unable to get him to join the formation, I cued him out of the arena, signaling the boy at the tunnel to rattle the door to get his attention. Henry heard and made his departure.

This whole misadventure didn't take more than a minute, but a minute is a long time in the arena and such delays throw things out of kilter. Big healthy lions bubble over with energy and only an optimist would expect them to sit still for any length of time. Two of the three in the abortive formation began taking pokes at each other, and the third was about to join this sparring match when I ran over and broke it up, cued the other animals off their seats and finally managed to finish the laydown.

At the next two shows Henry repeated the same performance more or less. And he was now becoming a two-way problem because, earlier in the act, he was holding up the formation of the big pyramid of lions and tigers. Henry, an animal normally so dependable he was often referred to as O.R. (Old Reliable), now balked at taking his seat in the pyramid, a formation that loses much of its effectiveness when one of the pedestals is unoccupied. During two of these pyramidal tableaux Henry jumped to the floor before the band could give the music cue that means "At ease!" or "Break it up!" and started moving around the arena behind pedestals while I strove vainly to coax him back into the pedestaled group.

The big cats don't like to have one of their number in motion behind their backs, consequently the ones on floor seats half turned around and tried to take swipes at Henry as he went by. This, needless to say, didn't improve the appearance of the formation. Henry might have been seriously injured by the animals that aimed these pokes at him; the only thing that saved him was that it is difficult for a lion or tiger—even one on a floor seat—to hit squarely and effectively a moving target behind its back, no matter how swift his paw action.

What I feared most was that one of the angered lions or tigers would jump off his pedestal and tangle with Henry, which would have been bad news for my bob-tailed cat, who was no match for any of the animals in the act. It wasn't a matter of courage, I felt, despite the dissenting views of others, including some experienced animal men. By disposition Henry was not a fighter and he would have been badly ripped— perhaps killed—in a real fight.

Although Don Hayman had been jesting when he made the remark that opens this chapter, I found myself looking to psychiatry for a solution. What was wrong with Henry? What had happened to his zest for performing? Some animals unmistakably enjoy performing and Henry had unquestionably been one of these. Now he clearly did not want to perform.

I can go even further than that. He actually did not want to be seen! Without his long graceful tufted tail he no longer looked like a lion and he seemed to know it. The mishap that cost him his tail had given him an inferiority complex. At least that's what I as a self-appointed big-cat psychiatrist had decided.

Meanwhile members of the circus staff who from time to time circulate among the cash customers to get audience reactions were reporting that spectators were asking one another what kind of animal the one with the stump of a tail was. He looked like a lion, these doubters agreed, but maybe he was some sort of halfbreed—or perhaps one of his parents was "a whatchermacallit, a kind of an animal with a short stubby tail which I used to know its name but I clean forgot it." And so it went, with more and more circus fans expressing their bewilderment.

The obvious thing to do, it seemed to me, was to take Henry out of the act. But because that was plainly indicated, was it necessarily the wisest thing to do? I wasn't convinced. Henry, before certain personality changes took place, used to live for his ring appearances. To try to document this and say with any degree of certainty why he once liked to perform would be difficult. I have pointed out that some animals appear to be applause-lovers—in fact, I have had a few that were such "hams" they would have repeated their tricks endlessly if they could have counted on my letting them go on and on.

The most common reason why animals like to perform is that they enjoy the exercise. I have handled only a small number of big cats that didn't like exercise, beasts that were genuinely lazy. Just as there are lazy people, there are lazy lions and tigers.

Henry was among those that enjoyed the exercise of performing twice a day (as a supplement to the daily exercise run in the arena). He was also a great pleaser; in "talking" to me, as he did fairly often when the act was over in the days before his accident, there was an eagerness that seemed to communicate, "How am I doing, boss?" Or, "Have you noticed how fast I now pick up my cues?"

In an effort to keep from overreaching myself in these interpretations I keep thinking of the Huxley cautionary reminder that the science of animal behavior is a young one. There isn't a great deal of provable information that one can quote with any degree of confidence in reaching a conclusion in this comparatively new field. Most of what we know is based on what "qualified observers" report. The word *qualified* is, I suppose, capable of different definitions and interpretations. I claim—correctly, I hope—that by reason of long experience and a deep interest in wild-animal behavior and motivation I am qualified. I became a cage boy at fifteen, an assistant trainer at seventeen and a full-fledged trainer a few years later. In the almost forty years I have served in that last capacity I have trained nearly two thousand lions and tigers. Not all of them became performers—a certain percentage had to be weeded out—but I have had an extensive experience with all of them. In addition to the lions and tigers, I have trained other cats such as ocelots, pumas, jaguars and black and spotted leopards. My observation of this assortment of felines has given me a well-rounded picture of the cat family, medium, small and big.

If my experience with this assortment of cats in general,

and almost one thousand lions in particular, taught me anything about animal psychology it had conveyed that Henry
wanted to be taken out of the act. From the standpoint of
Clyde Beatty, animal trainer, whose job it is to entertain
audiences, the problem of retaining Henry in the act or removing him was not an important one. However, from the
standpoint of Clyde Beatty, long-standing observer and student of animal behavior struggling to figure out what was
best for my bob-tailed lion, the problem was an interesting
one. The fact that Henry *seemed* to want to be removed from
the act did not necessarily establish that this was so. I have
seen inexplicable changes take place in animals and it was
because I was hoping for some kind of miracle that I decided
to keep him in the act a little longer. This would give me a
final clue as to whether he would be able to recover his erstwhile dependability and poise as a performer.

Because I found the problem fascinating and discussed it
at length with circus associates and other friends, I was the
recipient of many suggestions. One, made by a newspaper
friend, was that I try my hand at developing a document
that would be Henry's whole case history—a small book going
into all the ramifications of the case. There was indeed enough
material for such a work—for Henry was an endless source of
anecdotes whose interpretation would give insights into the
personality changes he had undergone—but I figured this
would amount to belaboring the subject, that the public would
not be *that* interested in this study of animal behavior, as
absorbing as I, a specialist in the field, found it.

Another proposal was that I arrange to have Henry exhibited
in the side show and billed as "the lion that got his tail bit off,"
with a barker telling the thrilling saga of the "hour-long battle
well nigh unto death" in which Henry lost his tufted appendage. Then, according to this plan, someone would circulate
among the onlookers to offer "for a dime, only ten cents, the
tenth part of a dollar," a leaflet telling in graphic detail the
story of the lion-tiger free-for-all—"one of the most gripping

in the annals of circus history"—in which Henry lost his tail and almost his life.

The more I thought about it the more convinced I was that my problem went beyond taking Henry out of the act or retaining him. It was really a question of whether Henry and I were to part company. Because if I took him out of the act I would have to sell him or give him away. Brand-new surroundings would help him forget his unhappy experiences.

While I was indulging in these final considerations, Henry's erratic behavior in the arena—a pattern I was now convinced would not change—made my decision for me. Two or three times I thought I had corrected that urge to hide from the other animals and just as I began hopefully wondering if Henry had at last lost his self-consciousness about his vanished tail, he would resume his hiding tactics. During one performance, in a frantic effort to get behind a pedestal fast, he forgot to look where he was going and hit the stout steel braces of the floor seat so hard he almost knocked himself out. It was all I could do to keep Maharajah, the big Royal Bengal tiger that was occupying the seat, from pouncing on him.

This was the last straw. Automatically I made two decisions: to take Henry out of the act before he got himself killed, and to give him to someone who would take good care of him. It would be unwise to let him remain with the circus—say, as a menagerie exhibit—after removing him from the act. Every time I came near his cage he would make a commotion as soon as he picked up my scent and he would present an ear to the bars for rubbing and/or scratching. Then he would start "talking" to me and if I know anything about "this young science of animal behavior" he would try to convey that he wanted to be transferred back into the act; for no animal I have ever trained liked exercise more or seemed to enjoy being near me so much.

At this point it seems appropriate to point out that it was my love of animals that originally got me started as an animal trainer. I have never heard of anyone deliberately setting out to be a member of my profession. It's something you drift into. As a boy of ten or eleven I had developed a knack for teaching dogs to do tricks and I used to say, I'm told, that I wanted to be an animal trainer when I grew up; I am told by the same people that, like most other boys of that age, I also wanted to be a policeman, a fireman, a railroad engineer, a movie star, another Ty Cobb or Christy Mathewson, a prize-fight champion and all the other things a boy of ten or eleven aspires to be.

When at the age of fifteen I unceremoniously left my home in Bainbridge, Ohio, to join the circus, leaving a note of explanation for my startled mother, I was motivated by a love of wild animals. I wanted to do some kind of work that would give me a chance to be near them. I was given a job as cage boy, which meant that my principal task was cleaning out cages—inelegant work, to be sure, but I was grateful for the opportunity. I was fascinated by the work of the animal trainer and his assistants, watched them in training sessions by the hour, and studied their every move. In time I asked to be given a tryout as an assistant trainer, although that is another story.

What I am trying to get across is that an animal trainer starts with a love of animals, and that it was because of the affection I had developed for Henry that the problem of deciding what to do about him had become so knotty a one. Otherwise the reader might wonder: why all this agonizing about Henry's future? The crack of the whip and the bark of a blank-cartridge pistol are so synonymous with my work in the arena that I am regarded by some—a small minority, I am glad to report—as a tough guy who likes to push animals around. It comes as a surprise to some that I love these animals and that the big cats and I have had a lot of fun together over the years. It's a strenuous life and I wouldn't call mine an unhazardous profession, but it has its compensations, as when you learn to communicate with these beasts of the wilds that you have taught to perform.

I finally gave Henry to a friend, the late Frank Walters of Houston, Texas, a man so fond of wild animals he traveled with me for weeks at a stretch, eventually becoming more familiar with the different aspects of my act and the personalities of my big cats than any circus fan I have ever known.

Walters, a man of means with generous impulses, periodically assembled enough acts to put on a circus for the benefit of Houston's underprivileged children. He, like so many others, had developed a fondness for Henry, and he saw to it that the bob-tailed lion was given professional care and exercised regularly. Walters reported that Henry was enjoying his new life and surroundings—(as a menagerie exhibit, not a performer)—and was his old spirited self again.

I have had an afterthought about Henry, something that hadn't occurred to me until I started working on this book. He was one of the few big cats I ever used in my act that didn't conform to the pattern governing the names we give lions and tigers in our show.

These names, generally speaking, are in two categories. One implies ferocity, the other the eminence of the lion and the tiger in the animal kingdom. Those who don't accept the lion as the king of beasts invariably select the tiger, so we are on safe ground in giving them both names suggesting sovereignty. This is not displeasing to our press agents, who believe a story about a big cat has more of a wallop if the animal has an impressive-sounding name.

In the classification designed to suggest power and ferocity there have been over the years such names as Volcano, Rowdy, Spitfire, Hellion, Fury, Demon, Monster, Stormy, Dragon, Tempest, Roughneck, Muscles, Paul Bunyan, Brawny, TNT, Colossus, Samson, Hurricane, Dynamite, Bully, Bluster, Atlas, Tough Guy, Cyclone, Hercules, Mighty, Explosion, Earthquake, Titanic, Bad News, A-Bomb.

In the classification suggesting either the regal or some form of supremacy or leadership, such names as the following have been used: Monarch, Emperor, Rex, King, Prince, Princess, Duke, Duchess, Count, Countess, Emperor, Empress, King, Queen, Rajah, Rani, Sultan, Sultana, President, Governor, General, Chief, Commander, Skipper, Admiral, Commissioner, Senator, Chairman, Chief.

Some of these names stuck, some didn't. Sometimes I give an animal a name only to find that the cage hands do not consider it suitable and call him something entirely different—perhaps to achieve a short cut, something that trips over the tongue more easily. To avoid confusion I occasionally switch to the name the cage hands prefer, unless it is too obscene. Now and then they select a name that couldn't very well appear in a family newspaper, though usually even their coarsest-sounding names have more point and a better ring to them than the conventional ones I have listed.

Getting back to Henry, it never occurred to anyone—even before he lost his tail and while he looked more like a lion—to give him a name in either of the categories I have mentioned. For instance, he simply never looked like Fury or Tough Guy. And as for the other group, Rex and Monarch and all such would have been complete misnomers. Whoever gave him the name Henry had an inspiration. It fitted perfectly. He *was* Henry.

I now turn my thoughts to Muggsy, a small lion who antedated Henry, and whose pugnaciousness earned him his name. My recollection is that he weighed a little less than Henry's 350 pounds and probably was the smallest lion I ever used in the act.

Like Henry, Muggsy avoided fights but for a different reason. Henry was a peace-lover. Muggsy was a war-lover but preferred to stay out of fights himself. To him a free-for-all in the arena was the greatest of spectator sports; he followed every detail with the avid interest of a baseball fan watching a world-series game.

When he thought things were too quiet in the arena, Muggsy seemed to suffer from boredom and probed for ways and means of starting a brawl and diverting suspicion from himself. At times he got away with such tactics, for he was fast and had a good poker face. But there were times when he was caught making the sneaky move that started the scrap. He was no coward and when attacked he would fight back. He knew all the stratagems of defense and fought to protect himself rather than try to inflict damage on a bigger adversary who could hurt him badly if he tried to take the offensive. He was fast and when he found himself badly overmatched he knew how to extricate himself and retreat behind a pedestal until things blew over. Occasionally after one of these encounters he wound up with a slight limp or a swollen ear, but he managed to avoid serious injury.

Muggsy was intelligent and could have mastered almost any trick in the act, but he did not have the size and imposing appearance that are so essential to an animal that does solo work. He was mainly a seat-warmer, that is, one of the banked array of cats that form the background against which the solo artists perform. I also used him in the laydown.

One day as Muggsy lay sprawled out in the laydown, I noticed that his head, instead of being on a line with those of the other lions, was almost two feet in back of theirs. At the moment I had my hands full trying to sell a tough lion the idea of lying down and joining the group; he seemed to prefer rushing me and banging away at my chair. Out of the corner of my eye I could see Muggsy edging back farther and farther until his head was on a line with the hindquarters of the animals on either side of him.

Before I could get the lion that was resisting me to lie down, Muggsy bit the lion to his left in the behind and raced behind a pedestal.

There was definitely something of the practical joker in

Muggsy's make-up, a sort of clownish bumptiousness that made it difficult for him to resist an opportunity to annoy a larger animal. The experienced trainer, though he may get an occasional laugh out of such prankishness, knows it is dangerous for a small animal to pick on a bigger one.

Without realizing it, Muggsy was trying to get himself killed. After he had gotten himself into a serious scrap from which I had a tough job extricating him, I took him out of the act and retired him to the menagerie tent.

Then there was Midnight, a black leopard, the most unusual animal of her kind I have ever trained. Although many years have elapsed since she was a member of a mixed group I worked for the Gollmar Brothers Circus, she lingers on in my memory.

Eventually I stopped using black leopards, which, pound for pound, are the fiercest and fastest members of the big-cat family. Their great speed and compactness—Midnight weighed about 175 pounds and was small and unspectacular-looking by comparison with a lion or a tiger—makes them a constant threat to the trainer. In using them the trainer finds himself taking great risks with little or no pay-off in the way of audience reaction.

So great is the black leopard's maneuverability in a comparatively small enclosure such as my arena that the unpredictable spring from a standing start—and it can be a tremendous one in the case of so prodigious and lightning-fast a jumper—is an ever-present threat against which there is no defense if it comes with sufficient suddenness.

I am grouping Midnight with Henry and Muggsy because the outstanding characteristics of these three cats were related in some way to the question of fighting. Henry hated combat and tried to get away from it; Muggsy loved a scrap and started as many as he could; Midnight disliked a fight as much as Henry but, unlike the bob-tailed lion whose philosophy it was to mind his own business, my black leopard tried to break up fights, an ambitious undertaking for so small an animal.

My act in those days consisted of seventeen animals—two lions, two tigers, two pumas, two polar bears, two Russian bears, one Himalayan bear, three hyenas, three leopards (two spotted and one black). It was as disparate an aggregation as any animal trainer has ever handled. Grudges inevitably develop in *any* group of animals; in as mixed a lot as the one I have just enumerated there were more real and potential feuds than I or any other trainer should have attempted to cope with. This was early in my career and I was trying to get somewhere in a field where the opportunities are limited. So when this four-legged miscellany was turned over to me by the Gollmar management, I readily agreed to see what I could do with them.

In a group of animals more nearly her own size Midnight could have held her own, for I've never seen a black leopard that wasn't fundamentally tough and vicious. She was smart and knew her own limitations, was aware that in a free-for-all she could easily be torn to pieces. Instinctively she watched for minor brawls that could lead to such a holocaust, and when they occurred she tried to break them up in her curious way, now and then meeting with success. For instance, one day toward the end of a performance one of my lions took a poke at a tiger on the floor of the arena. Before they had properly squared off, Midnight swept down from her high seat in one of her swift, graceful movements, dashed between the quarrelers and with one great leap was back on her high seat in the arena. The unexpected appearance and disappearance of the black leopard momentarily caught the attention of the lion and tiger and this interruption was all the time I needed to break up the potential fight.

Many times that year I struggled to figure out that animal's mental processes in the hope of being better able to control and protect her. In an act made up of animals more nearly her own size she probably would have had a different personality.

Perhaps instead of stopping or trying to stop fights she would have started them. For she had the built-in ferocity that all black leopards have. But, as I have pointed out, she also seemed to have a kind of judgment and common sense that kept her basic combativeness under control. Thus she knew enough not to become embroiled in brawls with animals that outweighed her two and three to one.

The more I think of it the more astonished I am that so small an animal, equipped mainly with speed and determination, was able to break up so many fights-in-the-making.

Because of her nervousness—induced largely by the presence of so many more powerful animals—I had my doubts as to whether I would be able to train Midnight to jump back and forth through a flaming hoop, the stunt for which I had her in mind. But, though she had her jittery moments, I had no trouble communicating what I wanted her to do. And once she had the cues fixed in her mind, she performed the trick perfectly.

But her nervous alarm at the first sign of discord in the arena continued, and because of this I knew that sooner or later I would have to take her out of the act. Someday this jitteriness in the presence of strife would betray her into trying to stop one fight too many. Inevitably one of the brawlers would seize her and she wouldn't have a chance. She had had several narrow escapes—in fact, one day she barely managed to elude a smash from the giant paw of a tiger that would have broken her neck if the blow had landed.

This nervousness also caused Midnight to make sudden lunges for me that would have knocked me down if I had not developed the habit of watching her every move. She had powerful shoulders for so small a member of the big-cat family, and there was great force behind these rushes. Several times I caught her on my chair; but there is no foolproof defense against so incredibly swift an animal. There came the day when in a lightning-fast, unstoppable assault she slashed both my arms. I was hospitalized and it required almost a hundred stitches to close the wounds. I had to remove her from the act.

I could not attempt to say with any degree of certainty what motivated Midnight vis-à-vis the other animals. It seems to me that that leopardess had a pretty good idea of what she wanted to accomplish. A peaceful relationship with the other animals was her only salvation in the situation in which she found herself, so she set out to achieve it. As indicated earlier, under different circumstances—perhaps in an act with smaller animals that she could dominate—she might have been a warmonger herself.

I have her pegged as a realist of the arena.

6. Building a Whole New Act—
Part One

Why I Broke with Ringling Bros.-Barnum & Bailey
— Good-by, Madison Square Garden — An Animal
Trainer without Any Animals — First You Find 'Em,
Then You Train 'Em

In the early 1930s *The Big Cage,* a book I had written with my present collaborator, was bought by Universal Pictures. I did not realize then that this would set in motion a chain of events that would alter the whole course of my career. At the time I was with the Hagenbeck-Wallace Circus, which was owned by the Ringling Bros.-Barnum & Bailey organization.

I was occasionally detached from Hagenbeck-Wallace to play what the front office called "the big dates"—among them New York and Boston—with the Ringling show.

It was an ideal arrangement. I had grown up with the Hagenbeck-Wallace performers, numbered many friends among them, and the H-W show was "home" to me. I also enjoyed the excitement of the big-city dates, especially the month to five weeks in New York.

I was thrilled by the celebrities who called on me in my dressing room in New York's Madison Square Garden—such people as Ernest Hemingway, Walter Huston, Ed Wynn, Gene

Tunney, Jack Dempsey, Floyd Gibbons (the foreign correspondent who scored one of radio's earliest successes as a
newscaster), the perennial Lowell Thomas, Joseph Medill
Patterson, founder and publisher of the New York *Daily News,*
and a number of men in various branches of newspapering
such as Grantland Rice, Joe Williams, Walter Trumbull, Bob
Considine, Heywood Broun, Bill Corum, Burris Jenkins, Hype
Igoe, O. O. McIntyre and Mark Hellinger, to mention just a
few. It was a parade of outstanding people in many fields—
famous writers, baseball stars and other sports figures, nation-
ally known stage and screen personalities, etc. It is exciting to
meet such people at any stage of your career, but when you
are still in your twenties it is doubly so.

A popular pastime today is to kid anyone who gets excited
about such things and to dismiss as a name-dropper the person
who mentions the famous people he has met. The fact remains
that I was thrilled by that parade of celebrities through my
dressing room.

Many of those people went out of their way to befriend me.
In addition to being entertaining, most of them seemed able
to carry on a rewarding conversation on a wide variety of
subjects and this gave me the urge to become better informed
myself—to broaden my interests and to stop looking at everything through the narrow, restricted lens of animal training.

It was an education to listen to some of these people. Hemingway, for instance. He had a way of relating wild-animal
behavior to some of the things people did, and the first thing
you knew he was off at some interesting tangent making a
point that was appropriate, not just dragged in. It's hard to
convey just what I mean. Everything he said seemed to have a
natural tie-up with my act and with life in general. There were
moments when the things he said were obviously designed to
draw me out, and I hope he was satisfied with my responses.

The motion picture of *The Big Cage* was the first of a series
of developments that in time resulted in my being prevented

from ever again appearing in Madison Square Garden, a Ringling monopoly.

This is how it came about:

When the picture was completed, those in charge of selecting attractions for the Radio City Music Hall in New York City previewed it and were enthusiastic. They informed Universal Pictures and me that they would be glad to exhibit it if I would make personal appearances. They felt that since I was well known to New Yorkers, it would help at the box office if I made these appearances. It never occurred to me that my employer, the Ringling organization, would have any objection. I figured that the movie would help the circus and vice versa. So, having no reason to believe that there would be any difficulty, I agreed to make such personal appearances as would not interfere with my matinee and night show at the Garden. The Music Hall and the Garden are only a few minutes apart by taxi, and since the Music Hall operated on a continuous-performance basis, it would be possible for me to appear several times a day, say a few words and be on my way.

The management of the big circus empire was undergoing changes, and John Ringling, who had always been friendly to me and had authorized my making that movie in the first place, was not around to support me when the representative of the financial interests that had gained control of the Ringling Bros.-Barnum & Bailey enterprises made the surprising ruling that I would not be allowed to make personal appearances. They took the position that my appearance elsewhere in New York would take the edge off my work at the Garden. I couldn't follow this reasoning.

When the Music Hall management was informed of the Ringling verdict, they decided against exhibiting the picture. It opened instead in a minor house.

One Universal executive expressed the belief that my employer's decision had done irreparable damage; it was his contention that it would get around in "the trade" that the Music Hall management had had a second thought about the picture and had decided it was not good enough for New York's leading motion-picture theater.

The arbitrary attitude of my employer was hard to understand. The controversial motion picture had yielded the circus considerable revenue. In those days the lions and tigers in my act were the property of the Ringling Bros.-Barnum & Bailey enterprises. Universal Pictures paid three thousand dollars a week for the use of the animals; they also paid all other expenses involved, including transportation of the animals from winter quarters in Indiana to Hollywood and back again, insurance, the salaries of the trained caretakers I designated, veterinarian bills, etc.

As the motion picture was made during the depression of the 1930s, when circus business was at a low ebb, the deal with Universal for the use of the animals was a lucky break for my employer, especially as it was a between-seasons operation. Instead of having to pay over two hundred dollars a day for the care and feeding of forty-eight lions and tigers (including the "spares" we had to keep handy for replacements), the circus had an assured income of three thousand dollars a week for the use of the animals. In other words, since I used the big cats in Hollywood for twelve weeks, the Ringling organization had an income of thirty-six thousand dollars from them instead of having to make an outlay of almost seventeen thousand dollars for their maintenance between seasons.

I felt that I had been the victim of a senseless lack of cooperation, and I had some caustic things to say on the subject. All I accomplished was to incur the wrath of top management.

To punish me for taking such strong exception to their ruling in connection with that controversial motion picture, management began leaving my name out of press releases. I found the situation amusing, since they continued to feature my name in lights on the marquee over the Garden's entrance. Under the circumstances, I could worry along without being mentioned in those mimeographed handouts.

The New York press continued to be kind to me. The coverage was personal—interviews and firsthand reports of my work in the arena—and I found it a constant source of amusement to be shown the circus press releases by reporters who came around to see me.

As much as I liked New York, I was glad when that engagement was over and I could return to the Hagenbeck-Wallace show, so ably managed by Jess Adkins, then the soundest circusman in the Ringling Bros.-Barnum & Bailey organization. Adkins, for reasons of his own, didn't like the way the Ringling enterprises were being run. And while he didn't have much interference in running the H-W show, he wondered whether he had much of a future in an organization that didn't have a first-rate circus executive at the top.

The following year—again between seasons—I returned to Hollywood to make another motion picture, *The Lost Jungle*. My relations with the Ringling front office were still strained, but I managed to get permission to make this movie.

In its issue of March 29, 1937, *Time* magazine gave me a cover story in which the following appeared: ". . . Another important result of the Depression was to disgust Clyde Beatty, who had built his cat act into the world's most sensational one-man spectacle during the lean years, with the miserably disproportionate $100 a week salary his friends whisper he was getting from Ringling in 1934." Some people didn't believe the story and said so, but it happened to be true. Not much money for risking my neck fourteen times a week. It came to $7.14 per performance.

This revelation proved an embarrassment, because after all I was supposed to be a "big star," if you'll pardon the expression. While I had no desire to create the impression that my earnings were fabulous, at the same time I did not want to emerge as a simpleton who didn't know how to handle his business affairs. Though the revelation created some awkward moments for me, I secretly admired the enterprise of

the writer who had somehow dug up the information about
my salary.

In the Ringling organization salary matters were strictly in
the province of the business manager's office. But I imagine
that if I had appealed to owner John Ringling before he left
the organization, he would have made an effort to do something for me. I had once thought of approaching him—we all
knew him fondly as Mr. John—but I changed my mind when
I heard that he was in financial difficulties. He had been unable
to meet interest payments on a bank loan of $1,700,000, and
not long afterward he withdrew from the company.

But on the whole my low salary was at least partly my
own fault. I don't recall that I ever made a wholehearted effort
to get what I was worth.

I have always loved wild animals and considered it a privilege to be near them. In those early days this almost amounted
to an obsession. My head was full of ideas for new tricks,
new formations, new routines; and I was having the time of
my life getting insights into the personalities of the different
lions and tigers. I couldn't have left any doubt in anyone's
mind that I considered my job a dream come true.

A newspaper interviewer—the source is a faded clipping in
an old scrapbook—contended that "Beatty is so crazy about
the big cats he would probably work for three squares a day
and a place to sleep." Which wasn't far from the truth.

However, the facts of life began crowding in on me and it
didn't take me long to find out that one hundred dollars a
week didn't go very far. So those movie deals were most welcome. It was disillusioning to discover that Hollywood writers
and directors seemed to think that wild animals could be
controlled more or less like actors, but when you need money
you can put up with a few disappointments.

It was surprising to read a screenplay and learn that at
this or that particular moment Lion A or Tiger B was to move
forward twenty-seven feet, turn left, step back twelve and a
half feet, roar and/or snarl, and then stalk Actor Whoozis in

the "typical jungle manner, baring his teeth and claws and lashing his tail menacingly."

In a situation of this kind I would promise to show the script to the animals, ask them to read it and get their reaction. If their response was unfavorable there would have to be some changes, I would point out. It occurs to me that maybe those screenwriters had read the hogwash about my so-called "hypnotic eye" that enabled me to get the big cats to do anything I asked except crochet and play the piano.

At the conclusion of the 1933 season I appeared in *The Lost Jungle*. There were scenes in which my lions and tigers roamed free in realistically improvised veld and jungle. The 1934 season would get under way a short time after the completion of the picture and I was anxious to head for Madison Square Garden, where we were soon due to open the spring season, and get my cats accustomed to performing in an arena again.

For three days prior to the matinee that was to be our first performance of the new season, I tried to get Sam Gumpertz, the new Ringling manager, to clear the way for the setting up of the "big cage," as my arena has come to be known. This meant being placed on the rehearsal schedule for specific periods.

Rehearsals were constantly in progress—all according to a prearranged timetable. And for some mysterious reason I was unable to get my workouts listed.

My act involves many props—a pedestal for each animal and considerable other equipment. First the heavy sections of the arena are put in place and clamped together, then the overhead safety net has to be installed. Next comes the assembling of the sections of the tunnel through which the big cats are fed into the arena. With so many different acts and routines on the schedule, a series of rehearsals such as I had in mind requires much advance preparation.

Request after request for rehearsal time, made through members of Mr. Gumpertz's staff, accomplished nothing. It began to look as if I would be lucky to wangle *one* rehearsal.

By eleven o'clock of the morning of that first matinee I still had not rehearsed my animals and had no information as to when I would be permitted to do so. I'm reasonably patient, but there is just so much pushing around a man can take. I got hold of Pat Valdo, the assistant manager, and asked him to tell Gumpertz I would not go on without a rehearsal.

Gumpertz was seated in a box watching the different performers rehearse. Valdo walked over to where he sat and delivered my message.

A few minutes later Gumpertz came storming over to where I stood on the hippodrome track chatting with fellow performers. He enjoyed kicking people around but never so much as when he had an audience. Striding belligerently up to me and poking me on the chest with his forefinger, he announced that I would put on my act at the matinee *without* a rehearsal. He was the boss and I would do as I was told, etc., etc., meanwhile continuing his tantalizing use of that finger to emphasize every other phrase.

This reminded me that I had a couple of forefingers myself. So, with my right-hand one, I poked him back in similar fashion as I announced for one and all to hear that I would not play that matinee without first giving the cats a good workout.

This started him shouting and in no time at all a number of performers and miscellaneous circus hands encircled us. Gumpertz became repetitious, angrily reminding me again that he was the boss and I would do as I was told or clear out. I told him I would do just that and he could work the big cats himself. With which I plowed my way through our impromptu audience, headed for the nearest exit and started down the street in the direction of my hotel.

My mind was full of unhappy thoughts—for instance, this rift meant saying good-by to Lillian Leitzel, Alfredo Cadona and other good friends in the Ringling show. In the midst of agonizing about parting with old friends, I had still another thought, a most practical one. My employers owed me five thousand dollars! Would they pay it or, on the ground that my quitting so suddenly had done them that much damage or more, would they refuse to pay it? (Perhaps a brief explanation of this debt is indicated. With my own money I had bought some animals for the Ringlings, and I had not yet been reimbursed. Hollywood earnings had enabled me to become their banker.)

As I entered the hotel lobby I smiled for the first time that day as I pondered this aspect of the money that was owed me: "Five thousand dollars is five thousand dollars. I'm not *that* mad."

Nevertheless, I started packing my bags as soon as I entered my room. A few minutes later there was a rap on the door. I had two callers—Fred Bradna, the Ringling show's equestrian director, and Gumpertz's assistant, Pat Valdo. Both had always been friendly. Bradna said, "The boss has changed his mind. You can have your rehearsal."

I let them persuade me to return to the Garden, although it would be a long time before I would forget the browbeating to which Gumpertz had subjected me.

By this time we were far behind schedule. But I simply had to have that rehearsal, a most thorough and painstaking one, to make up for the two or three the situation really called for.

My animals were completely rusty as far as arena work was concerned—during those months in the klieg-lighted veld and jungle of the motion-picture world I had been compelled to make some changes in my method of communicating with them—and it would be needlessly hazardous to switch them back to the business of performing for circus audiences without checking and rechecking all their cues, entrances, exits, etc., making sure they would take the right pedestals, and in general doing everything I possibly could to assure a reasonably good first performance.

In view of all these delays it was not surprising that the matinee started an hour late. Gumpertz was fuming at the conclusion of my rehearsal, which of necessity was a lengthy one. He accused me of stalling and deliberately holding up the matinee.

Actually I lose all sense of time when I am working with my animals. With lions and tigers in front of me, others to my right and left, and still others behind me there isn't much time for anything except intense concentration on the job in hand.

That final beef of Gumpertz's was the clincher. I made up my mind then and there to leave the Ringling organization.

If there had been any change in Gumpertz's attitude I might have reconsidered; for after all I had no quarrel with the Ringling firm itself. I was still nettled by the refusal to let me make personal appearances in connection with the proposed showing of *The Big Cage* at the Radio City Music Hall, but in that situation, as in the present one, I was opposed by an individual, not by the Ringling organization (although I must admit I was puzzled by their hiring such unreasonable managers).

Throughout this embattled engagement at the Garden, which proved to be my last one there, Gumpertz continued his pettiness, behaving more like a spoiled child than the head of a big enterprise. For instance, he instructed Roland Butler, chief Ringling press agent, to "cut down on Beatty's publicity." Butler, a close friend, told me the story himself. Gumpertz continued his vendetta in a press release announcing "the greatest animal act of all time" as the main attraction of the Ringling show the following year. A woman trainer would present "seventy-five lions and tigers in the most daring display of control over wild animals ever exhibited anywhere in the world." The woman chosen to perform this miracle was Dorothy Herbert, a bareback rider, who didn't seem to know any more about it than I did.

Dorothy was one of the ablest performers in show business at her own specialty, but she had never handled a wild animal in her life and had no desire to.

At the conclusion of that engagement at Madison Square Garden I rejoined the Hagenbeck-Wallace show. When I told the manager, my good friend Jess Adkins, about the bad time Gumpertz had given me, Jess said that that was typical of our new management. There was no sense in staying with an organization that thought Sam Gumpertz, who had had no experience in the field, was qualified to head a big circus empire. He had had a certain amount of success as a Coney Island concessionaire. He was reputed to know how to run a scenic railway, a tunnel of love, a merry-go-round and a ferris wheel, and how to get financial mileage out of a troup of gen-u-wine Egyptian belly dancers, but he was totally unfamiliar with the world of the big top. He was strictly an amusement-park operator.

One thing led to another and the first thing I knew I was conferring with Adkins and Zack Terrell, a mutual friend who had once managed the Sells-Floto show, about starting a circus of our own. We finally entered into an agreement to do just that at the conclusion of the 1934 season.

We acquired a spacious, rambling building in Rochester, Indiana, and took possession as soon as the Hagenbeck-Wallace show ended its tour of the country.

Despite some disadvantages, the building we acquired was suitable for our purposes. It had once been a repair station for railroad boxcars and coaches—an enormous one—and we would be able to move our circus cars over the tracks right into the building.

We didn't have much capital, having raised just about enough to get started, so this old building, which we were able to rent at a low figure, was a great find.

I selected for my own activities an area spacious enough to accommodate my arena, which I had standardized at a diameter of forty feet. The room was big enough to provide operating space outside the big cage, which meant I would be able to keep equipment there and still have plenty of space in which to move around. The main disadvantage of this arena area was that smack in the middle of it there was a circular post about two feet in diameter. In fact, I could not find any space in the building suitable to my purpose that didn't have one or more of these columns; so I would have to get used to training the recruits for my new big-cat act in an arena with a post in the middle. The animals would have to get used to it too.

As I have pointed out, the lions and tigers I had previously worked with were the property of the Ringling organization, and my job now was to find enough cats for the formation of a brand-new act. And it had to be done in time for the opening of the next circus season.

In fact, ours was an even more ambitious objective than that. We had sounded out the management of the circuses put on annually by the Shriners of Detroit and Cleveland to see if we could interest them in my act and other attractions we were planning. Each was a two weeks' engagement, the Detroit show starting the first of February, followed by the one in Cleveland.

In retrospect I realize what optimists we were to offer the services of a circus which so far consisted of the headquarters we had acquired and the circus experience of Adkins, Terrell and myself, which we would not be able to implement until we started some activity in that empty building.

We knew that we had many problems, but we acted as if they were nonexistent. We were too preoccupied with the future to stop and think that we might not be able to put together a whole circus in so little time. Some acts could be secured through talent agencies and edited to suit our needs, but an act such as mine—around which the new circus was being built, according to Adkins—would have to be built from scratch.

My first assignment would be to acquire as fast as possible the lions and tigers I would need. Terrell had organized and managed an animal-training exhibit at the Chicago World's Fair of 1933. The animals had been trained by the able Allen King and were known as King's Lions. He had not yet disposed of these animals. There were eight or nine of them, as I recall. They were healthy, good-looking animals and some of them, I decided, would wind up in my act, although under different circumstances I would not have used any of them. They had been taught by another trainer, and although King knew his business, I didn't like to use cats trained by someone else. I imagine King would have been just as wary of animals trained by me.

There are certain fundamentals that all trainers observe, but there are also many points of departure. An animal used to the cues and maneuvers of one trainer can be confused by those of another.

Moreover, in addition to specific cues, a trainer develops a kind of telepathy by means of which he communicates to the beasts what he wants them to do. This sometimes takes the form of body movements. For instance, if I want to flash to a lion seated near the top of the arena that he's due to start down, I get his attention by cracking my whip and then by a combination of body and arm movements I tell him to start descending.

The age of some of Terrell's lions also presented a problem. Two of them, for instance, were twelve years old. Lions live to be twenty-two and over—I remember one that reached thirty in a zoo—so at twelve those animals weren't really old. They were in vigorous health, lively, impressive-looking—the big black-maned variety that have since become so scarce—but they were much too old to unlearn what they had been taught.

Under normal circumstances I select as new pupils cats that are from two and a half to three years old. Sometimes I will use a four-year-old as a beginner, but only if he is so fine an animal and so intelligent that I don't like to pass him up.

It would be needlessly risky to use Terrell's twelve-year-olds. Lions have a way of "going bad" from about the tenth year on. Frank G. Bostock, the great English trainer, discussed this in a book published in 1903, *The Training of Wild Animals*. What he said over sixty years ago in a chapter entitled "'Going Bad'—Animal Instinct," is as true today as when he wrote it.

Here is a typical passage:

"What those who have charge of wild animals in captivity, and especially trainers, dread most among the large carnivora, is that inexplicable change of temperament on the part of the animal known in the parlance of the circus and the menagerie as 'going bad.' Lions are likely to go bad about the tenth year of life. . . .

"This 'going bad' may come in the nature of a sudden attack, or it may develop slowly. . . . An experienced trainer can usually detect the symptoms of this curious ailment."

I thought I could detect it in the unrelievedly sullen eyes and the occasionally twisted mouths of Terrell's twelve-year-olds. As badly as I needed lions, I quickly voted that pair out of the act.

I have a theory—and though it is only that, it is based on observation and study—that the "curious ailment" Bostock refers to is the menopause. In the case of Terrell's cats, a male menopause. I am convinced that lions and tigers of both sexes are subject to this phenomenon. It develops earlier in tigers than it does in lions.

This menopause factor is one of several reasons why I like to start a big cat at the age of three or four and use the animal for a maximum of five years, retiring him to the menagerie tent before he reaches the age of ten. Unfortunately, I have not always been able to achieve this objective. Had it been possible, I would have been spared considerable trouble, including some of the severest injuries I have sustained in the arena.

I quickly made it known to all the animal dealers and zoo officials of my acquaintance that I was in the market for lions and tigers. I was reasonably sure that I did not have enough time to build the kind of act I wanted. It would be difficult to get enough of the right kind of cats and train them as I thought the job should be done. But I would do the best I could.

One of my first moves was to communicate with Louis Ruhe and Ellis Joseph, leading dealers with whom I had done considerable business in the past. They informed me that they had animals they considered likely candidates. As busy as I was, I would have to see those animals. These men were dependable, but they were only superficially familiar with my work, and I could not expect them to detect signs which to a trainer spell trouble.

I made some purchases at the Ruhe and Joseph establishments. Neither had many animals on hand. While the Depression was not quite as bad as it had been, conditions around the country were still unsatisfactory. Zoos had stopped buying animals—in fact, some of them had an assortment up for sale—and the dealers didn't feel justified in keeping much stock on hand.

The familiar cry of zoo officials in those days was: "They're eating us out of house and home." Feeding lions and tigers is an expensive proposition—(not to mention the many other wild-animal appetites that had to be satisfied)—and in communities where there were municipal zoos there was strong sentiment for cutting operational costs.

Private and commercial zoos and so-called animal farms made big cats available. I made some purchases at the Detroit and St. Louis zoos. Another good source was the Jungle Compound at Thousand Oaks, California. The Selig Zoo in Los Angeles was another good source. Their main business was providing animals for use by the Hollywood motion-picture studios. The movie field had been hard hit and the Selig people had more hungry animals on their hands than they cared to feed. They sold me two lions and three tigers, all young ones. Although they were good to look at, healthy and mentally alert, I bought them reluctantly. For they had been reared in captivity. I knew from experience that animals fresh from the veld and the jungle make the best performers, but I was in no position to be fussy. I would have to take what I could get.

My friend Dr. Theodore Schroeder, head of the Detroit Zoo, was especially interested in my problem and did all he could to help. I had informed him that we also needed animals for our menagerie, and when he sold me an enormous, ill-tempered lion that later acquired the name Detroit, he assumed I was buying the animal for exhibition purposes. When I told him I planned to use this grumpy giant in my act, he looked at me in disbelief. When he realized I was in earnest, he shook his head and said, "I wish you wouldn't, Clyde," explaining that he regarded the animal as a potential killer. A remark of that kind, from an authority who was also a friend, should have stopped me.

But I desperately needed animals—big magnificent-looking specimens like this one—so I stuck to my purpose. I argued that I would be especially careful with this big handsome surly devil and see if I couldn't change his disposition. I took the position that all big cats are potential killers, and knowing that this one had a reputation for meanness, I would exercise extraordinary caution in handling him.

In this lion's favor was the fact that he had been raised in Africa. I already was stuck with too many animals that had been reared in captivity. My main concern was that this cat was six years old, young for a lion but a little too old for a beginning performer.

However, where else would I be able to find so huge and gracefully proportioned a lion—one that would look so spectacular in the arena?

When I thanked Dr. Schroeder for letting me have his

"monster," as he called him, he remarked, "We won't miss his appetite or his disposition." As we shook hands and parted, I predicted that this animal would make a fine top-mounter. It would take a lot of doing, but it could be done. My prediction came true, but for the record I am compelled to add that the good doctor had shrewdly sized up the "monster" he had sold me.

With the confidence of youth I felt I could keep this truculent creature under control. I suppose I couldn't afford to think otherwise. I was in a race against time to produce a new act for a new circus and if I flopped my position would be untenable.

Well, I managed to keep that spectacular monster under control for a few years, but eventually he went berserk and killed two tigers. I was lucky not to be on the casualty list myself.

But I mustn't get ahead of my story.

One of the lions offered by a zoo's curator proved to be the very one the Hagenbeck-Wallace Circus had given him the year before, a "picture animal" I had retired from the act because he had lost his speed and no longer performed with the gusto that is so typical of younger animals. When I reminded him of this he laughed and offered me a spirited, handsome five-year-old with the comment, "I hate to part with him, but there's one consolation. Of all our big cats he's the biggest eater." He was echoing Dr. Schroeder's sentiments in parting with Detroit. Never within my memory was the cost of feeding animals so important a factor in the zoo world.

In a comparatively short time I had assembled about thirty lions and tigers. They had been collected haphazardly and I would be extremely lucky if five-sixths of them proved adequate—just barely so, in some cases. This would not be the best act I could build, or anywhere near it. It would be the best I could produce under the prevailing conditions. Subsequently

I would make substitutions. That is, after we opened I would secure additional cats and keep training them as replacements until I had the group I wanted.

Meanwhile Gumpertz had been hearing rumors. The Hagenbeck-Wallace Circus, owned, as the reader recalls, by the Ringlings, maintained winter quarters and a permanent office in Peru, Indiana, which is only a short run from Rochester (in the same state) where we purchased the abandoned railroad building.

Gumpertz didn't pay any attention to the rumors until he heard about our acquiring that building as our training center and headquarters. He knew that I was a member of the Elks in Peru, so he telephoned the club's office to find out where I was living. He learned that I was the guest of my friend Paul Eisenberger at his home in Peru (where I stayed until I had a chance to rent a house near our circus-in-the-making in Rochester).

The circus season over, Gumpertz was back in his palatial home in Florida. From there he telephoned Eisenberger and asked him to tell me "not to do anything" until he had had a chance to talk things over with me. He would leave at once for Indiana.

For some reason which I could only guess at, Gumpertz made no effort to set up a conversation with me over the telephone. He could not have failed to remember that in our last meetings he had tossed some of his best insults at me and perhaps he feared that in retaliation I would hang up on him. If that was the case, he guessed wrong. I would have taken the call and told him I had made a firm commitment and that therefore my services were no longer available. This at least would have saved him a trip from Florida to Indiana.

When Gumpertz arrived at Eisenberger's home, I had no desire to see him but I agreed to step out and have a chat with the Ringling boss in his car.

Gumpertz began by saying he had heard I was thinking of

starting a whole new circus. Did I realize what that involved? He was sure I would abandon so impractical a scheme when I thought it over. How could my associates and I hope to put together a complete circus between seasons? It had never been done before. In fact, it had never been *attempted* before. And for a good reason. It was "downright impossible." If we were really in earnest about this thing we'd better reconsider before we lost our shirts. And on and on in this vein.

I tried to cut in and get it through Gumpertz' head that the die was cast, that I had made a binding agreement with my partners and that whether our plans were practical or not was now beside the point.

But the Ringling panjandrum rattled on, possibly hoping— at least early in the conversation—that the proposed new circus was all a bluff, or that, if we *were* taking the idea seriously, we had not yet gotten beyond the conversation stage. He might even have had second thoughts about the building my partners and I had rented for our new show. As yet there was not much activity in that big rambling edifice, which fact his Peru office must have reported. I had arranged for the acquisition of a number of animals for my new act but so far only a few had arrived. To a man of Gumpertz's mentality, even the arrival of *all* the animals would not be a clincher. He just couldn't imagine anyone leaving the Ringling organization.

Perhaps our acquiring this real estate and a few animals was just a device by means of which Adkins (who had also announced he was quitting the Ringlings) and I were seeking to force his hand.

Gumpertz yammered on. It was hard to buck that torrent of words. And harder still to figure out what really was going on in that curious mind. Apparently he thought that, regardless of what moves Adkins and I might have made, the door was still open—wide open.

I could hardly restrain a smile when he expressed concern over my future. If I needed any further proof of his insincerity, that was it.

I began to grow weary of this one-sided conversation. So, in another attempt to get him to see the light, I interrupted him in the middle of a sentence to tell him once more that he was wasting his time. The only difference was that this time I got a little more volume into my voice.

But he could no more be stopped than a rampaging bull elephant. ". . . Think it over, Clyde. You're making a big mistake. How in the name of common sense do you expect to get the animals you need on such short notice? It can't be done. Wake up, man!" Etc., etc.

Even the voluble Gumpertz could not keep up this kind of monologue forever. When he stopped to catch his breath I told him that, as far as I was concerned, the interview was over. "How many times do I have to tell you, Mr. Gumpertz, that I have made a commitment that I intend to honor?"

At last it began to dawn upon Gumpertz that perhaps I meant what I said. He changed his tactics. He began pleading. . . . "You can't walk out on us like this, Clyde. We simply haven't anyone to work your act."

I couldn't resist telling him he no longer needed my act. I reminded him of his announcement that the following season they would have that sensational act in which a woman trainer would appear with seventy-five—count 'em!—lions and tigers, "the most ferocious group of wild animals ever assembled in one arena."

Whereupon Gumpertz forced a laugh and said, "You didn't take that nonsense seriously, did you? That was just newspaper talk." He added a postscript to the effect that someone was always spreading silly stories of that kind. "You know how many crazy rumors get started in our business, Clyde. It's all part of the game." Etc., etc.

This was no time for mincing words. I told Gumpertz he was the "someone" responsible for that particular story. He had issued the instructions himself. Roland Butler had told me so.

Now Gumpertz began begging. It was pitiful. ". . . We'll

give you more money, Clyde. Tell us what you want and it's yours for the asking. You just can't walk out on us like this. I didn't mean those things I said, young feller. Everyone loses his temper once in a while. *Please*, Clyde, don't leave us. We'll be in a terrible fix if you do. . . ." And more begging and whining, tiresomely repeated, until I got sick of the man's voice.

I had reached the end of my endurance. What the situation now called for was an unmistakable clincher, one that even the incredibly stubborn Gumpertz would accept. With all the finality at my command I told him that I was irrevocably committed, that there was no way in which I could get out of the deal I had made with Adkins, and that even if there was I would not invoke it since I had decided that never again would I consider working for Sam Gumpertz.

That did it. He was convinced at last that I meant what I said. I stepped out of the car and he drove off.

Five years later George Hamid signed me up for the whole summer season on his Million Dollar Pier (as it was then called) in Atlantic City. One day Hamid told me that Gumpertz, no longer with the Ringlings, had joined him in his Atlantic City venture, having "bought in," as we say in the entertainment world.

I had been performing on the Pier with my cats for a few weeks before I realized that Gumpertz was associated with the Hamid enterprises. In fact, I didn't learn about it until Hamid told me that Gumpertz was working in the office of the Million Dollar Pier and had expressed a desire to see me.

Gumpertz, it developed, was in charge of the penny machines—an endless assortment of them—such as were familiar sights in the days when the penny arcades flourished. In addition to the machines that sold the public a cent's worth of salted peanuts, chewing gum or chocolate, there were a great many that were classified as "entertainment." You put a penny in the slot, gazed through a viewer and as you turned the crank you saw a few feet of a Charlie Chaplin film, a "bevy of beautiful bathing girls" (overdraped by today's standards) or perhaps a big moment from one of the prize fights in which Jim Corbett or Stanley Ketchell or Jim Jeffries or some other master pugilist participated.

Those machines, I understand, were good revenue-producers. There were many of them scattered throughout that huge pier and they were in constant use. They entailed practically no upkeep and yielded thousands and thousands of pennies daily.

While I had no desire to see Sam Gumpertz, I decided to do so since George Hamid, a good friend, had suggested it. So one day I called on my former Ringling Bros.-Barnum & Bailey boss at the business headquarters of the Million Dollar Pier.

He was seated at a long, flat desk counting pennies. As I entered he was stooped over rolling a paper wrapper around what was probably a batch of a hundred pennies. There was a great mound of coppers in the center of the desk and elsewhere on it were many of the finished rolls. And on the floor beside him there was a rather large sack that must have contained a few hundred dollars' worth of the copper coins.

Gumpertz was so absorbed in what he was doing that he didn't hear me enter. When I greeted him he looked up and we shook hands. This wasn't the assertive Gumpertz I once knew, but neither did he seem dispirited.

"Sorry we had all that trouble," he said. This was followed by a reference to "the good old days at Madison Square Garden." I couldn't remember any "good old days" when Gumpertz was around, but I said nothing.

Whatever pleasant memories I had of the Ringling management had to do with the period when John Ringling—the beloved Mr. John—was in command.

I found myself thinking of the pre-Gumpertz days when I was attacked by Nero, the rampaging lion discussed in Chapter One, and wound up in the hospital for three months. In those days circus contracts stipulated that the performer did his act at his own risk and that the management was not responsible "for any injuries sustained or medical bills incurred as a result thereof."

This was before I had made any money in Hollywood and at a time when my salary was a hundred dollars a week. My hospital and doctors' bills ran into thousands of dollars and I would have had to borrow money to pay them. Although my employer was not legally obligated to pay a dime of this expense, Mr. John arranged to have the Ringling Bros.-Barnum & Bailey business office pay all those bills. If my accident had occurred during the Gumpertz regime, it would have kept me in hock for a long, long time.

I left Gumpertz's office on the Million Dollar Pier feeling sorry for him, which didn't make any sense, since I never had any reason to like the man. Yet somehow I didn't like to see the former general manager of the Ringling empire reduced to counting and wrapping pennies.

Actually it was wasted sympathy. Gumpertz was well-fixed financially and he seemed to feel he was still in show business.

Which reminds me of an old circus story. An elephant caretaker, in charge of a herd of twenty, was worn out from the long hours and hard work entailed in cleaning up after the animals when they developed a persistent dysentery. When he returned home late one night in a state of near-collapse and complained to his wife about his daily ordeal, she said, "Why don't you chuck the job?"

Startled and hurt by her suggestion, he exclaimed, "What! And give up show business?"

I resisted the temptation to kid Gumpertz about something that had happened shortly after I left the Ringling organization and they had made it known that they were looking around for someone to take my place. About this time there appeared on the scene a woman who claimed to be an experienced animal trainer. She made still another claim, one that appealed to the whole Ringling publicity crew, men who knew a colorful story when they saw one. It was this woman's contention—

and she produced an assortment of clippings from foreign newspapers to "prove" it—that she was the daughter of Rasputin, the Russian peasant whose talent for intrigue had enabled him to get himself accepted as adviser to Czar Nicholas II in spiritual matters (he claimed to be a monk) and in affairs of state. She announced dramatically that she had inherited her father's hypnotic eye and thus would be able to perform miracles as an animal trainer.

Gumpertz ordered that she be given a tryout. She almost got herself killed and that was the end of "Madamoiselle Rasputin" as an animal trainer. For a brief period she appeared in the Ringling show's "spec" at the Garden. The spec is the colorful parade with which all circuses open, and its name is derived from the word *spectacle*. She didn't last long, however, as the newspapers were far from convinced that she really was the daughter of "the mad monk," and very little publicity resulted.

I was afraid that if I brought the matter up it would have an adverse effect on Gumpertz's penny-counting, perhaps confusing the bookkeeping of the Million Dollar Pier, something I wouldn't want to do to my friend George Hamid.

Before long the headquarters we had established for the new circus was a scene of great activity.

My arena was set up in the big room with the pillar in the middle, and I began studying the new layout. I would have to keep the location of that post eternally in mind to avoid backing into it or getting pinned against it by one of the cats.

I walked from cage to cage looking over the candidates for my new act—good material, on the whole, considering how speedily they had been assembled. There were a few tigers whose eyes were too close together to suit me and one that proclaimed his bad temper by flattening his ears against his head if you tried to get his attention by calling to him through the bars of his cage; and there were a few lions with long narrow heads, the kind that can be so troublesome. But on the whole I was lucky to be able to recruit so many good-looking, young, powerful cats on such short notice.

Working one at a time, I began their training.

The first step was to teach them the difference between right and left. When I run a new animal into the arena through the tunnel leading from the cages, I watch to see whether, once he leaves the chute, he moves to the right or the left. Some seem to gravitate naturally to the right, others to the left.

If after studying several entrances of an animal I am convinced he prefers to turn to the right, I train him to understand that this is how he is to enter the arena regularly. But of course if I wind up with too many right-siders, it becomes necessary to train a certain number to enter left. Instinctively some of the big cats do, but it is never a fifty-fifty proposition, so considerable drilling has to be done before it is fixed in the minds of the different animals which ones are to enter right, which left. Once this is definitely determined and each animal understands which way he is to turn on coming out of the chute, there seldom is any need to teach this lesson over again.

Once I got my new class to know the difference between right and left, I began the task of "seat-breaking." To give the reader an idea of what is entailed, I will describe how I "seat-broke" King, the most regal-looking of my newly acquired lions, who came by his name when a bystander observed that he could visualize this animal seated on a throne with a crown on his head.

The tall, high-legged pedestal familiar to circus-goers is not introduced at the beginning. It would be too easy for the animal to crawl under one of these pedestals and knock it over. They are made of heavy metal and if one came down with a bang on a beginning performer, it might make him forever "pedestal-shy," as we say.

The first step is what is known as block-seating. A "table" is formed by placing four heavy blocks of wood together, each roomy enough to seat a lion or a tiger, and this unit is placed flush against the bars. Then I communicate to my trainee that I want him to seat himself on the "table." One by one the blocks are removed until only one remains.

Sometimes the response of the trainee is only partial when he is motioned toward the single block for the first time—that is, he merely braces himself against the block seat, his fore-paws resting on the edge of it. The next move is to get him to clamber up, which is usually not too difficult to do.

The first time King leaped up on the block seat he seemed genuinely pleased with himself. The lack of confidence his eyes had earlier reflected was gone and he regarded me benignly. I stroked the top of his head with the light buggy whip I some-times use in these elementary classes, trying to convey "Well done!" He seemed to get the message, tilting his noble head to one side and giving me another friendly look.

While I always start the seat-breaking of any animal by teaching him to get up on a block seat, I also have regular pedestals, of different heights, in the arena. Once a pupil has been block-seated, it is fairly easy to get him to try one of the regular pedestals. When he finds he can go scampering from pedestal to pedestal until he reaches the highest perch in the arena without anything happening to him, he begins to de-velop confidence in his new surroundings.

Pedestaling King proved rather uneventful. He seemed to enjoy racing up and down these heavy metal platforms. After doing it a few times, he looked around at me as if to say, "There's nothing to it, boss."

On one of his descents from the topmost seat he came down too fast, failed to land squarely on one of the pedestals and jumped off when it started rocking. The pedestal toppled over and hit the floor with a bang, King retreating to the other side of the arena and remaining huddled there, his expression con-veying something like, "Gosh, look what *I* did!" I righted the pedestal, ran the buggy whip gently over the animal's head and cued him for another ascent. Up and down he went with joyful abandon like a big house cat that has discovered a new form of entertainment and is determined to get as much fun out of it as possible.

Only a few difficulties developed during the seat-breaking of my new class. One of these involved Lady, who had a tendency toward nervousness and overexcitability. Everything about her reflected that she understood what I sought to communicate to her and that she was trying to respond.

I had enjoyed block-seating her. She picked it up quickly. I motioned her up and down the block and she seemed to be getting fun out of this little game.

But the following day when I tried to switch her from the block seat to a pedestal she became nervous. She overleaped as she aimed for the top of the pedestal with its long metal legs. She was unhurt, but so plainly flustered I maneuvered her to the door leading out of the arena and signaled an assistant to open it. Soon Lady was back in her cage.

Later that day I had no trouble getting Lady to leap to the top of her designated pedestal. She purred contentedly as she sat there. She seemed to enjoy this perch and for at least ten minutes showed no interest in being cued down.

Although I was battling time, I could not afford to rush Lady off her roost. It seemed to give her a feeling of security to sit there on the same seat that earlier in the day had eluded her.

I had been working at a furious pace, and in slowing me up Lady had unconsciously done me a favor. I touched her back gently with a light buggy whip and ran it across her fur. Her pleased expression seemed to say "Do it again," which I did several times while she slanted her head first to one side, then the other. We developed a good working relationship then and there—as good a one, that is, as is possible between a trainer and a member of the unpredictable big-cat family.

In training a new animal the first principle to observe is not to work the pupil too long at a time. When I can't get one of my freshmen to do my bidding in a few minutes, I dismiss him and give him a chance to relax. Then I work on him again in about an hour, meanwhile trying to figure out why he didn't respond the first time.

Sometimes I decide that the fault is my own. I believe, with shameless immodesty, that I can communicate with wild animals as well as anyone, but there are times when I forget to practice what I preach—that there is as much variation in the mental processes of animals as there is in humans. Which is another way of saying that what works with one animal may not work with another. For instance, Animal A may respond to a hand cue that mystifies Animal B, who can be made to execute the desired maneuver only by means of a voice cue or perhaps a combination of hand and voice cues. Other animals respond best to a combination of a soft whistle and set movements of my body.

When there is resistance, I prefer the noisy kind. Nine times out of ten the beast that manifests his displeasure by roaring or snarling makes less trouble in the end. Such an extrovert sometimes accompanies his noisy demonstration with a swipe at my chair, thus taking it out on that appurtenance instead of me. His rebellion is frank, out in the open. He is merely disobedient, a privilege I concede to any lion or tiger new to the arena. Some like to perform, some do not.

It is best to dispense with those that do not like to perform once you are sure you have the situation properly analyzed. Sometimes an animal that has the right disposition for a performer does not comply with the trainer's wishes because the trainer has not yet found a way of communicating to the creature what it is supposed to do. Some of my early noncooperators became fine performers once I corrected mistakes I had made in handling them.

Quiet, sullen resistance is the danger signal the experienced trainer watches and takes seriously when it continues long enough.

Another example—(I have mentioned others elsewhere)—of the folly of generalizing about wild animals is the fact that some of these quiet resisters turn out to be good performers.

Most of them, however, do not, and the ones that seem definitely unhappy about the idea of performing are best retired to the menagerie, where they serve a useful purpose as exhibits.

The animals in our new show—elephants, giraffes, camels, zebras, chimpanzees and other anthropoid apes, bears, lions, tigers, leopards, etc.—would constitute a traveling zoo. Many of the small towns we would play are far removed from the nearest big city where there is a zoo, and the only chance the children in these communities have to see live versions of the wild animals they have seen pictures of and read about in their schoolbooks is in a circus menagerie. This is as true today as it was 30 years ago when we were organizing our new show. Some of my finest-looking lions and tigers have wound up there after demonstrating a convincing dislike for the routine of performing.

One factor that I find amusing is laziness, which is discussed in detail in Chapter Eight, involving Bruno, the laziest lion I have ever known. A handsome animal before he developed a big sagging belly, Bruno did not like to exercise. His main interest in life was his daily fifteen to eighteen pounds of horse meat and the long nap he took when his meal brought on drowsiness. He was no different from some fine-looking people I know who have the same loathing of exercise—fine-looking, that is, until they developed Milwaukee goiters, to swipe a phrase from a newspaper friend. In developing my new act I weeded out a few big cats that were plainly lazy and earmarked them as menagerie exhibits.

So a rebellious nature is not always the explanation of an animal's unwillingness to do a trainer's bidding. Sometimes it is merely laziness. Bruno, for instance, was so lazy he never took advantage of the daily exercise run in the arena. His practice (until I realized the folly of trying to exercise him) was to find a comfortable spot and stretch out like some maned grandfather, not seeming to realize that this was no way for a young lion to act.

Time and again I am asked how I finally arrive at an appraisal of an animal. Perhaps *finally* is not the right word, because you never arrive at any final conclusion about *any* of the big cats. The best the animal trainer can hope for is to be 80 per cent right about a lion or a tiger.

There are certain basics I observe in working with an animal new to training. First I let him get used to finding his way through the tunnel into the arena and back again to his cage. I study him from outside the arena as he makes these inevitable return trips. Occasionally I crack my whip as a means of getting the animal to turn around and face me so that I can gauge whether he is nervous or not.

If I find that the animal is relaxed I know that I can begin quietly edging my way into the arena. I start by sitting on the edge of a pedestal, then I move around slowly and let the animal get used to my presence. When he realizes that I have no unfriendly intentions, any nervousness that may have seized him when I made my entrance vanishes and he gets used to my presence.

My race against time went on. Once I had my animals seat-broken—(the painstaking, laborious work involved is merely hinted at in the foregoing)—I had quite an assignment ahead of me. Following the seat-breaking I would have to teach the big cats to form the so-called pyramid I had developed and which proved so popular in the Ringling and Hagenbeck-Wallace shows. This consists of cuing the cats to take certain seats in the arena, one series slanting up to the right, a second slanting to the left, and both coming to a point at the top where I pedestaled a magnificent six-hundred-pound lion.

When the pyramid is formed, the spotlight is played upon it, the trainer takes a bow, and almost without exception there is a big burst of applause. For this formation is a spectacular sight when it comes off perfectly.

Occasionally the applause is accompanied by laughter, as when the top-mounter gets fidgety. The animals are trained to remain motionless for a few seconds as they hold this pose and nearly always do. There is, however, something involved in the business of being top-mounter that makes an animal restless, playful, inordinately curious, or what you will. At any rate, the lion—in my act it is always a lion—that draws this highest perch in the pyramid requires a great deal of training.

(In some big-cat acts the top-mounter is a tiger. There is nothing uniform about animal training except a few of the things done in the earliest stages of training. For instance, Dave Hoover, Pat Anthony and other capable trainers have their own ideas of how certain results and effects are best achieved.)

Even the best-trained top-mounter sometimes embarrasses his trainer. I once had one—a handsome devil—who occasionally spoiled the dramatic effect of a pyramid of motionless lions and tigers by turning around on his pedestal and facing the audience when he should have been facing me. After a while he became known around the circus as "The Treasurer," the theory being that he was counting the house. I loved that lion, was secretly amused by his lapses, and did nothing to correct this curiosity or whatever it was that impelled him to look around and present his back to me as he stared out at the audience—amiably, I should add. He was a great performer and I was afraid I might break his spirit if I tried to combat his practice of "counting the house" which he indulged now and then. Circus associates of mine contended that a house-counting top-mounter humanized my act, which made me feel better about the whole thing.

After experimenting with several lions I selected as the top-mounter for my new act the one mentioned earlier in this chapter that I had purchased from the Detroit Zoo. I picked him because he was huge and magnificently proportioned. Besides he was not fidgety like the other lions I tried out, was spectacular in repose.

"Traffic control," as I call it, is all-important in teaching the lions and tigers to execute the pyramid. The animals are cued to take their places in a specific order. Thus the top-mounter takes his seat first, the animals nearest the top on the right and left sides of the pyramid go next, until they are all pedestaled, the ones occupying the floor seats (the base of the pyramid) taking their places last.

In my race against time I had to do this formation over and over again until I was sure that each animal knew the seating order. Otherwise there could be a lot of embarrassing confusion. For instance, one day the animals that sat near the top didn't pick up the cues fast enough, with the result that they were milling around on the arena floor when the rest of the pyramid had been formed. They couldn't get to their seats because the pedestals they would have to ascend were already occupied.

I kept drilling my new group until I got them to the point where they were letter perfect or as near to it as one can hope for. Once they had mastered this formation they seemed to enjoy doing it over and over again. The growing interest in the mental processes of animals and animal psychology in general tempts me to speculate on what was going on in the minds of those big cats as I kept them repeating the pyramid. I will not make any silly claim that, bent on pleasing me, they were happy because at last they were able to execute this maneuver to my complete satisfaction. I believe their composite thinking must have been more along this line, "Gee, this is great exercise!"

My race against time became nerve-racking when, in terms of how long it took me to seat-break the animals and teach them the pyramid, I started figuring out how much time I would need to accomplish the rest of the job. This entailed schooling a lion in the art of globe-rolling and teaching a tiger to do the rollover trick; and training at least one lion and one tiger to jump the hurdles. And there were many other things to be taught. As the days came and went—in what seemed such rapid succession I could hardly keep track of them—I found myself thinking more and more of the dead-

line I had to meet and wondering whether I would be able
to meet it.

I understand there is a French saying to the effect that "*impossible* is not a French word." I was young and determined
enough to decide that *impossible* wasn't an American word
either. And when Adkins and Terrell, my partners in this new
circus venture, asked me apprehensively, as they did now and
then, whether I would have the act ready on schedule, I invariably told them I would. Nobody ever said "You bet!" in
more reassuring tones, though doubts often crossed my mind.
Had I promised more than I or any other trainer could possibly accomplish in the allotted time? . . . But I kept such
doubts strictly to myself.

Racing the clock while putting together a whole new animal act is not good for the nerves. Mine are pretty steady, but
I doubt it was ever intended that I should put them to the
test of working night and day at the difficult business of
teaching wild animals to perform.

There were times when I was so exhausted I wondered
whether I could go on. Then a nap would revive me. When
you're really tired you can rest anywhere—even on a cement
floor if you soften it up first with whatever happens to be
handy as padding. You can't be very elegant around training quarters. Practically every square foot of space is in use
and the only way you can create any room for a quick snooze
is to push things out of the way.

I had accomplished a great deal in a few weeks, and while
I had a long way to go, my natural optimism routed my doubts
and I was betting on myself to finish on time unless illness
interfered.

Years ago I saw a vaudeville act in which a comedian impersonated a prize fighter in training. At one point he said,
"I will now punch de bag ten t'ousand consec'ative times."
Whereupon he punched the bag three or four times, commenting, "Dat'll give you de idea." To give the reader an idea

of what the trainer is called upon to do in training big cats new to the arena is all I have tried to do in this chapter.

In the next chapter, in which this same race against time continues, I will attempt to show what was entailed in teaching these same animals a more advanced trickology.

Wild animals are an inexhaustible subject, so the job of making performers of them is never dull or boring. At this writing I am not so much interested in what a lion or a tiger can be taught to do, however striking it may be as a piece of showmanship, as I am in the insights into animal behavior that I get by studying the reactions of the different animal personalities—and, as I said earlier, no two of them are alike.

It is in studying the reactions of these different big-cat types that I get much of my fun as an animal trainer today. It was a lot different in those days when I was building a whole new act. Then my main interest was in getting the animals to perform. I was too young and too preoccupied with achieving success to be overly concerned with the whys and wherefores of animal conduct. Today it is a consuming interest.

One way of finding out how the cast of my new-act-in-the-making was responding to training was to watch them eat. Daily at feeding time I took a look and was reassured by what I saw. With the exception of two tigers, they started eating as soon as their slabs of meat were shoved through the food slots at the base of the cages.

It developed that the two that seemed uninterested in food were not suffering from loss of appetite. They were types—not uncommon—that seldom eat when anyone is watching them. When they were without an audience, their chunks of horse meat—a daily fifteen to eighteen pounds for each—disappeared, and nothing remained except a few scraps of bone.

I also watched to see that the animals drank their water. They need a rather liberal amount and I was pleased to see them empty their large water pans.

The water disposed of, some of the animals began throw-

ing the pans around much in the manner of playful children.
Up and down the long row of cages you could hear these
heavy metal receptacles banging against the sidewalls and
floors.

If a lion or tiger wasn't throwing his pan around, it was
because he wanted to have another drink. They indicate that
they want a receptacle refilled by running their paws around
it and licking it.

Of the equipment I carry into the arena with me—a metal-
reinforced chair, a whip and a blank-cartridge pistol—the chair
is the most important. That understanding observer Ernest
Hemingway figured this out for himself. A student of bullfighting, he quickly related my use of the chair to the toreador's use of the cape.

My own particular school of animal training is more than
a matter of tricks and formations. Once I can get a big cat
used to keeping his eye on the chair—one of the fundamentals
on which I concentrated in building my new act—I can maneuver him around the arena and get him to fight me. In a
circular enclosure such as mine this gives the audience an
ever-changing picture and a much better idea of the animal—
his majestic look, his speed, the suggestion of great power.
When I am in good form the animal is really fighting the
chair, not me.

There are few occupations more dissimilar than that of the
bullfighter and the big-cat trainer. But there are a few anal-
ogous points. The toreador executing a proper veronica, for
instance, keeps the bull's attention on the cape just as I, in
manipulating into a variety of movements and stances a lion
that is fighting me, put on my best show when I can keep
his gaze fixed steadily on the chair.

So, over and over again, in the headquarters at Rochester,
Indiana, where we were organizing a whole new circus, I
worked on my big cats until they responded to the chair as I
wanted them to.

A relatively small number of trainers have been seriously injured or killed in a profession that is centuries old. One of the reasons is the effectiveness of the devices employed to engage the attention of the animals.

7. Building a Whole New Act—
Part Two

The Big Cats Now Ready for Higher Education –
Equilibrium on a Round Rolling Surface – The Roll-
over – A Rebellious Tiger and an Undignified Retreat –
A Race against Time in the Best Tradition of Old-
Fashioned Melodrama – We Finally Open

G LOBE-ROLLING IS a major step forward in the career of a
big cat—lion or tiger—that is learning to perform. When I
start an animal on such advanced work, it is a definite sign
that he or she is thoroughly schooled in the ABCs. It means,
in other words, that my pupil has mastered the fundamentals
and is ready for more complicated studies.

Automatically I eliminate, when I consider new candidates
for globe-rolling, any beast that has displayed extreme nervousness under stress, or doesn't have a good sense of balance.
Even if the animal has displayed exceptional intelligence and
a capacity for quickly mastering the basics, should he also
show signs of overexcitability I reserve him for a role that does
not require the cool restraint that is so essential a part of the
make-up of a successful globe-roller.

Having selected my pupil, I must next "barrel-break" him.
An animal is not expected to tackle so difficult and elusive an
object as a globe without some preparation. This involves the
use of a barrel-like cylinder whose surface is covered with a

thick matting that enables the animal to dig in with his claws and keep his footing.

The barrel is controlled from outside the arena by means of ropes. At first the recruit is merely expected to get used to his new perch. Therefore the barrel is kept stationary in the beginning. The idea is to accustom the animal to one thing at a time. It would be asking too much to expect him to get used to his new perch and a rolling motion simultaneously.

When the pupil is thoroughly at home on his cylindrical roost, the barrel is moved forward a foot or two at a time by means of the ropes. At this stage there still is no rolling motion. The idea is merely to get the animal accustomed to moving forward on the barrel.

Next the barrel is placed on a "skid," or track, and rolled forward a foot at a time. A heavy block is placed on the skid at the point where I want the barrel stopped. The idea is to achieve a slow and steady gradualism in teaching the animal to balance himself on this rolling object. If I pick the right animal, instinctively he will start moving his feet in a manner designed to help him keep his balance. When his footwork is good enough to enable him to keep his equilibrium for a foot or two, the block is moved forward to give him a chance to balance himself for a yard or a little more.

Sometimes this is too much for the pupil and he goes sliding off the cylinder to the arena floor; but the big cats are intuitive in a situation of this kind and almost without exception land gracefully on their feet, so deftly softening the impact of the fall that they aren't even shaken up.

After several days the trainee learns to balance himself for a distance of approximately four or five feet or a little more. The big cat that keeps his feet stationary when the cylinder is in motion cannot hope to keep his footing. Oftener than not my future globe-roller instinctively moves forward with the roll of the barrel and in trying to keep up with it succeeds in remaining aboard it. When this happens often enough,

[27]   A lion and a tiger sparring for position in a beginning fight. In the next picture . . .

[28]   The combatants are settling down to some infighting. The lion is unconcerned as his adversary grabs at his heavy mane. Note the lion's right forepaw, which suggests a prize fighter about to deliver a haymaker. A second later, that "fist" lands and sends the tiger, stunned and demoralized, crashing against the bars of the arena.

[29] From left to right, I am flanked by Fred Ringler and Walter Fuller, friends of long standing. Fuller, who is with the Detroit *News,* has written eyewitness accounts of some of my most exciting moments in the arena. Ringler is a former Detroit drugstore proprietor whose show window was once invaded by one of my lion cubs under comic circumstances. Both men figure in Chapter Three.

[30] A section of the "pyramid" described in Chapter Six.

S. H. Ringo Photo, The Virginian Pilot

[31-32]   It is essential that the big cats concentrate on me, as in the first photo. In the second, the attention of the animals has been caught by the movement of heavy props outside the arena at the very moment they should be watching what I am doing and getting used to a new rollover tiger I am breaking in.

Batjac Productions Photo

[33]   This shows how the cameramen are protected when motion pictures of my work are made. The tiger on the pedestal is not yet accustomed to its new surroundings. To keep it from jumping down and hurting itself by banging into unfamiliar objects, the animal is held in place by means of a rope controlled from the outside. When the shooting starts, the rope is removed. Its slackness in this pictures means that we are about to start shooting.

[34]   Here I am with Nero, the lion that almost ended my career when I was still in my twenties. (See Chapter One.) The accident, a freakish one, did not reflect the true nature of this lion, one of the most extraordinary animals I have ever trained. If not for the ministrations of Dr. Stephen D. Malouf of Peru, Indiana, who is still practicing medicine there, I would have lost a leg.

[35-36] RIGHT: One of
the gentlest tigers I have
ever trained.
BELOW: The killer type.
This tiger killed a cage
boy.

Mary Kennedy Photo

he develops a knowledge of how to keep his footing on a rolling object.

The equipment I carry is my chair, always useful if an animal decides to attack, and the light buggy whip. This I play lightly on the hind legs of the animal as a reminder of my presence. It has the effect of keeping him moving his legs forward, and this is the surest way of aiding him to keep his footing when the cylinder is in motion.

Once the trainee begins to feel at home on the cylinder, he is ready for a try at a regular globe, although, in the beginning, this also is covered with matting as an aid to a surer footing. The globe used is a heavy one made of solid wood, three feet in diameter. This, like the cylinder, is placed on a track. At the start the globe is permitted to have no play and the animal is cued to mount it as though it were a regular pedestal.

When he has grown used to this new perch, he is put through the rest of the routine that was outlined in connection with the matted cylinder. The block holding the globe stationary is moved until the big wooden ball has a fair amount of play. When my new globe-roller has learned to balance himself with the sphere in motion over a distance of a few feet, the block is moved forward a greater distance.

Suppose you try out three different cats for the role you are trying to fill. Candidate A, who is cooperative in the beginning and seems a cinch to learn the trick fast, may bog down as the lessons proceed and develop a dislike for this particular assignment (and later on prove a happy and dynamic performer in another). Candidate B may develop a liking for the role but may perform so slowly and methodically in these training sessions that it is easy to appraise him in advance as a performer who will not excite audiences. Candidate C, who at the start fights me every inch of the way to the accompaniment of his angriest snarls, roars and black looks, may, after I have solved the riddle of how to communicate with him, prove to be the best and most reliable performer.

To me the most poignant aspect of animal training involves the big cat that is doing his best and, realizing he isn't quite bringing off what you want done, gives you one of those appealing looks that seems to say, "I *almost* know what you want me to do. If you'll just be a little more explicit I'll go the rest of the way. In other words, Mr. Beatty, this globe-rolling business is all right—and so are some of those other tricks—but would you mind briefing us a bit more clearly? We know you're in a hurry but maybe you've overlooked something you should have told us."

That the reader may see the picture more clearly, let me say that the starting-point of our operation is near the arena bars, with the animal's back toward the bars. I cannot devote myself exclusively to keeping the globe in motion—for I must watch the animal every second of the time and be ready to meet an attack—and in the main it is the job of the attendants outside the arena to keep the sphere going by means of their rope controls.

One of the novice's most natural reactions is to stand stiffly, bracing himself, to keep the globe from moving. The attendants at a signal from me keep slowly forcing the issue, and automatically the animal, in his struggle to keep his balance, moves the wooden ball forward. After a series of rehearsals of this kind the pupil begins to develop the knack of balancing himself. Some animals are instinctive balancers and readily pick up the trick, while others learn only after much effort has been expended by the trainer.

When the next stage is reached, the assistants and their controls move out of the picture. At this point the track on which the sphere moves is sloped slightly downward. I stand in front of the balancer so that he moves toward me. Once he is able to keep his balance, the slope is done away with and I devote myself to cuing him to keep the ball in motion by the proper propulsion of his feet.

This trick mastered, the matting is removed from the big wooden sphere, which has a smooth surface, and I begin the task of getting my pupil used to the slick footing. In most cases, if he has really learned the principles of equilibrium, this can be accomplished in three or four drills. The first trial with the smooth, uncovered globe is a test of whether I have properly schooled my trainee in the rudiments. If an animal, after a series of tries, shows no capacity for coping with the new situation, I know that I haven't succeeded in getting him to understand how to keep his footing on a revolving object, and I start him all over again, going through the whole laborious process once more.

My final task—and this comes only after virtual perfection in maintaining his equilibrium is achieved by the globe-roller —is to get the animal to perform his feat of balancing at an elevation of five feet. The ball and track are placed on supports of this height, for unless the globe-rolling trick is performed at an elevation, most people in a circus audience will be unable to view it properly.

Finally I had a globe-roller trained for my new act—a gracefully proportioned, bright-eyed Royal Bengal tigress who became known as Seleika.

So *that* phase of my race with the calendar was over. I picked Seleika because she reminded me so much of Duchess, a fine tigress I had trained when I was with the Hagenbeck-Wallace show. Both animals had beautiful heads whose markings were almost identical and both were eager students who wound up as enthusiastic performers.

I always think of Seleika as the tigress whose face took on a sheepish look whenever something went wrong—for instance, when she skidded off the smooth surface of the big wooden ball the first time she tried to balance herself on it after I had removed the matting.

But the facial expressions of wild animals can be misleading. I learned from experience that Seleika, whose look after such a misadventure seemed to say, "Sorry I goofed, pal," might be thinking something entirely different. Still wearing the sheepish look, she was capable of slashing at me with a claws-out paw, usually wrecking a leg of my ever-present shield, the kitchen chair, as she did so. Yes, the expressions of wild animals and their behavior don't always match.

Whether the big cats are capable of deliberately assuming deceptive facial expressions I don't know. That is one the scientists will have to figure out, perhaps someone in the Department of Animal Behavior at the Museum of Natural History.

Duchess also had resorted to that sheepish look, accidentally or by design. Several times she made determined lunges at me while sporting the selfsame meek, submissive look. But I developed a great fondness for Duchess when she became one of my most willing performers. She seemed to be thoroughly enjoying herself as she deftly maneuvered the smooth wooden ball across the track.

Audiences always applauded her efforts and she apparently appreciated their response. She was one of those animal "hams" who find applause stimulating. I am thinking of the times when she simply did not want to stop, seemingly spurred on by new bursts of applause.

The only time I had any serious trouble with Duchess, the fault was mine. The oversight of an assistant was responsible, but the blame rested with me because I am supposed to check everything.

One day we were giving a performance in a small town in Wisconsin. It had been raining hard all morning and the big wooden ball used in Duchess's specialty had been soaked. In playing one-night stands it is very difficult, with all the work there is to be done, to prevent props of this kind from occasionally lying around outdoors, but the attendants had strict instructions to examine all my working props before they were placed in the arena and to dry any of them that were wet or even damp.

I make a practice of inspecting the arena before each performance, to make sure it is properly set. My investigation on this particular day was very hasty because the driving rain-storm had delayed the rearing of the big top and we were all behind schedule and working like demons to be on time for the matinee—for after the first downpour the skies began to clear and it looked as if we had a fair chance for a "house."

All went well with my act that afternoon until Duchess's turn to perform. She leaped to the top of one of the pedestals that supported the skid and from there on top of the wet globe. The treacherous surface was something entirely new to her, and, slipping before she could balance herself on top of the wooden sphere, she went toppling to the floor of the arena. She brushed past me in her descent. I got out of her way in a rush, for in a situation of this kind it is not unusual for a tiger to attack. To my complete surprise the amazing animal, seemingly undaunted by the accident, which would have put most tigers in a fighting mood, ascended the pedestal again and was back on top of the globe in no time at all.

By now I realized that the wooden sphere was wet, and I would have gladly excused Duchess from her duties. But she didn't want to be excused. She wanted to perform. In a re-markable exhibition of equilibration, the tigress reached the end of the skid (which, of course, has a protective barrier to keep the ball from going off into space). As she neared the end, I thought she was surely going to fall, but after a game struggle she managed to maintain her balance.

I could hardly believe it when Duchess reached the end and started the second half of her job, which consisted of roll-ing the wet and slippery ball back to the starting point. But the feat was too difficult for even so nimble a cat. Suddenly she slipped, and in her effort to right herself she lost her bal-ance completely. In a last frantic effort to regain it she went over the side of the "track," carrying the ball with her. Down went tigress and globe to the floor of the arena with a crash. As they fell, I ran over to do what I could to keep the animal from being injured by the moving sphere (which had to be solid for a stunt of this kind and therefore heavy). But Duchess, the alertest and nimblest of cats, leaped clear of the hefty ball as I came up. It rolled toward me and banged against my legs, knocking them from under me.

Before I could get to my feet, Duchess came tearing at me and this time there was no hocus-pocus about her facial expression and general demeanor. She was enraged, as her bared teeth, ears flat against the head and lashing tail attested. I fired my blank-cartridge revolver and she backed away sufficiently to give me time to scramble to my feet. With the aid of that ever-helpful shield, my chair, I succeeded in getting the tigress back on the pedestal she occupied regularly.

I regretted this experience, for Duchess was an intelligent, responsive animal and I wanted to keep her good will—to as great an extent, that is, as anyone can hope for the good will of a cat animal. Fortunately, she promptly forgot the incident and continued her career as a zestful, applause-loving performer.

There is something spectacular about a big cat rolling a globe or a cylinder. To this day I feature a huge lion rolling a cylinder five feet high and two feet wide across the floor of the arena. It's still good for a round of applause.

Before I leave the subject of globe- and cylinder-rolling, let me say that the most skilled animal of all, in the performance of this feat, is the bear. But this is not surprising, as a bear's hind legs are built in a way that makes it much easier to perform the trick than it is for a lion or a tiger. In fact, an intelligent bear, with his ability to stand upright, can be taught to mount a globe and keep it in motion with his hind legs alone, whereas I have never seen a cat that could perform the feat without employing all fours. I have had as many as three bears in my arena rolling globes at the same time, and I consider this less difficult to accomplish than it is to teach any one of the great cats the same trick.

I was amused by the tumultuous applause that resulted when a bear featured in the Moscow State Circus that toured the United States in 1963 did the globe-rolling stunt. A big handsome animal, it made an impressive appearance and the crowd thoroughly enjoyed its antics.

As told in Chapter Ten, I worked a bear act before I became a big-cat trainer, and gave it up when I discovered that the public did not seem to realize that bears are dangerous. My "spotters" in the audience reported that to most spectators the animals in this long-ago act of mine seemed more like animated teddy bears, that no one seemed aware that bears could make trouble and had mauled and even killed trainers; so I decided to cast my lot with lions and tigers. For the public was at least aware that they weren't teddy bears or the feline equivalent thereof.

If I ever again appear in a bear act I will dress up as a Russian.

When Adkins and Terrell originally assigned me to the building in which I was to break in my new act I had only one objection. As mentioned in the previous chapter, the only room big enough to accommodate my training arena was supported by a big circular column about two feet in diameter. That pillar had not proved an unsurmountable obstacle, but it had frequently been a nuisance.

Somehow that post-marred arena symbolized our whole venture. It was a gamble to work in such an enclosure, but after all wasn't the whole undertaking one big crap-shoot?

We were gamblers, my partners and I, and we had plenty of nerve—or perhaps it was blind, unreasoning confidence— in arranging for a nationwide tour of a circus that had not yet been organized. Fortunately we were all well known in circus circles and we experienced no great difficulties in lining up bookings. But as we watched the clock and calendar and wondered whether we had allowed ourselves sufficient time, we did plenty of mental fingernail-biting. As the main attraction it was up to me to live up to what they had promised or come reasonably close.

Some years earlier I had perfected a trick—the tiger rollover—that had made a hit wherever it was shown. I recall that when I first performed it in Madison Square Garden it was the subject of much comment, and two New York newspapers devoted whole stories to it. It provided the photographers with many opportunities, and they soon made a practice of shooting it from every conceivable angle. They used to tell me that although I might not realize it myself, the rollover was never the same twice.

What they meant was that although the broad outlines of the trick were the same, the tiger's execution of it varied in accordance with the animal's mood. This resulted in pictures in which my rollover cat ran the gamut of facial expression all the way from the quietly benign to the utterly ferocious, with intermediate moods well represented.

The rollover consists of signaling a tiger off its pedestal and getting it to lie down on the floor of the arena. Then I hand-cue it to roll over on its side until it has made several full turns in an uninterrupted series.

Sounds simple, no? After all, it's merely the big-cat version of what many a dog owner has succeeded in teaching his pet to do.

The dog owner, of course, can grab hold of his pet and manipulate it to indicate what he wants it to do. Unless he wants to lose a hand or an arm, the tiger trainer cannot do this. He has to teach his pupil by suggestion and this requires a much subtler means of communication.

To perform the rollover for my new act I picked a bright-eyed, well-proportioned Royal Bengal that qualified from the standpoint of intelligence and looks. But even so this animal would not have been my first choice if I had had a less temperamental candidate available. All tigers are more or less temperamental. This one I had classified as overly so. He was too swift a mood-changer, an animal just a bit too unpredictable for comfort. One minute he would seem perfectly relaxed, a minute later, for no apparent reason, he would appear to be nervous, overwrought.

The first order of business was to run this animal into the bare arena—no pedestals or other equipment, no other animals. Then I gave him a vigorous exercise run. After a workout of this kind an animal lies down. When I felt he was sufficiently rested and relaxed, I began teaching him the rollover.

I attached a light buggy whip to a long pole which enabled me to reach the tiger at a distance of ten feet. By touching his feet lightly with the whiplash, and by a combination of hand and body movements—expressive gestures rather than clearly defined cues at this stage of the game—I conveyed to the animal that I wanted him to move over on his side. Once I got him there I began the process of teaching the next steps.

One day as I touched this tiger's hind legs and paws in the manner just described, he scrambled to his feet and came lunging at me. I stopped him with my chair and as I shook him off he charged again.

The look in this trainee's eyes, the distorted mouth, the lashing tail and the ears flat against the head were clear indications that he meant business. So I retreated behind the center post, meeting the animal again with my first line of defense, the chair, as he lunged forward as before in an effort to find an opening. That post, which I had cussed out many times when it got in my way, now proved a godsend.

After I deflected the animal a few times with the legs of the chair, he gave up. This is typical of the tiger. If he doesn't achieve his purpose in the early stages of one of these bouts, he retreats. The lion is different. Once he commits himself to an attack he is far more determined and much harder to shake off.

While I was still breaking in my rollover tiger, my good friend Eddie Stinson, for years manager of Detroit's Shrine Circus, turned up in Rochester to see how things were going. Annually his organization put on a two-week show which has become a local entertainment fixture. He called to see how we were getting along and whether he was justified in report-

ing back to his associates that they could count on us for a
mid-February engagement. He was also committed to informing the Cleveland Shriners who annually produced the Grotto
Circus, a two weeks' engagement at the conclusion of the one
in Detroit, whether they thought they could count on us.
Stinson's report was all-important, as it meant an advance of
at least $25,000 in connection with those two shows if he was
happy about what he saw. He asked very few questions. One
of them was, "Clyde, will you have a rollover tiger?" I assured
him I would and that seemed to clinch it. That stunt, he told
me, was considered the climax of my former act, and when I
assured him I had an animal that would be able to do it
satisfactorily, he took my word for it. When you're betting
on yourself, you might as well go all the way.

The whole thing seemed to hinge on the rollover, which
when I originally performed it in Detroit became one of Stinson's favorite conversational topics. I resolved then and there
that I would work on my rollover tiger until he was letter
perfect, or as nearly so as possible. There was a lot to do before
he could be counted upon to perform with full effectiveness.

Adkins, Terrell and I were grateful to Eddie Stinson for
overlooking the confusion that greeted him when he arrived
at our training quarters. We had not yet had a chance to make
many concessions to orderliness, and all sorts of animals
intended either as menagerie exhibits or for use in a variety
of acts had started to arrive. Stinson, as he wandered about
that big rambling building we had acquired, might find
elephants tied up where broken-down boxcars were formerly
patched up or he might walk into the big room Adkins had
selected as his office and find a camel staring at him.

At any rate, Eddie had faith in us and that enabled us to
get off the ground. We didn't have much capital and the
advance he provided enabled us to produce a better show.

I went back to work on my rollover tiger. All I had accomplished so far was to get him to lie down and roll over on his

side. There was a lot more to do and as I set out to accomplish it I was grateful that the tiger that had chased me behind and around that pillar—(a fine place for the "death-defying Clyde Beatty," as the circus posters had so long proclaimed me!)—seemed to have forgotten his attempt to attack me.

There was nothing unusual about this. I had not made an issue of the attempted attack, so he forgot it as fast as it happened. Tigers are like that.

I kept reminding myself that, even though I was operating under pressure, I must not work any particular animal too long at a stretch. I stuck to this rule, but toward the end of our race against time I found it necessary to return to my training of the different animals at odd hours—often late at night—and this stepped-up frequency made some of the big cats irritable.

I have had many years to think of those days when I had to throw a whole act together in record time, and in retrospect I am surprised the animals did not make more trouble for me than they did. A lion or a tiger roused from slumber to rehearse at one o'clock in the morning can hardly be expected to be cooperative. Yet most of them were.

The few that resented night work almost wrecked my plans. One of them—an understandably peeved lion—hit my chair so hard a smash with his clublike right forepaw that he completely demolished it, and I retreated behind that pillar (a welcome sight for the second time!) with nothing in my hand except a piece of the chair's curved back. On my way to my retreat I managed to pick up a pedestal and thus could defend and extricate myself. From that day to this I have never wakened a slumbering beast. Let sleeping cats lie is as good an adage as the more familiar version.

As I reached my final week at training quarters—which was my last chance to do whatever brushing up remained to be done—it was obvious that I would have to break my record of the previous weeks for getting along with a minimum of sleep. There had been nights prior to this homestretch period when I had had to settle for five hours. Now I would have to settle for even less.

Once I got that rollover tiger accustomed to lying down in an empty arena, I tackled the next phase. I seated him on a pedestal and taught him to descend to the arena floor in a slow jungle stalk and to lie down on his side at a cue from me. Then I indicated that I wanted him to do a series of rollovers and to come to a halt when I so signaled.

After a while I got him accustomed to lying down in any designated spot and doing a perfect series of rolls.

The most difficult aspect of this whole maneuver is to sell the tiger the idea of following me as he descends from his seat and I start stepping backward. As he slowly approaches me and I keep backing away as he picks up my hand cue and lies down on the arena floor, what is uppermost in his mind is that he is vulnerable to attack by the other cats. For of course the final phase of this trick is to get him to perform it against the whole banked group of pedestaled lions and tigers.

This cannot be achieved until the rollover tiger has complete confidence in me.

The big cats instinctively distrust each other, and it is my task to convince the animal performing the rollover that he can count on my protection.

This is a difficult sale to make. The first time an animal exposes himself to attack in this fashion his apprehension is obvious. From his reclining position on the floor he keeps looking up to take in as much of what is going on as he can. His main concern is what he cannot see—that is, the animals behind him. So I move around cracking my whip at the cats on their seats in an effort to convey to the animal stretched out on the floor that he has nothing to worry about. For there I am, everlastingly keeping an eye on those creatures he is suspicious and afraid of.

This has proved to be sound psychology. The animal doing

this solo on the floor never ceases to be wary, but in time his extreme nervousness passes and he performs the rollover with a seeming disregard for the fact that Tiger A or Lion B, with whom he has been feuding, could leap down and snap his spine with one well-aimed bite.

To some of the cats I am another animal, a formidable one they don't seem to be able to figure out. True, I am one against many, but one that puzzles and awes them because I am a creature equipped with advantages no other animal has: that something I use as a shield (the chair), that long snakelike device (the whip) which makes that cracking sound, and that other noise-maker (the blank-cartridge revolver).

I am not only an animal equipped with these appurtenances, but they are all detachable and quickly re-attachable, a pretty puzzling business.

Occasionally an animal attacks and injures me, but when I recover and return to the arena and retain my attacker in the act, I seem to sense—and the animal psychologists will have to decide whether I am right—that I have impressed my cats anew.

Perhaps I should say it's like winning a poker hand against stronger cards. There's a lot of poker-playing in my business. All trainers start with a love of wild animals and a talent for communicating with them, but they must go on from there to become convincing bluffers (to which an overconfident manner, even a bit of swagger, contributes mightily).

Bluffing, as I started out to say, is as important in animal training as it is in the card game it so often reminds me of. A lion or tiger fully aware of the relative might of the big cats and mere man would make short work of *any* trainer. Thus animal training might be described as the art or science of keeping wild animals from learning the facts.

Returning to my rollover tiger, whenever I was called upon to remind him that I was his protector, and did so in the manner described, his nervousness would vanish and so would the restlessness of any animal that might be contemplating trouble. Those that stood up when they should have been seated were the ones that gave me the most concern. By the time I carried out my whip-cracking bluff a few times, the standees would move back and sit down.

Step by step I put together a whole new act. It was not as good as it would be a few months hence, but it would play well.

In fact, its inadequacies would inevitably provide audiences with unexpected thrills. What I mean is that an animal that just misses being adequately trained—and I would have to open the season with some in that category—can put on an exciting performance when he "forgets his lines" and either resents being prompted or is too confused and flustered to respond. The most predictable reaction of such an animal is that he will try to attack his trainer. What the audience seldom sees is the close-up of the disturbed creature's expression that tells me what to expect.

This reminds me that one of the most important qualifications of a trainer is to be able to read the faces of his animals. Some of them are deadpan artists, looking more or less the same regardless of whether they are aroused or not. That is, on the surface they *seem* the same. But the educated eye of the veteran trainer detects little signs that tell him the score— a stiffened tail that had been relaxed the moment before, a just barely discernible twisting of the mouth or an angry look that vanishes as fast as it developed—none of these portents accompanied by the roaring and snarling usually associated with an animal about to go on a rampage.

I have had assistants who would have been much more valuable if they had had the faculty of reading animal expressions more accurately. An aide, to be fully effective, must also be able to recognize quickly each and every animal. I have had assistants who couldn't tell them apart—intelligent, conscientious young men who had somehow strayed into the wrong business.

I have never seen two lions or two tigers whose expressions and markings were identical. There are look-alikes among animals just as there are among people, but the experienced animal man can tell at a glance which is which.

Well, we opened in Detroit and the reception we got was most gratifying. The faded newspaper clippings in an old scrapbook are pleasant reminders of the overflow crowds and their enthusiasm.

I recall that up to the morning of the day I entered the arena to give my first performance under the auspices of the newly organized Cole Bros.-Clyde Beatty Circus, I was polishing up my act. (The Cole Bros. name, an old and respected one in the circus world but dormant since the last Cole brother died, had been acquired from the heirs of the family.)

I had rehearsed night and day until it was time for our circus train to start loading and leave for Detroit, and though I had had very little rest during that final week of our drive to put a whole new show together between seasons, I was so excited by what we had accomplished in so short a period that I forgot to be tired.

Once we had settled down to our training grind in the abandoned railroad building in Rochester I rented a furnished house there. It was mainly a place to sleep. I returned to it at the oddest hours and there were nights when I worked so late I didn't see any point in returning at all, settling for a place to sleep at training quarters.

The irregularity of my movements was puzzling to the lion cub I had installed in the house as a pet. He and I had become good friends, but as I became more and more deeply involved in the business of creating a whole new act, I had less and less time for him.

He was as fond of sleep as any of the cubs I've given the

run of my home (wherever it happened to be), yet he had a way of dozing off with one ear cocked so that if I returned at midnight or later, he would rouse himself and give me as enthusiastic a greeting as a drowsy little lion is capable of.

During the 1936 season my associates and I, after two highly successful seasons with our new show, cooked up an idea that was considered revolutionary in circus circles. We would invade New York!

Time magazine said in the article mentioned in the preceding chapter that the Ringling organization "was accustomed to opening their season every year with no rival in sight." Their show had done so "ever since 1919, when the Ringling and Barnum & Bailey outfits joined forces. With Ringling Bros. and Barnum & Bailey still in Florida winter quarters last week, this tradition was shattered when Cole Bros.-Clyde Beatty moved into the Hippodrome, became the first important tent show in a generation to challenge 'The Greatest Show on Earth' not only by playing New York, hitherto practically a Ringling monopoly, but playing it before Ringling got there. The last circus that tried to slide into Manhattan under the Ringling shadow was Sells-Floto."

This article, which had been written by someone who knew the facts, went on to say that the Ringling organization "stifled this competition in a characteristic fashion." They bought up not only Sells-Floto but the other four circuses that were touring the country and might be tempted to try New York engagements—Hagenbeck-Wallace, John Robinson, Sparks and Al G. Barnes.

The story also mentioned that I had made $40,000 the year before, which compared favorably with the $100 a week I had been receiving from the Ringling people. But what thrilled me most was that I now *owned* part of something. I had always put everything I had into my work, even when I was receiving a pittance for my efforts, but I discovered that I could muster a still greater enthusiasm as animal trainer *and* part owner.

Business was so good at the Hippodrome that our engagement was extended to eight weeks, a long run for a circus, particularly one that was playing New York for the first time.

Adkins, Terrell and I had not endeared ourselves to the Ringlings by demonstrating that their powerful organization could be successfully fought.

Ours being a tent show, we prefer to play under the big top. In fact, today we are by a wide margin the biggest circus in the country operating under canvas. But occasionally we like to play in an auditorium in New York, Detroit and a few other big cities.

My associates—Jerry Collins, Frank McClosky and the late Walter Kernan—brought our circus to New York shortly before Christmas of 1962. (Adkins and Terrell had retired many years earlier.)

The day after we arrived to open a five weeks' engagement at the Coliseum, we found ourselves in the midst of New York's longest newspaper strike. The result could have been a calamity. Although there were no newspapers, normally our main reliance for publicity, we did reasonably well. The attendance would have been considered only fair under normal circumstances, but we did much better than we thought possible under the conditions that prevailed.

I recall how eager we were to find out whether, after an absence of so many years, the New York press would show any interest in us. They did—the day before the newspaper blackout. We were particularly thrilled by a story with pictures that dominated the front page of the *World-Telegram & Sun*. Then came the strike.

One of these days I hope to return to the Coliseum. But not in the spirit of reviving old rivalries and dissatisfactions. The present-day Ringling organization has no relationship to the one that gave me a bad time in the 1930s. In fact, they are most friendly. And I hope they will not mind my disclosing that only a few years ago they asked me to rejoin their circus in a starring role and made me a most flattering offer.

8. The Lazy Lion, and Other Stories

John Helliot and His Baiting Technique – Can You
Buy a Lion's Good Will? – John and I in a Strange
Jungle Where a Bear Goes Berserk – A Pampered
Lion Turns Bad – Salute to a Great Old-Timer

Bruno was the laziest lion I've ever known. He had a natural lassitude that was brought to a peak of perfection by John
Helliot, the laziest animal trainer I've ever known.

John was my assistant and he and I had become good
friends. A long-time veteran of the steel arena who had
reached his peak many years before and was now coasting,
John had had broad experience with the big cats and he and
I had many interesting conversations. And occasionally an argument.

John was an exponent of an earlier German school of training whose methods had long since been supplanted. One feature of it involved the business of getting balky animals to perform through the promise of rewards, just as an overindulgent
parent might promise little Johnny a new pair of roller skates
or a bicycle if he stopped throwing spitballs at his teacher.

John gave me a hurt look every time I kidded him about
his "bribery policy" by way of expressing my opinion of his
practice of using tasty little chunks of meat, suspended from
a stick, to coax the big cats into doing whatever he had in

mind. Since the early stages of training are an involved, step-by-step procedure, by the time John had done much work in any training session with a new trainee that animal had been the recipient of a number of tidbits and would sometimes hold out for more before recognizing the next cue.

John was Hungarian by birth, but he had lived so long in Germany that he was far more of a German than a Hungarian. He spoke German fluently and had picked up English rather handily, although his accent and sentence structure combined to make him sound like one of those German comedians who flourished in musical comedy a number of years ago. I was recently reminded of John when I heard Jack Pearl in a revival of his Baron Munchausen routine on television. Helliot could have served as an understudy for Pearl.

One night John began sputtering as I renewed my joshing criticism of his practice of trying to buy the good will of the big cats with his little rewards of meat. I argued that it would take all eternity to train a lion or a tiger by this method, and that when you had him trained you would have to continue bribing him to keep him performing. Sooner or later the other animals would expect similar tributes, and if they didn't get them they would rebel. I took the position that John's method was practical only when you put on a show with one animal at a time in the arena, as was once the custom in Germany.

John had a dual role. He was my animal caretaker—a knowledgeable one—and he also put on a small animal act prior to mine, a sort of curtain-raiser in which he had himself billed as "Herr Helliot." He figured that the "herr" business immediately proclaimed him as an import, his reasoning being summed up like this: "By dis time, Clyde, I got a pooty goot idea vot you *Ameikaners* like. Imported goots. Dot's me. I'm imported straight from Europe." However, the unfolding of history has a way of changing a man's mind, and subsequently John decided he would rather be known as Mr. Helliot.

John was a devoted friend, dependable and kindly. Professionally I thought more of him as a caretaker than as a trainer, and although this occasionally nettled John, it didn't interfere with our friendship.

For a man I think of in terms of chronic lassitude, John Helliot somehow managed to get a reasonable amount of work done. He took excellent care of the animals, which he accomplished by becoming an executive. Not caring much about ministering to the needs of the big cats himself, John organized the cage boys so that they did nearly all his work as well as their own. His philosophy was that if anybody was going to be overworked, it might as well be the young camp followers, usually cage boys, who had talked their way into their jobs by insisting that their big goal in life was to be near wild animals and look after them. That was my story too when I was a cage boy. Practically everyone who holds such a job hopes some day to be an animal trainer or at least an assistant trainer. There is no limit to what a dedicated cage boy will do to demonstrate that he loves wild animals and wants to learn everything there is to know about them. I was so painfully earnest about this myself when I broke in as a cage boy at the age of fifteen that if my immediate boss—the chief caretaker—had insisted that I work two shifts a day, I am certain I would have agreed to do so, and probably would have thanked him for this added opportunity to get acquainted with the animals.

One of the things that tickled me most about John was that he carried one of those folding camp chairs around with him and was not infrequently seen unfolding it as he beckoned the cage boys to join him for a staff meeting. John carried out meticulously my instructions that the animals' cages be kept immaculate, and when he found any signs of negligence he called a summit conference of his aides and gave them hell.

But most of all I enjoyed watching John when he was training Bruno, the lazy lion mentioned in the opening paragraph of this chapter.

I recall returning to training quarters after an absence of a few days and finding John, seated on his chair in the middle of the arena, addressing the sprawled-out Bruno. "Vell, Bruno," said John, "you must feel pooty goot now from dot long rest, so now ve do a little vork."

Bruno didn't stir. (I was watching from outside the arena, and John apparently was unaware of my presence.)

"Dot's right, Bruno, rest yourself goot. Den ve vork." John picked up a newspaper and started reading.

After a few minutes of this he cast the newspaper aside and announced again it was time to "get done some vork." Bruno, comfortably stretched out on his side, yawned. Then his trainer issued a command that the lion would have found somewhat contradictory if he had been able to understand it: "Hurry up, Bruno, take your time."

This was too much for me. I started to laugh and John looked up and spotted me. "How are things going, John," I asked.

"*Ganz goot*, Clyde, *ganz goot*." Then there was a big sigh, followed by a fervent, "*Gott sei dank*."

When he had finished thanking God, which he did several times, he added a Jack Pearlism to the effect that everything was going "schvell, zimply schvell." Since John and I disagreed on so many phases of animal training, his view and mine of when things were going "simply swell" varied widely.

"Bruno doesn't seem very peppy to me, John."

"Don't you vorry, Clyde. I get him in goot shape for you. Choost vait and zee. He make zimply vonderful performer."

Bruno was a handsome animal, but he had been reared in captivity and had never forgotten the fondling and petting that had been his due as one of the cutest of cubs. As I have pointed out elsewhere in these pages, animals that begin their careers as pets seldom make good performers. Some of my associates thought I had a closed mind on this subject, so I was determined to see what could be done with Bruno. If I could make a performer of him, it would tone him up physically— (indolent animals become obsese and develop ailments that exercise can correct or prevent)—and it would also give me one more good-looking animal that I could count on for arena work.

Outwardly Bruno was five hundred pounds of languid amiability. But this did not mean that he wasn't capable of reverting to type and causing trouble. I felt this possibility would be minimized if I could help him overcome his sluggishness. Laziness in animals is a progressive thing and I didn't want Bruno to become so hopelessly unenergetic that he would grow snappish when I or anyone else tried to get him to stir himself.

He was so allergic to exercise he was almost unreal. I had seen laziness in animals but nothing to match Bruno's, which, plus his chronic boredom, made him a bit of a comedian.

As an amateur psychologist I felt that this animal's lassitude, which had become more and more pronounced, had been stimulated by that of his trainer. Just as there are lazy people, there are lazy animals, and the surest way to make them lazier is to subject them to training methods such as John Helliot's.

It took John several weeks to train Bruno to do the sit-up on a floor pedestal as a prelude to getting the animal to do the same trick on the high center pedestal of the pyramid. This involved selling the lethargic lion the idea of moving from a floor seat to a high one, which meant negotiating a series of pedestals of graduated heights. This took much pleading and wheedling, but John managed to get him up there by means of these begging procedures, in the course of which he made liberal use of those handouts of beef chunks and their built-in persuasiveness. Having reached the top of the high seat, Bruno sat and rested from this effort for a full minute while John in plaintive tones coaxed him to "zit up." Well, Bruno finally sat up and there is no doubt that he was a spectacular sight as he erected himself on his hind legs, his forelegs stretched straight upward. He held the pose just long enough to show he could do this trick, then abruptly returned to a sitting position to rest from his labors.

"Vell done, Bruno! You goot boy. Now you choost zit there a vile and take it easy."

Whereupon John unfolded his camp chair, sat down and lit a cigar. Bruno, deciding not to "zit there," came slowly down, and stretched out on the arena floor, facing the trainer. Then he began to do some mugging, which John evidently understood to mean that the animal wanted something. "Votcha vant, Bruno?"

"Maybe he wants a cigar, too, John," I suggested. "Why don't you give him one?"

John ignored me, his gaze fixed on Bruno, who was going through the pantomime of eating.

It hadn't occurred to John until that moment that even this pampered animal would want anything further to eat for a while. But what the big cat wanted was now quite obvious.

"I choost remember, Bruno," exclaimed John. "You do such nice zit-up and I forget to give you zum candy." Whereupon he fed the listless lion some more of those choice beef bonbons.

John made a practice of talking to Bruno as though he were another person. He thanked his trainee for being so "villing" and promised not to get him "too veary and vorn out."

He hardly acknowledged my presence the day of Bruno's first "vorkout in the zit-up." He confined himself to urging me to stop "vorrying," assuring me again that he would make a good sit-up lion of Bruno.

I had my doubts, but I was perfectly willing to let John see what he could do. I had a fine sit-up lion in the act, but he was a scrappy cuss and I feared that sooner or later he might overmatch himself and suffer an injury in a fight; and then it would be good to have an understudy around.

From the standpoint of appearance Bruno would make a fine substitute. He had the size and the weight and he was gracefully proportioned. There was no doubt in my mind that audiences would find him an impressive sight as he stood perpendicularly stretched out until his upraised paws almost touched the protective netting overhead. The question was whether I could get him to do it with the quick responsiveness without which this particular stunt had no impact on crowds.

I decided to try him out in a rehearsal. He needed a good workout—a whole series of them if I hoped to keep him from growing fat. I had noticed the beginning of a slight protrusion around Bruno's stomach, and if it continued to grow he would no longer be a "picture animal."

It didn't take me long to discover that Bruno was not attuned to my methods of training. It took me several minutes to get him to sit up. My regular sit-up lion achieved this pose in a few seconds, and even with the encores most audiences sought by means of continued applause, the whole business took only thirty or forty seconds.

To complicate matters, when I finally got Bruno to sit up, he swiftly broke the pose. Moreover, it was obvious from his behavior that he expected to be rewarded with those edible bribes by means of which John wheedled him into watching for his cues and executing them properly.

I decided to break Bruno of his begging habits, his own particular version of a dog yipping for extra food. I agree with the policy of the leading veterinarians and zoo officials that it is best to feed the big cats once a day and that there should be no exceptions to this rule.

Bruno got sassy when I ignored his begging, and he began losing his amiability. He was too downright lazy to bother indicating his displeasure by means of an all-out thunderous roar—(this meant getting up off his haunches and filling his lungs to capacity)—so he confined himself to such sitting-down protests as howls and snarls that didn't require much energy. His philosophy seemed to be: "If Herr Helliot can feed me little extras, why can't you?"

I subsequently tried out Bruno a few times as a background lion in one of the banked formations of big cats against which the solo performers did their stuff. One day I caught him asleep on his pedestal, his head rocking ever so slightly yet noticeably, and I woke him before he toppled off. Bruno had almost as great a talent for dozing off in a sitting position as he did lying down. I figured that if he couldn't stay awake during a simple tableau, he was not cut out for show business.

In all the time I had known this lion and tried to make a performer of him I had never seen him shed his laziness except at feeding time. When his slabs of meat were shoved through the feeding slot in his cage, he would grab them with a burst of energy that he never displayed at any other time.

Herr Helliot was sad when I informed him that I had given up trying to make a performer of Bruno. "He's a goot lion, dot Bruno," said John sadly. "You give him one more chance, yes?" If I did I would "zoon zee" the animal's "goot zide."

Regretfully I told the good herr that I found Bruno an interesting study in animal behavior but that I would have to retire him from my act until such time as I decided to perform in slow motion. "Why don't you use him in *your* act, John?" I asked.

Normally, John would have jumped at this suggestion because he and Bruno were great pals. After much discussion he agreed to place the lazy lion in his own act, but somewhat reluctantly because it amounted to admitting defeat. He had insisted from the beginning that he would be able to convert Bruno into the understudy I needed for my sit-up lion.

John did not give up easily. Even when he must have been convinced that I had made up my mind about Bruno and would not change my mind, out of pride he continued to plead the lazy lion's case.

Our last conversation on the subject found me saying something to this effect: "John, you old fraud, you've spoiled that animal. He was a slowpoke to begin with but you slowed him up further." This was designed to draw John out on his favorite theme, that everything in America was "rush, rush, rush." He could be genuinely funny as he sputtered out his indignant comments on the mad pace Americans set in everything they undertook, which he dismissed as "zimply zilly and shtupid." Once, in the midst of one of these attacks on U.S. hustle and bustle, the good herr, exhausted by his strenuous expostulations, unfolded his ever-present camp chair and sat down to rest from his labors. I was in agreement with John that the pace in many areas of American life was "simply silly and stupid," but having spent as much as three to six months to train a single animal, I didn't include myself in the indictment.

I loved that Hungarian and that lazy lion and occasionally I would sneak up on them while they were carrying on a "conversation." John used to tell stories about the Old Country and Bruno would listen a while, then let out a yip, which meant, "A few more of those choice meat chunks, please." Poor John! He couldn't even get Bruno to "listen" without bribing him.

In time Bruno became hog-fat and developed belly sag. A once handsome lion was now misshapen and looked more than twice his age, which was only five and a half.

One day Nat Levine of Republic Pictures, with whom I had made a movie deal, called on me while we were on tour. John, who fancied himself as a chef and liked to play host, invited us to join him for dinner, which he would cook himself. It would be a chicken dinner, the good herr informed us. He had an old German recipe for chicken soup which he claimed was unbeatable. That would be the first course.

Nat and I were invited to watch John do his cooking. We were a little startled when we saw our host and chef drop some chicken legs into the soup pot with the dirty-looking chicken feet still attached. I told John I had never heard of anyone using the feet of the fowl in making chicken soup. "Dot's the best part," he insisted.

I wondered whether John had not been too lazy to chop the feet off. It was hard to tell whether he or Bruno was more accomplished in the fine art of the easiest way. John had smoked his ever-present cigar down to a stub while cooking and I watched carefully to see that he didn't drop the butt into the soup pot as the easiest way of complying with a long-standing circus rule that all smokables must be extinguished before being discarded.

Whenever I find myself in a conversation on animal behavior—and I'm sure the reader realizes by now that no subject interests me more—I mention some of the odder animals I have trained (or tried to train) and inevitably I get around to talking about Bruno and John. That pair always fascinated me and always will. Both were studies in lethargy. Which had had a greater influence on the other?

Even though it is not a common trait, if I could solve the riddle of laziness in the big cats I would be able to unlock a number of related mysteries.

When I originally met John Helliot I was a cage boy and he was a full-fledged trainer. He was nearing the end of his career as a trainer at the time mine was beginning. He was most encouraging but expressed disappointment over my unwillingness to adopt his techniques. He thought I had a flair for handling wild animals but that I made my job needlessly difficult by not using certain short cuts, including the baiting method described earlier. He never lost faith in his belief that you could earn an animal's "good vill" by means of those little bribes of choice chunks of meat used as either an inducement or a reward, or both.

John had sustained a number of injuries during his heyday as a trainer. Both his arms had been badly chewed and he had lost an eye. Yet it was impossible to get him to concede that perhaps his baiting method had its shortcomings. I took the position that no matter what method a trainer used he could not wholly avoid accidents. But I felt that John's policy of bribery needlessly complicated things. These little tokens were habit-forming, and it is quite possible that John had been attacked by animals that were annoyed and frustrated by their inability to convey to him that they wanted to be rewarded at a particular moment when he was concentrating on an important trick and unaware of their wishes. At such a moment he would have been compelled to ignore their begging even if he had noticed it.

But so great was John's affection for wild animals that he would defend those that were his responsibility regardless of what took place in the arena. *Yah, yah,* that big unsightly scar on his right arm was the work of an angry lion. "But if ve shtop and tink about such things," John argued, "ve vill remember dis: if dot lion vas really out to get me I vouldn't be here now to tell the shtory, Clyde. Choost vy dot Hans chewed up my arm I vish I knew. Pecause Hans he vas a goot lion. Vatever it vas dot got him all vorked up I don't know, Clyde, but he never vent on the varpath again. So, like you *Amerikaners* say, let pygones be pygones."

John was quite a philosopher, one who never forgot old ties. Though, as the reader knows, I disagreed with most of his training methods, I admired his loyalty to the people who had taught him his profession in the Old Country. He had been able to earn his living at it all his life, and now that he was preparing to retire as a performer, his knowledge of animals and how to care for them would be a saleable commodity.

There was one aspect of John's slow, deliberate method of training that was an asset. In the early stages of training the big cats, it is important to be extremely patient and take as much time as is necessary to teach them the fundamentals. Few trainers were better equipped than John to "seat-break" new lions, for instance.

After I convinced John that he would have to abide by my methods and abandon his baiting tactics, he proved most helpful in seat-breaking young lions that I was training as replacements for older ones, and in teaching them other fundamentals. (John was then exclusively a lion trainer, so in those days I did all the seat-breaking of the tigers myself.)

John knew that lions could be seat-broken without bribes. He had seen me do it. But even after he had seat-broken several lions for me, admitting that the technique I had developed made "baiting" unnecessary, when he worked his own act he resumed his old practice of rewarding his lions with food extras. He was probably right, too. Once you start a practice of this kind you get the animals used to it. You can't make a new policy stick unless you start with a whole new set of animals.

How many stories come to mind regarding dear old John! One has to do with a favorite lion of his that he had named August—(he pronounced it *Owgust*)—a big light-maned cat that had been born in captivity, raised as a pet and allowed to roam free until it reached the end of its cub days and had to be caged as a safety measure.

An animal of this kind can seldom be trained for major work in an act like mine, but he can play an important role in a "quiet" act such as John's, in which the trainer poses with his animals in a variety of groupings. The "posing" act, which depends on animals reared in captivity as pets, has been very successful in Europe. It has also had some success in the United States, although the American public seems to prefer acts—at least in the big-cat field—that feature animals from the wilds that are only partially trained and whose primitiveness registers at once.

Herr Helliot and August, the lion I just mentioned, had become great pals, John having never once disciplined him. August was one of ten males the good herr presented in an appealing act at the peak of his career. One day—"choost like dot!"—a fight broke out among the lions after John had waltzed through most of the act and had only a few more "poses" to do.

John made a practice of entering the arena with a long stick in his left hand and a whip in the other. The theory of the stick was that it was a pacifier. It gave an animal something to chew on when he came at you with too much of a rush. The principle is the same as that involving the chair I always carry into the arena, except that the legs provide *four* pacifiers. When one is snapped or knocked off, you have three left.

John, in an effort to get those lions to stop fighting, brandished his stick and cracked his whip. In doing so he happened to reach August with one or the other—he wasn't sure which, but it wasn't much of a blow. This, you will recall, was the animal that had never been disciplined. August, according to John, gave him the most reproachful look he had ever seen on a lion's face. John, feeling badly about having hit his pal, exclaimed, "Exkoos me, Owgust, I didn't know it was you." This story has been handed down and still is told in animal-training circles.

It was because of such occurrences that some people came to regard John as a clown of the steel arena. This was understandable because of his German-comedian delivery. When he didn't sound like Jack Pearl, he was a dead ringer for Sid Caesar's Professor Schnickelfritz.

Actually, John was one of the best of the old-time trainers. And in addition to having a vast knowledge of wild animals and a warm, understanding feeling for them, he was as courageous a man as the animal-training field has ever produced.

When I was asked to make the motion picture *The Lost Jungle*, mentioned earlier, I stipulated that John, who had reached the end of his career as a performer, accompany me as general consultant. It was a good arrangement for both of us. John needed the assignment and I was glad to have so experienced a wild-animal man handy for almost any kind of chore.

The jungle in which the action took place was a Hollywood creation, a place so "lost" that nobody had the remotest idea where it was. All I knew was that it was wild country where you could find *any* kind of animal, which gave the director a chance to throw together species that were normally continents apart. If you emptied several zoos and threw the animals together at a water hole you would have an idea of what one of the "big" scenes was like.

Since practically all species were represented, it wasn't surprising that we had some performing bears. One day John was giving one of them a workout when the animal suddenly turned on him and sank its teeth into his right knee. A representative of the American Society for the Prevention of Cruelty to Animals, who was standing by with a loaded gun, came up close, aimed at the animal's head and was about to pull the trigger when John pleaded with him not to shoot. In the meantime the bear kept on biting and John was messed up from his stomach down.

I was not on the set when this happened, but I got eye-witness accounts from several people. All agreed that the attacking animal—enraged for some unguessable reason—was so determined to mutilate John that the strenuous efforts made to drive him off with shovels and two-by-fours seemed to have the effect of further infuriating instead of discouraging him. He could not be made to loosen his hold. John again protested—in a noticeably weaker voice for his strength was waning—when the man from the humane society raised his gun a second time and was about to fire.

A Western was being filmed on a nearby set and someone got the idea of sending for a cowboy who was handy with a rope. In addition to the phony cowboys who don't know a horse from a zebra and a lariat from a clothesline, every Western had a complement of real cowpokes who knew how to handle a rope. One of these men was summoned and he quickly had a lasso around that vicious bear's neck. But by the time they pulled the animal off him, John was in bad shape. He wound up in a hospital and remained there for several weeks. For a while it looked as if he might never be able to walk again without a limp; but the injuries to his legs did not prove as serious as originally diagnosed, and John walked out of the hospital on legs that functioned normally and he announced that he was ready to tackle his next assignment.

Typically, John blamed himself, not the bear. "Clyde, I tink maybe dot day I got hurt I vork dot pear too long, *nein?*"

It was not in John Helliot's nature to blame an animal for

anything. He had overworked that bear, the resultant accident had been his own fault, and that was that.

John, always amusing, said he was puzzled by the behavior of the A.S.P.C.A. man. He had always thought that this organization (whose work on the whole I greatly admire) was dedicated to protecting animals from people, not the reverse of that proposition. I don't recall just how John put it, but that's the gist of what he said.

I *do* recall his adding something along this line:

"Ven someone from one of dose cruelty societies vants to shoot an animal instead of a people, den I know the vorld is shtanding on his head. If dot guy from the cruelty society knew vot he vas doing, he vould have shot *me* for overvorking a pear. Den I bet dey give him a medal and higher vages."

The greatest blow to John's pride came when the gluttonous Bruno, that incredibly lazy lion of his, "turned bad." With the possible exception of me, Herr Helliot regarded Bruno as his best friend. And then Bruno, chief beneficiary of John's baiting technique—who had in fact grown fat on the extra food he had wheedled out of his trainer—attacked John and might have killed him if an alert cage boy had not handed him an ammonia "gun,"—a syringe which if properly aimed at an attacking animal enables the trainer to escape to the safety cage while the slowed-up animal, trying to catch his breath, is pulling himself together. The ammonia did Bruno no harm; in fact, not much later he was his ever-hungry self again.

(In the 1930s the ammonia gun was in common use. It is seldom used any longer. Such a device, if one is to rely on it, has to be in readiness at all times. Ammonia corroded every type of syringe I experimented with, so I decided against relying in an emergency on a device that might or might not work.)

I had often told John not to be surprised if some day something happened to make him change his mind about Bruno.

So when the greedy beast turned bad, I was careful not to say anything in the I-told-you-so category.

I said nothing and neither did he. Knowing John as I did, I'm almost certain that if I had made an unkind remark about the animal on which he had lavished so much affection, he would have rushed to the big cat's defense. And he would have figured out a convincing-sounding angle.

For as far as wild animals were concerned, John Helliot was the attorney for the defense. It was not in his nature ever to be their prosecutor.

When a man has a comedian's delivery such as John Helliot's, there are those who don't take him seriously. To me he typified a kind of greatness—a love of wild animals I have seldom seen equaled and never surpassed.

9. From an Animal Trainer's Notebook

The Head-in-the-Lion's-Mouth Trick – How It's Done
and Why It Shouldn't Be – The Big Cats on the Tightrope – How Old Is Animal Training? – And Sundry
Other Items

W̲HAT ABOUT that business of sticking your head in a lion's
mouth?" people used to ask me in the days when I performed
that stunt. In fact, there was a time when men in my field
were supposed to go in for that brand of showmanship. If they
didn't, they weren't considered animal trainers.

This is a stunt I never liked, one reason being that it has an
element of phoniness. Still another reason is that it is one of
those so-what routines.

When you've done it, what have you accomplished? Perhaps
those who are not interested in or entertained by animal acts
would say the same thing about *any* trick or formation the
trainer does. But at least there are stunts and tableaux in
which the trainer is able to demonstrate that the wildest of
wild animals can be taught to concentrate, pick up cues and
do things that are an affirmation of the Darwin-Huxley thesis
that the higher mammals—with special reference to the big
cats—are thinking creatures. And, when these stunts and formations are brought off effectively, they also give people who

are fond of animals an ever-changing view of them in action that they could not get any other way.

No matter how much I downgrade that head-in-the-lion's-mouth business, people insist on knowing how it's done. The whole business is so silly I feel foolish discussing it, and my only excuse for doing so is that it is as much a part of animal-training history as pulling rabbits out of a hat was in the heyday of the vaudeville magician.

I am always amused when I look at an old circus poster proclaiming the daring of The Great So-and-So who "fearlessly puts his head in a lion's mouth." I've known some pretty reckless trainers, but I have never known or heard of one crazy enough to stick his *head* inside the mouth of a lion. What the trainer does who is supposed to perform this feat is to put an inch or two of his *face* between the open jaws of the animal in a manner and at an angle suggesting that his whole head is about to pop in.

First, however, certain precautions are taken. The trainer's right hand rests securely on the lion's upper jaw and his left hand holds the lower jaw firmly. The second the trainer feels the slightest pressure on either hand indicative of a possible clamping together of the jaws, he withdraws his face—not his head, for his head, remember, has never actually been inside the jaws—and only rarely is there any kind of mishap. I do not know of a single instance of a trainer being seriously injured during the performance of this trick.

And I don't recall a single complaint from a spectator to the effect that the trainer had not literally done what the publicity said he would. This is because the trainer's withdrawal of his face is almost too fast to follow. It is a case, to paraphrase the old shell-game adage, of the face being faster than the eye.

In this connection I am reminded of a former animal trainer, a European who performed creditably abroad. While lecturing in this country he told perfectly preposterous stories, which he featured as the main part of his lecture, about the head-in-the-mouth stunt. He even told tales of trainers whose heads had been snapped off while they were performing the prodigious feat. Encouraged by misguided admirers, he told taller and taller tales, until he was finally branded as a faker. Yet he was an authentic trainer who had risked his life in the arena for many years. His imagination had gotten the better of him, and he had succeeded in discrediting himself and the interesting but unimportant stunt he was trying to glorify.

Anyone who is honest about animal training will admit that the trick in question can be worked only by stacking the cards. Only a lion that has been raised in captivity as a pet can be used.

This being the age of home-study and do-it-yourself, there may be among my readers some who are taking correspondence courses in animal training. To any such who are thinking of trying the head-in-the-mouth business, let me say a cautionary word on another aspect of this ancient trick. Think twice before you try it if you are allergic to halitosis. Most lions have it, even the healthiest ones. So if unpleasant breath offends your nostrils, better keep this stunt out of your repertoire.

Have you ever seen a leopard or a puma walk a tightrope?

This trick is no longer in my repertory but whenever I discuss it with circus fans they show a lively interest and that is my excuse for dealing with it in these pages.

I'll begin by confessing that the so-called "tightrope" isn't really a tightrope. It is a strip of tough, tested hickory to which rope has been nailed on either side. However, I do not feel especially apologetic about making this admission, for it is something of a feat to teach a wild animal to walk across even this broadened version of the tightrope.

In the first stages the animal's job is not very difficult. His assignment then is to walk across a board six inches wide.

Many cats are natural balancers, so I don't claim much as a teacher of equilibration. The really difficult task in the case of such animals is to make them understand that you want them to walk across the board.

Once my cat succeeded in walking the six-inch board with regularity, I started him on a four-inch board. Then I cut the width down to two inches. Good old resilient hickory was the wood I always used. It has a way of giving without snapping. Experience taught me how to choose my hickory, and I developed a knack for recognizing the most pliable kind, with the result that I never suffered the humiliation of having a piece of it crack under the legs of one of my feline balancers.

Two-inch hickory is the narrowest I could safely use. It was to the sides of this wood that the rope was nailed for the "tightrope" act.

Early in my career—when I was with Howe's Great London Circus—I was assisting a trainer who was teaching a leopard to walk the tightrope. My boss, instead of working the stunt in the center of the ring, from pedestal to pedestal, hooked his tightrope, so-called, from one of the bars of the arena straight to another bar about twelve feet across, cutting off a section of the circular arena and making of it a sort of elliptic space inside of which I was required to stand. My job was to watch there, stick in hand, and discourage the tightrope walker whenever he showed any signs of jumping from his ticklish perch.

The first time the animal was sent across the "rope" he behaved himself, and my boss and I thought we weren't going to have any trouble with him. The next time, the leopard, after walking the first half of the rope with an almost smug calm, suddenly jumped from his hickory roost straight at me—and he might have messed me up if I hadn't been alertly watching his every move. Even in those early days I didn't quite trust the big cats, and I ducked with a nice sense of timing as he sailed into the near-ellipse in which I stood. I didn't lose any time scrambling for the wide-open spaces of the main arena.

In the light of my subsequent experience I believe the

trainer who let me stand in that cut-off space—it was little bet-ter than a trap—was an old fool. And I was a young fool for doing his bidding.

I once had an act performed with five leopards and five pumas. The management kept demanding new thrills and I finally worked out a stunt that involved a leopard springing onto my back from a pedestal ten feet high about fifteen feet away. The animal I tried for this trick was Dixie, one of the nimbler-witted of my spotted cats.

I started by cuing Dixie to jump from the ten-foot pedestal to a slightly lower one, with a broad padded top. Then I cued her to leap from this high seat to one with a still smaller top. This new pedestal reached to my shoulders, the height to which I wanted to accustom Dixie. In the trick, as planned, I would turn my back on her and stoop over slightly and she would leap for me, landing with a front paw on each shoulder. I would grab these forefeet as she landed, to keep her poised on my back.

In the early days of this trick I wore a heavy turtle-neck sweater that protected my neck, and over the sweater a leather coat with a high collar. Before long I had Dixie working so that time after time she made a neat landing on my back. In fact, she was performing so zestfully I couldn't help feeling she was enjoying herself. Many animals, as I have said else-where, seem to get pleasure out of their arena work. With the movement of my back which was Dixie's cue to jump, this animal now regularly leaped into action with a positively happy abandon.

One day, about a week before Dixie was to perform her trick before an audience for the first time, we were having another of our rehearsals. The attendants set the arena, and Dixie and I prepared to go through our routine. She fairly bounded up the graduated pedestals, forming a sort of arena stairway, that led to her ten-foot perch. I walked off to my post in the center of the ring and turned my back on Dixie as I had done dozens of times before. Then I bent over slightly and gave the movement of my back that was her cue. She jumped, but misjudged her distance, and landed a bit short. As she struggled frantically to keep from sliding off my back, which she had barely reached, I grabbed quickly for her slipping paws and just managed to reach them. In a strenuous effort to keep her on my back (I knew that an unhappy experience at this stage of the game would affect her future work and possibly set me back weeks) I gripped her paws too hard. In some way or other I had let go of her right forepaw. Holding on mainly with her hind claws, which by now were well embedded in my leather coat, she swung around with her right paw and just succeeded in reaching my right eyebrow and the side of my nose. At the same time she managed somehow to find the back of my neck with her teeth, though luckily for me she was not poised for a deep and telling bite.

When attendants drove Dixie off with prods, I started taking inventory of my injuries. My right eye was full of blood, and not knowing the true nature of the injury I began to wonder whether I was going to lose the eye. The ripped eyebrow pained and smarted and that didn't help my morale. Such is the power of suggestion that when I placed my hand over my left eye I was sure the right was fading fast. When the doctor turned up a little later I learned, to my relief, that the eyeball had not been damaged.

The injury to my nose wasn't serious either, but to this day a red streak shows there in cold weather, where Dixie slashed me. And when the hair on the back of my head is pushed up, the scar left by the leopard's teeth can be seen. This injury also proved minor, although it might have been fatal if the animal had been set for a real attack.

All things considered, I was pretty lucky. The most unfortunate aspect of the whole experience was that it resulted in a definite setback for Dixie as a performer. I nursed her along until she was doing her leaping act before audiences, but she never once performed before a crowd with the spirit she showed in rehearsal before the accident.

Nothing that happened early in my career affected me more than this experience. I wasn't sure in those days what Dixie's loss of spirit meant, but it saddened me. I was certain that she had had no intention of harming me—that the injuries I sustained were due to a combination of panic and her frantic efforts to get hold of something that would keep her from falling.

In the light of what I have learned in the intervening years, I believe that Dixie suffered a loss of confidence in me—not enough to cause her to rebel and refuse to perform, but sufficient to make her wonder whether the same thing might not happen again. She was a fine cooperative animal but quite understandably lived in fear of another mishap, and it's my hunch that that is what gave her work thereafter a mechanical, lackluster quality.

It is quite possible that when she didn't land properly on that unfortunate day, I was not standing exactly where I should have been and that therefore the fault was mine.

At any rate, I was deeply moved when that joyous animal suffered a loss of spirit.

Putting a wild animal over a hurdle is a trick that circus audiences have endorsed for years. An eight-foot hurdle is the tallest I have ever used. This is not much of a jump for a lion or a tiger.

In an enclosure such as mine where there is so much equipment, including the big floor pedestals that encircle the arena, and where therefore only a meager running start is possible, it is not desirable to use a really high hurdle. Even a low one thrills an audience, which gets a fine view of a big cat sailing through space regardless of the hurdle's height.

The trick is not impressive unless the animal used is a big, powerful specimen, and that is what usually creates problems.

Persuading five hundred pounds of lion or tiger to go over a hurdle is no simple matter.

The first rule I observe is not to attempt to put a big cat over a *solid* hurdle. Wild animals have a fundamental sense of self-protection, and before they can be taught a trick, they look for some way of gauging the possibilities. In the hurdle trick, therefore, a barrier is used through which the performer can see what is on the other side.

I recall a serious accident that took place when an inexperienced trainer tried to get a spirited lion to jump over a "blind," or solid, barrier. Unfamiliar with the technique that calls for the use of a hurdle that enables the animal to see at a glance what is on the other side, the trainer used forcing tactics when the lion refused to budge, prodding him with a pole and yelling at him excitedly. Despite which the animal simply would not leap over the barrier, and when the trainer kept forcing the issue he got himself badly mauled.

People often ask me when animal training started. My collaborator and I put a researcher on the job in an effort to learn the answer, but it seems to be one of those things that is hard to pin down in terms of specific dates.

We found ourselves going farther and farther back in history until the trail led to Ptolemy VI, son of Cleopatra, who was the sixth king of the Macedonian dynasty of ancient Egypt. Ptolemy died in 145 B.C. Just as we were prepared to say that animal training started with Ptolemy VI, we discovered that his mother, that woman who seems to have had a hand in everything, had had something to do with animal training before her son figured in it.

Let me explain. History reveals that Ptolemy VI used lions in many of his parades to celebrate religious occasions. Other animals were also used. In one of these parades twenty-four conveyances were drawn by elephants, sixty by oxen and twelve by lions.

Ptolemy became king in his infancy, but Egypt flowered

under his regent, the aforementioned Cleopatra, who, it develops, used lions to celebrate religious occasions while her son was still in his infancy.

Anyone who knows anything about lions needn't be told that it would be impossible to get them to pull a vehicle unless they had first been trained to do so. In fact, this seems to me to be one of the greatest of all training feats, one calling for complete mastery over the animals. Diligent research turned up no information on how these lions were trained or by whom.

The fact remains that only an animal trainer—a truly great one—would be able to get twelve teams of lions to pull vehicles of *any* kind. To begin with, the cats would have to be harnessed, a feat in itself—and they would have to be taught to concentrate on the job in hand instead of picking fights with one another, which is second nature with the big cats when they have such close access to one another.

I can't think of a feat of modern animal training that is more impressive than the work of the trainer or trainers who served Ptolemy and/or Cleopatra over two thousand years ago.

It rarely comes to pass that two circuses play the same town the same day. But this happened to me some years ago in Flint, Michigan, with amusing results.

The Hagenbeck-Wallace Circus, in which I had been featured for several years with my big-cat act, was in town, and so was my own show. The H-W circus was then operated by my friend Howard Bary, able publicity director for our present circus.

The newspapers in Flint and nearby towns had a lot of fun with the publicity battle that followed. The H-W show starred a man they billed as "The Great Blockaman," who claimed to be a master hypnotist who could "hypnotize man or beast." He had an animal act in which four lions appeared. It was his contention that he controlled them by means of his "hypnotic eye." He announced that, if given the opportunity, he would hypnotize every animal in my act—I then worked thirty-five lions and tigers—and, this accomplished, he would hypnotize me.

Blockaman, a big bushy-haired man who looked like P. T. Barnum's wild man of Borneo, also announced that he would bring me and my animals out of our trances in any order the audience might designate. In the meantime, if the public doubted his powers they were invited to see him work his magic with his own lions at the Hagenbeck-Wallace Circus, now showing at . . . Get your tickets now! Come early and bring the children. Seeing the great Blockaman will be an experience they will never forget. So hurry, hurry, hurry!

I admired The Great Blockaman's gall, but I knew enough about his limitations as an animal trainer to feel safe in publicly offering him $100,000 if he merely agreed to step into my den of cats and put them through a few of the ABCs of animal training—pedestaling them, for instance.

Our show took a full-page ad in one of the papers to make these and a few other representations and to hurl other challenges and defiances in the best tradition of circus warfare. Blockaman never showed up.

The so-called hypnotic eye, as applied to animal training, is a myth that refuses to die. Early in my career, imaginative writers endowed me with such powers. Although I have made several public disclaimers—the first as far back as 1933—occasionally someone still connects aspects of my work with hypnosis.

This tendency probably started as a result of the "stare" trick which I originated many years ago. This involves letting a lion come very close to me, his face not more than a foot from mine, after which I "stare him down." Having done this, he backs away, then turns and trots off. It's a trick that audiences like, judging by their applause. They are particularly enthusiastic if the animal is a spirited one which, prior to the "stare" routine, has battled me hard.

The answer to this trick is very simple. For some reason which I have not been able to figure out, lions don't seem to want me to look them steadily in the eye. It makes them uncomfortable, so they quickly give up meeting my gaze. There are those who think that in this phenomenon there is something to be learned about lion character. If there is, I have seen no supporting evidence. All I can vouch for is the seeming discomfort of the lion when I look him straight in the eye.

I have given this fact considerable thought in the hope of establishing a psychological point or two, but I cannot claim any success for the simple reason that every lion I have used in the "stare" stunt has reacted in more or less the same way. The only point of departure I can report is that one lion might start backing away after meeting my gaze for ten seconds, another might put up with my stare for twice that length of time, but they all withdraw in approximately the same manner and trot off to a pedestal or leave the arena if the cue calls for that.

Tigers, on the other hand, do not seem to mind my staring at them. They stare right back. I never could find a satisfactory answer to this—that is, the difference between the lion's and the tiger's reaction—but that's the way it is.

Nothing seems to escape the eye of the lion.

One day I had just run the animals into the arena when one of the lions started rooting around in the dirt. We had reared the arena in the area where the lot on which we were showing was at its smoothest. But that lion had noticed something. He started tugging at it. A quick glance revealed that it was a few inches of sacking that blended so perfectly with the dirt in which it was imbedded that it was hardly noticeable.

I tried to drive him to his pedestal but he ignored me and kept tugging away until he had yanked a whole burlap sack out of the ground. He raced around the arena with it between his teeth while other lions tried to take it away from him. I couldn't restore order and get on with the act until I had taken that bag away from its discoverer.

Another time we were showing on a lot that we afterward learned had once served as the refuse dump for a nearby town. So neat a job of filling in and leveling had been done that you would never suspect that this had once been the town dump. There was only one clue—and one of my lions found it and with typical curiosity got busy investigating. Discovering a small black patch imbedded in the dirt, he started working away at it, throwing dirt in all directions with his powerful paws. Then he began tugging at the black substance with his teeth and the first thing you knew he had succeeded in pulling an old discarded automobile tire out of the ground!

And then he wanted to play with it. Other lions came over to take a look; then one of them tried to take the tire away from its discoverer. I couldn't get the act going until I gained possession of that tire and removed it from the arena.

It is getting harder and harder to find the right kind of lot or field on which to erect our tented city as we move from town to town. And when we are playing one-night stands, as we do most of the time, we wind up now and then on a surface that has flaws we either did not notice or accept with our eyes open; because there are times when we do not have any choice.

A few hours before the matinee starts, the ground is reinspected and the more obvious flaws are corrected, but in moving from place to place as often as we do we inevitably run into difficulties involving the terrain on which we must set up the big top, the menagerie and side-show tents, etc.

I remember the day a few inches of rag caught the eye of one of the lions—and when he yanked it out of the ground it proved to be only a scrap, not more than half the size of a woman's handkerchief. Yet I could not get that animal to attend to business until I had cued him away from that rag he had unearthed so that I could pick it up and hand it up through the bars to an attendant outside the arena.

But before the animal decided to relinquish that insignificant scrap of rotting fabric, which he kept slapping around with his paws, seemingly trying to determine if there was any life in it, he had held up the act longer than the animals involved in the burlap-sack and rubber-tire incidents.

And in none of these instances was orneriness involved. Lions are born investigators. Whenever they see anything that seems to require investigation, they get busy at once with their sleuthing.

Occasionally an incident of this kind involves a tiger, but nine times out of ten it is a combination of the eagle eye of the lion and his insatiable curiosity that is responsible.

Sometimes there are factors other than curiosity involved in these investigations. One of these is sheer animal instinct.

In 1963 we were playing in a small town where the circus had been set up on a field that was full of green things growing—grass, weeds and an assortment of small shrubs and plants. The greenery was at its lushest in the area where the tunnel from the cages to the arena had been set up.

As the animals—both lions and tigers—came through, they started sniffing the ground and occasionally one of them would yank up a green mouthful and start chewing. It was a job to keep them on the move because most of the cats wanted to stop, smell and do some nibbling if their nostrils confirmed that they had found what they were looking for; so traffic through the tunnel was slow that day and the cage boys had quite a job keeping the animals from lingering too long over their discoveries.

It developed later that there was some wild mint growing along the tunnel pathway. What is commonly known as catnip is really a form of mint, and all felines love it, from house cats to lions and tigers.

In England the plant known in the United States as catnip

is called catmint, in recognition of its minty flavor. And probably because of that more explicit name, the reason why felines are so fond of what Americans have always designated as catnip is better understood in Great Britain.

There are so many details that have to be checked!

For instance, sometimes a lion or tiger does not finish the fifteen to eighteen pounds of horse meat he is fed daily. Occasionally when this happens he hides what is left over—usually under his straw bedding.

One of the jobs of the attendants is to be sure, before the animals are sent into the arena to perform, that no meat has been secreted anywhere in the cages.

One of my lions that had succeeded in hiding a chunk of meat under a layer of straw was about to take it with him shortly before the start of a performance when an alert cage boy caught him in the act and prevented him from carrying it out of his cage into the arena. If that animal had succeeded in getting that fairly sizable piece of horse meat into the arena, inevitably he would have been challenged. Other animals would have tried to take it away from him, and a free-for-all might have resulted.

My left ear was not functioning properly—I wasn't hearing things as sharply on that side as I was on the right—so I took my problem to a doctor. He examined me and told me I had developed what has become known in industrial circles as a "boilermaker's ear."

The report of a blank-cartridge gun will bring to attention a lion or a tiger whose mind is wandering. When a big cat is not paying attention to me, I can't very well communicate what I want him to do, so teacher has to fire his gun to get Johnny—or whatever the big cat's name is—to look at the blackboard.

Occasionally, too, I do this "blanking" for reasons of showmanship. The drama of certain situations that develop in the

[37]   The story of these lion quintuplets, born not many months after the world-famous Dionne quintuplets, is told in **Chapter Three**.

[38] Among my big cats are some that become restive while my spinning tiger is performing. At this moment I am under a strain, as I have to keep an eye on the spinner and at the same time be ready to whirl around fast and confront an enemy of the performer (neither within the camera's range) that is about to leap down from his seat, according to a shouted warning from an attendant outside the arena.

[39-40] This lion cub, most lovable of the pets I have had over the years, lived for automobile rides. He preferred an open car, but my only photo of him seated in one is fuzzy. . . . As a cub, the lion shown in the picture below was the gentlest of creatures. Petted by too many, he became the equivalent of a spoiled child. Some years later he turned vicious and went berserk in the arena. Animals born in captivity seldom make good performers.

[41-42]   ABOVE: Teaching a tiger to roll a cylinder.

BELOW: Main difference between this photo and the one above is that it shows how a lion uses his tail as an aid in balancing himself. How big cats are taught to roll globes and cylinders is explained in Chapter Seven.

Bob Eginton Photo

[43-44]   ABOVE: Affectionate cub drapes a forepaw over its mother's shoulder.

BELOW: When I try to rehearse this mother—Princess, who is discussed in Chapter Three—two of her cubs jump on her in an effort to get her to play with them.

[45]   I am persuading this lion to get up on his pedestal. He isn't offering as much resistance as he seems to be. He roars his defiance, then
clambers up, a favorite gambit of many a big cat, particularly those
that seem to get the most enjoyment out of performing.

[46]   The first stage in training a tiger to jump through a flaming hoop. This is a Sumatra tiger, darker hued and not as big and spectacular as the Royal Bengals from India, which I prefer for most tricks and formations.

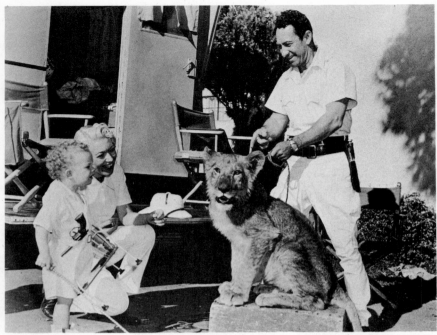

[47-48] Mr. and Mrs. Clyde Beatty, Clyde, Jr. (then three), and lion-cub friend. The photo at right shows the same group minus the cub, as they look today, nine years later.

arena is heightened by the bark of a gun. So the blank-cartridge pistol serves two purposes, one practical, the other purely for effect.

Since I fire the gun with my left hand, it's the left ear that takes the punishment. The doctor advised me to give up using the gun.

"Will it save the ear?" I inquired.

I was told it wouldn't, that the damage had been done. So I didn't see any point in dispensing with a helpful, if not indispensable, device.

If I had abandoned the gun I would have had to rely more on whip-cracking, an even more effective attention-getter, though not as effective from the standpoint of showmanship.

There is nothing new about jealousy among wild animals. This subject has been dealt with by zoologists, animal psychologists and others, so I do not feel that I am introducing anything new in bringing it up.

From personal experience I can cite a number of instances of one animal being jealous of another, but there is one that stands out above all others I have observed. It involves two of my star performers—Prince, my present rollover tiger, and Frisco, my spinning tiger; and it has developed into the bitterest feud between two animals that I can recall.

On all counts Prince can be considered my chief solo artist. When he does the rollover, everything else stops and he becomes Mr. Big—and he seems to realize it. An enthusiastic performer, he responds readily to the cues that start him rolling over and over.

It is unquestionably true that many of the observations one makes about wild animals can at best be no better than unprovable analyses. But careful study of the behavior pattern of a specific animal, as I have studied Prince day after day, convinces me that here is a cat that enjoys being the center of attention—more so, I believe, than any other animal I have ever trained.

His response to applause is—at least to me—unmistakable. And when he is at his electrifying best and giving one of his dynamic performances, I could keep him doing those rollovers indefinitely—or at least as long as the crowd felt like applauding.

Insofar as it is possible to detect self-importance in an animal, Prince has it. I can reach no conclusion, after watching him as closely as I have, other than that there is a bit of swagger in his make-up, a suggestion of strut and bumptiousness in his stride.

I'd like to add to my earlier statement that Prince enjoys being the center of attention. It would be more accurate to say that he would like to be the whole show.

Prince has frequently shown what can only be described as contempt for Frisco, who, as my spinning tiger, also does a solo bit, although it is not built up in the act as dramatically as Prince's more spectacular appearance in the rollover.

Time and again while Frisco is twirling round and round like a tiger top, Prince looks on sullenly and restively and frequently has shown signs of being about to spring at the animal with whom he does not seem to enjoy sharing the spotlight. A number of times I have maneuvered Frisco away from Prince's pedestal when the rollover tiger seemed about to pounce. But it is impossible to intervene in time in each and every type of situation that develops and twice I was unable to keep the determined Prince from attacking the spinner—in Philadelphia in May 1963, and in Salisbury, North Carolina, in April 1964.

In Philadelphia, Prince succeeded in catching Frisco from behind as they were both leaving the arena after the act, and ripping him down the thigh. I had to call in a veterinarian and have Frisco stitched up.

The Salisbury incident took place during a performance and was potentially more dangerous. While Frisco was doing the spin, Prince jumped down on him from his pedestal, grabbing the spinner by the left hind leg and pulling him against the side of the arena. Aided from the outside by Red Hartman, my assistant, I was able to separate them.

It was fortunate that Prince dragged Frisco against the bars, which made it possible for Hartman to stick a pole in the aggressor's mouth and break his hold. Had the combatants remained anywhere near the center of the ring, it would have been extremely difficult for me to break up the fight.

Frisco was not as seriously injured as he had been in Philadelphia, but the incident shook me up and gave me more to think about than the earlier attack. It is Prince's seeming determination to get Frisco that troubles me, and I may have to remove one or the other from the act.

Frisco has never forgotten that first attack in Philadelphia, and ever since has tried to keep an eye on Prince while doing the spin, which is extremely difficult to do. Several times when he saw the rollover tiger standing up on his pedestal as if poised for a leap when he should have been seated, Frisco slowed down his spin—and on a few other occasions when he sensed trouble, he cut the spin short to play it safe.

Frisco is a remarkable animal. He has not the slightest illusion about Prince's animosity, and under the circumstances I would understand his behavior if he grew balky and put up resistance when I brought him off his pedestal to do the spin. But never once has he balked. Like many another tiger I have used before him in this twirling routine, he seems to enjoy the role of whirligig; but it is my responsibility to protect him and at this writing I am thinking of ending his career as a spinner or Prince's as a rollover artist.

For the time being there is peace, but with the first sign that Prince is planning another attack I will have to make a quick move.

The more I think about Prince's behavior the more convinced I am that this situation is the wild-animal equivalent of what is known among humans as professional jealousy.

There is a vast difference between these two tigers. After Prince injured him painfully in Philadelphia, Frisco, had he been the vengeful type, would have attacked his adversary while the latter was so vulnerable as he lay stretched out on the arena floor during the rollover. But not once has Frisco shown that anything like this is on his mind. He remains seated on his pedestal during the rollover, and never shows any signs of restiveness while his foe is performing.

It isn't fear that prompts Frisco to refrain from attacking Prince when the latter is doing the rollover. Frisco is not afraid of Prince. On the one occasion they had a chance to fight on even terms—it was when they were being shifted and the panel separating their cages had been removed—Frisco had Prince on the defensive and would have given the rollover tiger a bad time if the fight had not been stopped.

Arena feuds are not uncommon in the world of animal training, although the one between Prince and Frisco has lasted longer than any other I can recall.

Queenie, a Royal Bengal, and Ma'am, a Sumatra tiger, were another pair of animals that kept a feud going in my arena for some time. Queenie was larger than Ma'am, but the difference in size was not as great as usual in the case of two full-grown tigers of these species. In most cases the Royal Bengal is a much bigger animal, but Ma'am was unusually large for a Sumatran.

When these Sumatrans are tough, they are mighty tough. Ma'am was like that.

I added Queenie to my tiger group when Ma'am was already a member of it. Ma'am made it plain quickly that she did not like Queenie. In this case, however, I know with a reasonable degree of certainty what started the feud. It was the fact that I had given Ma'am's pedestal to Queenie. Such shifting had never caused dissension in the arena before, and I did not realize that I was starting trouble. Dozens of times previously I had changed a tiger from one seat to another without incident.

As Queenie's position in the tunnel was ahead of Ma'am's,

the royal lady reached Ma'am's former seat first. During two successive performances the rowdy from Sumatra made straight for her old pedestal and yanked its occupant down. The fights that followed might have proved serious if I hadn't been able to break them up quickly. Whatever edge there was in these brief skirmishes was on Queenie's side. She fought back vigorously and dealt out as much punishment as she took.

Clearly the only thing to do was to switch Ma'am back to her former seat. This I did, but she had now developed so much animosity for Queenie that the move accomplished nothing.

The third time Ma'am attacked Queenie she was sent banging against a pedestal and she left the Royal Bengal alone for several days. Then one day when I was exercising the tigers in the arena the feud broke out again.

As usual, Ma'am was the aggressor. She made a sudden rush for Queenie, who was cagily taking in developments over her shoulder. When Queenie increased her stride, Ma'am foolishly thought it meant she had the Bengal on the run. With a spurt, the roughneck from Sumatra caught up with the animal she had singled out for persecution and made a leap for her.

Queenie was prepared. She suddenly whirled around, and with her back protected by the bars of the arena, advanced to meet the foe. A noisy battle followed, in which Queenie paw-clouted Ma'am several times, forcing her to retreat. Little actual damage was inflicted by either beast, but the violence of Queenie's counterattack left Ma'am reeling and bewildered.

Ma'am was forever sticking her chin out. She had as much pugnacity as I have ever seen in a tiger, but not enough fighting ability to back it up. She was a game but not a wise fighter. She had a genius for overmatching herself and almost invariably was defeated. She had a few draws to her credit, but, to my knowledge, not a single victory. Yet she persisted in picking fights.

One day during a performance one of the lions made a spring for Queenie and got her down. This was too good an opportunity for Ma'am to pass up, a chance to cash in on another animal's efforts. Ma'am leaped from her pedestal straight at the felled tigress. But she had hardly lashed out at Queenie when two big lions jumped from their pedestals and dashed over to join the squabble.

In the free-for-all that followed, Queenie—a wise and calculating fighter—managed to wriggle free and get away from her assailants, and when the Royal Bengal was gone, Ma'am found herself with three lions to fight! Before I could break up the scrap they did a pretty thorough job of cuffing and mauling her. She was lucky to get off with the superficial wounds the lions inflicted.

Later, Ma'am lost two more decisions to Queenie, who was subsequently removed from the act so that she might have cubs. The cubs were a success, and I decided to keep Queenie out of the act and thereafter use her exclusively for breeding purposes.

Two years later a situation developed that necessitated my temporarily restoring Queenie to the act. For five successive performances following Queenie's restoration, Ma'am behaved herself—so well, in fact, that I began to wonder whether she still remembered the animal she had habitually picked on two years before. And then one day the fun began—at a time when I had a right to feel quite reassured.

The act was over and the animals were leaving for the tunnel that led back to their cages. Queenie was off her pedestal and well on her way to the tunnel door when it suddenly occurred to Ma'am to attack her. Queenie, a believer in preparedness, had never taken her eyes off her old enemy from the time I put her back in the act, and she was characteristically looking over her shoulder when Ma'am elected to declare war again.

Queenie increased her stride as Ma'am made a lunge for her. As the Bengal disappeared through the tunnel, Ma'am in hot pursuit and now only a few yards behind, I yelled to the attendant at the tunnel door to partition off Queenie. The tunnel is a sectional affair with a series of doors by means of which the animals can be separated.

The attendant wasn't quick enough. I could tell by the commotion in the tunnel that Ma'am had caught up with Queenie and that they were locked together.

I rushed out of the arena and dashed around to where the struggle was going on inside the tunnel. Through the three-inch openings between the boards of the type of chute then in use, I could see that this time Queenie was determined to pay Ma'am back for all her dirty work. It took the combination of all the blanks in a freshly loaded pistol and the vigorous prods of three arena attendants to separate the combatants.

Queenie came out of the battle with only a few unimportant nips and scratches, whereas the ever-beaten Ma'am emerged with a bad limp. Her left hind leg was chewed and torn, and it was several weeks before her injuries healed and she could walk normally again.

That cured me. I had had enough of Ma'am. I transferred her to the menagerie and never again took a chance on her as a performer.

What creates feuds among animals? Is it much different from the factors that create feuds among people?

When I built my zoo at Fort Lauderdale, Florida, I picked a parcel of land that had lake facilities. One of the advantages of this was that on a hot day my big cats would be able to splash around in the water and cool off.

I had a group of thirty lions at the time and had them partitioned off with an iron fence so they could have their own swimming and wading area. The fence was placed at a point that was deep enough to give them swimming room and at the same time prevent them for getting the footing that would enable them to jump over.

As far as that lake was concerned, most of the lions contented themselves with flopping around in the water when the sun was at its hottest. Only one of them was a dedicated swimmer—Bessie, a spirited young lioness.

Bessie, a born explorer, one day discovered a rather big underwater opening in the fence where the metal had rusted out and fallen away. It was big enough to accommodate her, and she swam through it and began cutting capers in the water about a dozen yards beyond the fence.

I kept a family of black swans on that side of the barrier, but Bessie was so busy swimming she seemed unaware of them. She was wholly preoccupied with the business of cavorting in the lake without such silly restrictions as fences.

A picture that has never left me is that of the other twenty-nine lions lined up in their enclosure at the water's edge, a puzzled expression on their faces as the happily splashing lioness disported herself, their look practically saying, "What does that nut think she's doing?"

I always kept a rowboat handy. Getting into it, I started after Bessie, fearful that if she swam too far out it would complicate the task of getting her back where she belonged. I was also concerned about the interest the baby swans were now showing in the lioness, swimming up fairly close for a good look at this stranger that had invaded their part of the lake. It was not until then that Bessie showed any awareness of their presence. She started heading toward them to do a little investigating of her own, her expression friendly and her manner indicating nothing beyond curiosity. But I quickly placed my rowboat between the lioness and the swans to be in a position to do something about it in case Bessie changed her mind and decided to play rough.

The water was deep where Bessie was now operating, so she couldn't possibly get a footing with her hind legs, and the chances of her being able to get at me in the boat were slim. There was a possibility that she would be able to upset the boat if she could manage to bring her forepaws into action, but I was able to keep a decent distance away from her and did not consider myself in any danger. Using an oar as a means of communicating with her, I started heading her back in the right direction. She had had a good swim, she was getting tired and she offered no resistance.

Meanwhile the baby swans had discovered the opening through which the lioness had passed and they glided through it to the other side, where the lions were still lined up watching Bessie. The lions were wholly unaware of the presence of the birds—or, if they noticed them, showed not the slightest interest in them.

The mother swan, when she saw where her babies had gone, started paddling furiously after them. An angry swan ruffles its feathers, spreads out its wings and tail, and, hissing continuously, fairly flings herself at a foe. This poor distracted mother, fearful for her brood, lunged at the nearest lion. In a few seconds she was dead. The lions, paying no more attention to her as she lay there crushed and dismembered than a person does to a fly or a mosquito he has swatted, were soon lined up at the water's edge again watching me steer Bessie back where she belonged.

The baby swans, unmolested, swam back to their side of the lake.

It was one of those tragedies one never forgets. This happened twenty-five years ago, yet all the details are still vividly fixed in my mind.

I have made reference elsewhere, in another context, to Rajah, a handsome young tiger that I use in my present act, and the gentlest, happiest and most amusing tiger I have ever trained.

Even the healthiest animal—and Rajah answers to that description—occasionally suffers a loss of appetite. Once—only once—I had this problem with Rajah.

It is customary in zoos and circuses to feed a live chicken to a big cat as an appetite reviver. If this sounds barbaric, let me say that death, in a situation of this kind, usually comes even more swiftly than in the case of poultry killed for home consumption. It is practically instantaneous, happening as fast as when a live rabbit is fed to a python in one of the zoos that exhibit these huge reptiles.

When George Scott, my head keeper, placed a fat hen in Rajah's cage, the big tiger acted as if this was something he had been given to play with and, in his typically gentle manner, started toying with it. He stroked the chicken with a paw, claws retracted, then got himself in a posture suggestive of a house cat about to spring at a rubber mouse or some other plaything designed to amuse pets.

At first the hen was frightened and emitted a series of blood-curdling squawks; then when she saw that Rajah showed no signs of playing rough, she relaxed, began to feel at home and started examining the cage, even helping herself to a drink from Rajah's water pan.

The next day when Scott made his early morning inspection of the cages, he found Rajah and the hen fast asleep on the straw bedding, side by side!

Rajah's appetite returned in a few days and once again he was consuming with unmistakable relish every bit of his quota of eighteen pounds of horse meat daily.

The hen that Rajah wouldn't eat wound up in Clown Alley, where Eddie Dullem, chief clown of the Clyde Beatty-Cole Bros. Circus, who has a talent for improvisation and a way with domestic animals and birds, developed an entertaining comedy bit featuring that fowl. The bird was adopted by the clowns as a mascot and became a favorite with them.

While there are many basic similarities among the big cats, there aren't any two that are precisely alike. In the case of Rajah, you do not have to study him to see the difference. He is *obviously* different.

For instance, normally a male tiger purrs to attract the attention of a female in whom he has developed an interest. Not so Rajah, who purrs because it is something he enjoys doing.

Occasionally he even purrs when I am cuing him in the

arena. And it is not unusual for him to do it as a sort of greeting when I pass his cage before or after a performance, which I do daily. And when, in addition to a vocal hello, I snap my fingers as a kind of secondary greeting, his purring is at its happiest.

The more I think about Rajah the more remarkable he seems. He doesn't conform to any pattern. For instance, I have trained over nine hundred tigers and he is the only one I have never seen or heard do any snarling. I'm not sure what this proves, but it seems a fact worth recording.

In fairness to the great family of striped cats I suppose I should add that the tiger that snarls occasionally is merely doing what comes naturally. No animal can be expected to be perpetually good-natured—either in captivity or in its natural surroundings. The Rajahs of the tiger world happen so seldom they are almost freaks.

Just as I expect people to be grumpy now and then, I expect the big cats to have their moments of irritability. When such moods prove to be more than momentary, I check to see if anything is wrong. Sometimes a toothache is responsible, or a splinter in a paw, or something of that sort.

As a means of minimizing the trouble he can get himself into, I send Rajah into the arena last. This protects him from animals that might want to take a poke at him from behind. Which, because of Rajah's disposition, would put him at a great disadvantage. He might easily mistake a real attack for a playful gesture, treat it as such and get himself roughed up in the process.

But it is almost impossible to anticipate everything. Occasionally on entering the arena Rajah playfully leaps at Frisco (of the Prince-Frisco feud) from behind. Frisco, good-natured himself except where Prince is concerned, understands Rajah and doesn't strike back.

In a situation of this kind Frisco is more concerned with watching his enemy Prince, who in turn is watching him, in which I find no peace of mind, because there is a potential here for a free-for-all. So I am currently trying to get it through Rajah's head that he is no longer to spring at Frisco (who, I almost need not add, could under certain circumstances become an easy target for Prince).

Once, when Rajah suddenly jumped at Frisco from behind —much like one boy trying to scare another for the fun of it— Frisco leaped high in the air and almost gave Prince the opening he was looking for. Though I am not optimist enough to think that Rajah, as intelligent as he is, understands all the angles, he's beginning to get it through his head that his pranks are troubling me.

Rajah, at three and a half, is reasonably close to being the big-cat equivalent of the young man who refuses to grow up. My problem in training him from this point on is to teach him to conduct himself in his relations with the other performers in a manner best calculated to protect him, and to prevent needless brawling in the arena.

And this has to be accomplished without breaking Rajah's wonderful spirit. Nothing should be permitted to change that playful tiger's happy disposition.

While I am making progress in teaching Rajah the facts of arena life—the most important being that he must learn to curb his exuberance when surrounded by so many roughnecks —I find it necessary to keep an eye on him constantly, and sometimes this gets to be quite a strain. The easiest solution would be to remove him from the act, but he would no longer be Rajah if I did. Despite an occasional show of nervousness when he gets too close to a lion, he loves to perform.

As a trainee Rajah was a delight. I keep no records that enable me to state with any degree of certainty that this or that cat learned the fastest, but relying on my memory, which is pretty good, I'd say that I "seat-broke" Rajah faster than any other animal I have ever trained. He seemed to know immediately what I wanted him to do. And once he did he kept "telling" me, insofar as it is possible for an animal to communicate with his trainer, "This is fun. Please let me do it over and over again."

When I graduated him from a block seat to a regulation pedestal, he was in heaven. Up and down that pedestal he went, having a good time and also trying to please me, as evidenced by the eagerness with which he looked up at me after a few of these ascents and descents. Having earned the approbation he was seeking—a gentle stroking of his head with the light buggy whip I use during seat-breaking—he would want to get going again, which he would indicate by standing up on the pedestal. To keep him from going on endlessly with that up-and-down business, I would cue him out of the arena.

Earlier I pointed out that more than any other animal I have ever trained, Rajah "talks" to me. He is forever trying to tell me something by means of purring and other movements of his lips—and also by what I read in his eyes. Most of the time, these days, he seems to be asking for more work (he would call it play if he could speak); some of the time he seems to be saying, "Please keep me away from those lions." I have never seen any indication that Rajah is a coward. If he *had* to fight I believe he would—perhaps first placing himself at a disadvantage by means of a few playful probes designed to determine if he really was in a scrap.

It all gets down to this: Rajah just doesn't like lions. Once one of them took a swipe at him, and he sustained nothing more than a few scratches. That didn't seem to bother him so much as the fact that the big maned creature seemed to get mad for no apparent reason.

At this writing Rajah has a seat in the arena that he seems to like better than those he previously had. He is as happy as ever and more relaxed. And he doesn't seem as worried about the lions as he once was. I can't very well take in every detail of what goes on, but when I catch Rajah looking over at the nearest lion, I look over in that direction too, and that seems to give my favorite tiger confidence. From here on my main job is to see that he never has occasion to lose that confidence.

One day, thinking it was time for Rajah to learn still more of the facts of life, I tried to mate him to Princess, mother of the two fine litters discussed in Chapter Three. But Rajah would have none of her. In fact, he seemed positively scared to death.

Rajah is very much like a young man who is afraid of girls. But like most young men—the normal ones—he will overcome his fears. For there is no question about his masculinity and his normality. His problem is that he is a bit bashful, a late starter.

Once he gets used to girls I expect Rajah to give me his first peevish look, one designed to transmit:

"I've been thinking things over, Boss. And I wonder if you tried hard enough to teach me what I've been missing."

When a normally manageable lion or tiger—one that is usually not troublesome—has a sudden change of disposition, I watch him carefully. If there is a mounting irritability, the first thing I do is stand outside his cage while he eats his next meal. If I notice that he is chewing on one side, I have good reason to believe that he has a toothache.

Merely from the standpoint of the humane approach the animal must be given relief as soon as possible. And from experience the veteran trainer knows that an animal in pain can be needlessly dangerous, can even go berserk.

When I am reasonably sure that one of my animals has a toothache, my first move is to anesthetize him. This is done by means of an inoculation in the hip administered from outside the cage. I use only a small amount of medication—just enough to keep the animal "under" for about fifteen minutes, which allows sufficient time for an examination and a few other steps that have to be taken.

Veterinarians are not always available when such situations arise—and usually those that have not had zoo experience prefer not to minister to the big cats. For this reason I have had to familiarize myself with the most modern methods employed by the experts in alleviating all sorts of aches and pains and treating a variety of ailments to which the big cats are subject.

In the case of a toothache, once the animal is under anesthesia, with the aid of an assistant I pry the jaws open and keep them apart by the insertion of a block of wood. In my last experience of this kind I found that my patient—a lion— had broken off one of his big tusks and that the nerve was exposed. I immediately gave him a shot of novocaine to deaden the area involved.

By this time the animal was beginning to stir, so I gave him another hip inoculation designed to keep him quiet for an additional fifteen minutes. It is not considered safe by veterinary surgeons to keep a big cat "under" for more than an hour, and I have always lived up to this.

If the tooth affected is one of the big tusks, I use a heavy type of forceps in making the extraction; if it is one of the smaller teeth, I use a pair not much different from those you have seen in your dentist's office.

When I make one of these dental explorations, I never know with any degree of certainty what type of condition I will discover. If I find a tooth that looks chalky white, I'm reasonably sure that ulceration is responsible. Sometimes this calls for an extra dose of novocaine to make sure the animal will suffer no pain when I make the extraction. In a case such as this I feel my way, and if the animal shows the slightest sign of feeling what I am doing, I inject more novocaine into the gum area involved.

Once in pulling a tiger's tooth I found it had broken off so close to the gum line that I had to lay back the gum with a surgical instrument in order to get at the stump and be able to grip it solidly enough to loosen and extract it. The gum then had to be sewn together. On this occasion I was fortunate enough to have the services of a veterinarian who had performed similar operations in zoos.

In another such situation—this time involving a lion—I had

to do the gum-stitching myself, since no professional services were available. I am now a pretty good amateur veterinarian, and I am glad to be able to report that the results were satisfactory.

It is heartening to see the change in disposition of an animal that has been relieved of its dental misery. After an extraction I place my patient on a special diet until I am reasonably sure that the post-operative soreness is gone. According to the severity of the case, this might be a liquid diet—say, about three quarts of milk into which a number of eggs have been beaten —or a preparation of that kind to which I add ground meat or —in milder cases—a straight diet of ground meat.

If the tooth extracted is a big tusk up front—one of the deadly weapons which the big cats in their native haunts use for killing—the animal's ability to chew his food properly will not be affected, for most of the real chewing is done with the back teeth.

I invariably take an animal out of the act until he has completely recovered from dental surgery, using an understudy to perform in his stead.

I would hate to have to establish this scientifically, but there are times when I get the impression—a clearly defined one, it seems to me—that a big cat is trying his darnedest to communicate some such sentiment as "Thanks very much" after I have relieved him of pain. I'll never forget the exuberance of one particular lion, on whom I had performed a tough extraction after he had suffered considerably, when I turned him loose in the arena a few weeks later to see if he seemed well enough to return to the act. He raced around the ring like an athlete in training for an Olympic tryout. Round and round he ran, and when he had exhausted himself he stretched out at my feet like a household pet and gave me as tender a look as I ever got from Lucky and Timber, my favorites of the many dogs I have had over the years beginning with my boyhood days. But knowing how changeable the big cats are, even that kindliest of looks did not mean that I would be able to relax my vigilance in my future relations with that animal, a proven roughneck whose basic primitiveness was intact.

The importance of inspecting my big cats regularly cannot be overemphasized.

One day I was moving along the rows of cages taking a look at the animals when I came upon a lion that was sitting on his haunches and shaking one forefoot, then the other. Then he alternately stuck these feet in his mouth, bringing laughter from spectators who were wandering around the circus grounds before a performance, as circus fans frequently do.

It *looked* funny, and I didn't blame those people for laughing. But it was not a laughing matter. From long experience I recognized the situation for what it was. Burs had gotten between the toes of this animal and had made him decidedly uncomfortable. He had apparently picked them up in one of the fields or lots where we had been showing, either on the way to the arena or in the enclosure itself. In addition to causing pain and discomfort, burs sometimes lead to infections, so, with the aid of assistants I got busy at once removing them and with an antiseptic solution cleaning the places where they had lodged.

Those people who thought the lion who had stuck his feet in his mouth was a comedian left to join the crowd in the big top before I had a chance to explain the true situation to them.

In 1933 a motion-picture fan magazine speculated on how Universal Pictures had managed to get people to "double" for me in the filming of *The Big Cage*. There was really no need to speculate, as the facts had been published on December 12, 1932, in an article, from which the following is taken, by the Hollywood correspondent of the New York *Times*:

"The custom of 'doubling' for stars confronted with dangerous stunts in their pictures was reversed this week when

Clyde Beatty, star of *The Big Cage,* which he is making at Universal, substituted himself for minor players when it was necessary to enter the cages of some fifty lions and tigers. As a star, Mr. Beatty's contract provides him with a double. But . . . he not only plays his own part but those of others when the script calls upon the various characters to enter the cages."

Even if doubles had volunteered for this work, I would have been compelled to turn them down. In my field the unpardonable sin is to permit an inexperienced person to come face to face with wild animals whose fighting instincts are quickly aroused by a confrontation with a stranger.

10. Before They Trusted Me with Lions and Tigers

I Was a Bear Trainer—A Shaky Debut—A Polar Bear Loose in the Indiana Snows—A Tiger-Bear Fight—Substituting for a Lady "Animal Charmer"—An Assortment of Bears, including Himmy, Who Learned about Electricity

WHAT ARE bears doing in a book about the big cats?

All the big-cat trainers started with lesser animals. For instance, Herman Weedon, Jack Bonavita, Pete Taylor and Chubby Gilfoyle all began as bear trainers. So did my original mentor, Louis Roth. So did I.

Although I was not aware of it at the time, what I learned in handling bears was to prove an important factor in my subsequent success as a big-cat trainer.

At the age of fifteen I was a cage boy with Howe's Great London Circus, an American enterprise despite its British-sounding name. By the time I was a little over sixteen I was as talented a cage boy as ever wielded a metal dung-scraper or gave a thirsty bear a fresh pan of drinking water. These skills did not exactly qualify me to put on a bear act, yet when I heard that our bear trainer had asked for a leave of absence to look after a pressing personal matter, I jokingly said to Louis Roth, our chief animal trainer, that I hoped he would consider me as a fill-in.

To my astonishment Roth replied that he had been thinking of making that very suggestion himself. He had noticed that I regularly watched the bear act, even making notes of some of the things the trainer did, and that whenever he (Roth) had discussed the different tricks and formations with me, I had sounded as if I knew what it was all about.

Roth's confidence in me was a bit frightening. He was a big man in his field, one of the great trainers of the time, and I was somewhat fearful that I might have given the impression that I knew—or thought I knew—more than I did. If that was so, it was not because of any salesmanship I used. I was unsure of myself in those days and was ready to tell him I was half kidding when I had offered my services. Which would have been true enough, as my application for the job could only be described as tentative.

Louis Roth, in a day when even so small a group was considered phenomenal, had put together a five-lion act and had won acclaim in many of the best circus towns in the country. He had also successfully presented a five-tiger group. And now, with Howe's Great London Circus, he was presenting an all-leopard act, a bigger group of cats than he had ever worked before, though I don't recall the number. But I do remember it was a fine act that became very popular.

Roth had also trained our show's polar bears and had himself taught the trainer who was now going on leave.

A talented, many-sided man, Louis Roth. Not many trainers in the history of the profession had been able to develop so wide a variety of animal acts.

And a kind man too. He had taken an interest in me from the time I had joined the Great London show and had done just about everything he could think of to make me feel at home. Equipped with common sense, he had not hesitated to kid me when I must have seemed too much of an eager beaver—for instance, when I talked as though nothing in the world mattered except wild animals and animal training. He predicted that when I grew up I would learn that there was a lot more to life.

Despite which, he himself seldom discussed anything but animal training, and when he saw fit to include me in the conversation I joined in eagerly.

Long afterward Roth told me that he didn't regard my bid for the bear trainer's job as halfhearted. He said he was impressed by my healthy respect for the animals. He told me that most of the young men who applied for jobs as trainers and assistant trainers made a great point of telling him that they weren't "afraid of anything on four legs." He cheerfully admitted that he had had many moments when he was "scared to death," that a good trainer learns to conceal such thoughts and by outbluffing the animals manages to get them to carry out their assignments.

He also told me that he had noticed early that I loved animals. This was not a feeling that could be faked, he said. Either you had it or you didn't. You could not successfully communicate with these primitive creatures unless you had a deep affection for them, he maintained. That was the first requisite, and I had it. Nothing he said made me feel quite so good or gave me so much confidence. I didn't lack faith in myself, but I had sense enough to know that even though I was a reasonably understanding observer of what that bear trainer did in the arena, I could hardly call myself an animal trainer.

A great many years have come and gone since Louis Roth made his comment about applicants for jobs as trainers. I am thinking about retiring within the next few years, and having been quoted to this effect in the press, I have received a number of letters from young men who "want to learn the business" and eventually take over my act. Most of these applicants try to impress me with their fearlessness, whereas a little intelligent fear would be more impressive.

Louis Roth, if he were still alive, would be interested to

know that today's applicants for animal-training posts, like those of a vanished era, seem to think that the principal qualification is an almost reckless daredeviltry.

Roth asked me if I knew the routine of the polar-bear act. I told him I did.

He was reassured. He felt I *must* know it after watching the act so many times and studying it from every conceivable angle outside the arena.

Even if there had been time for a rehearsal, I doubt whether Roth would have held one. In retrospect I realize that he didn't believe in giving a candidate for a tough assignment too much time to think about it. If he knew you could swim, he believed in throwing you into the choppiest surf and betting you'd be able to swim back to shore—and standing by to rescue you if necessary.

I must have been a strange sight when I put on the uniform of the man I was supplanting—he was very tall and somewhat on the portly side, though he preferred to be known as "stocky." He wore one of those ornate outfits that resembled the dress uniform of a high-ranking general in a mythical musical-comedy kingdom, and when I put on the jacket it looked like an overcoat on me. I was slender and a little under average height, so when I tried on the trousers I found myself flopping around in them as though they were part of a clown's get-up. That fancy jacket came down so far I figured I could wear my own pants without anyone being the wiser.

When I told Louis Roth that I knew the routine, I was telling the truth—that is, I knew it from outside the arena. I didn't realize that when I stepped inside and stood facing those enormous bears—a few weighed almost one thousand pounds and the others not much less—I would get confused and forget what to do. I was like a kid scheduled to speak on graduation day who could rattle off his speech before the event but forgot his lines when the big day came.

I had prided myself on knowing each animal's distinguishing features, yet when I was in there facing them I couldn't tell one bear from another.

I had come to realize that polar bears were intelligent animals, and I still remember the expressions on their faces that made it plain they knew I was not their regular trainer. They were puzzled, as if to say, "Who the devil is he?" My gold-braided visored hat flopping around on my head, almost coming down to my eyes, must have contributed to their puzzlement.

How would I get started? I didn't know and began to wonder what I had gotten myself into.

I remembered Roth's warning that I would get into trouble if I touched Satan with the whip, but which one was Satan? He was the one with the meanest disposition, but how could I tell him from the others? *Now* they all looked alike. Five or six were Satan's size and had his general build.

So I decided not to touch *any* of them with the whip. Customarily the whip was used lightly and served merely as a device for reminding the bears what they were to do next. Satan resented its even touching him, and since he was known to be a tough customer, I decided I would just wave the whip and see what would happen.

The bears, ignoring me, worked the act themselves. It was not exactly a crisp performance; my only contribution was that I knew when to get out of the way.

A feature of the act was the so-called "bear slide." Bears get a great kick out of sliding down a smooth surface, and if early in the act I had hooked up the ladder by means of which they approached the top of the incline from the rear, they probably would have devoted the whole performance to climbing up and zooming down.

Actually I had forgotten this part of the act until my eye chanced to light on the ladder. I went over and picked it up and discovered I didn't remember too well how to hook it up, but I finally managed to put it in place after quite a struggle.

The bears—they are the only animals I've worked with whose curiosity matches that of the lion—gathered around me like a group of inquisitive people and watched me put the ladder in place. As I wrestled with it and finally fastened it to the gadget that would hold it firm, my floppy hat fell off and was trampled underfoot.

After the bears had slid down the incline for at least twice the number of minutes normally allotted for this stunt, I unhooked the ladder and stumbled off with it.

The bears performed the next few tricks on their own, and then it was time for the big finish—(that much I remembered!) —which consisted of one of the group ascending a big globe and, while standing erect, working it across the arena with his feet, a familiar bear trick that goes back to the early days of animal training. What gave the stunt a particular punch in our show was the fact that the animal that performed it was huge and looked a mile high standing up.

But while I remembered what the grand finale was, I hadn't the faintest idea which animal performed it. So, brandishing my whip and hoping for the best, I waved the whole group toward the big wooden sphere and walked them past it, hoping that the one that had been trained as a globe-roller would mount it and do his stuff. First he would have to ascend the pedestal that stood next to the big ball, then plant himself squarely on the round surface and start doing his stuff. Fortunately this expedient worked and the first thing I knew the right bear was manipulating the globe across the arena floor.

To my surprise, Louis Roth was satisfied with my debut. It developed that he had expected me to get rattled and make a lot of mistakes. The big test was whether I would panic after those mistakes and leave the arena before the performance was over, defeated and half scared to death. Those polar bears are terrifyingly big to a novice at close range, and their size alone, Louis said, licked most beginners.

One of the wisest moves Louis made before sending me in

was to remind me that polar bears had maimed and even killed trainers and that I must err on the side of caution, even at the risk of looking foolish to the audience. "Don't use any forcing tactics," was how he summed it up. He would be standing in the safety cage and if I got into serious trouble he would dash in to extricate me.

What else could anyone ask? Nevertheless, I was scared during most of that first performance. When I had those lapses of memory, I wondered whether one of the more vicious bears, confused by my erratic behavior, might not take it into his head to grab one of my arms or legs—a favorite bear gambit —and start gnawing away at it before my mentor could rescue me. But these moments of doubt and fear would be followed by a kind of blind determination to stick it out.

Although Roth was satisfied with my first appearance, he also told me that I had been lucky. The next time I entered that arena I would have to behave as if I were in charge; it would not be possible to "stagger through" (as he put it) future performances.

Don't ask me how it happened, but it's a fact that when I went in for my second performance I remembered everything I was supposed to do. The stage fright that had dulled my memory was gone, and I had no trouble recalling the details of all the routines and the order in which I was supposed to present them.

If Louis Roth had jumped on me after that first wretched performance, which a less understanding man would have done, that probably would have been the end of my career as a trainer—that is, both the beginning *and* the end. I've always been grateful to him for realizing that a ragged first performance should not necessarily be considered typical of what one can do.

I had only one disillusioning experience with Louis Roth. Impressed by the glittering array of medals he wore on his colorful, military-looking uniform, I asked him to tell me their

history. Since he seemed so proud of them I assumed they
had been presented to him in connection with his work—
perhaps in Germany, where he had begun his career.

Roth seemed surprised and puzzled by my question and
asked whether I really didn't know how he had acquired those
medals. When I insisted that I hadn't the faintest notion, he
said that perhaps it wasn't surprising after all; for I *was* very
young. Then, to my amazement, he told me that he had had
the medals made!

I said nothing, but he must have noticed my disappointment
because he went on to explain that if a man was an outstanding
trainer he was entitled to medals. There was no reason why
he should not present them to himself if no one else saw fit
to do so. He added that in the not too distant future I would
be a first-class trainer and would be justified in having some
medals struck off too. He said there was something spectacular
about the way they shone when the spotlight hit them and
he had been informed that this frequently brought admiring
comments from the audience.

Since I began with a bear act and my work with these animals led to my entering the big-cat field, it seems appropriate
to report a few more of my experiences with them, beginning
a few years after the foregoing took place.

I suppose there are as many practical jokers as ever, but they
seldom single me out for their antics any more. During those
long-ago days of my first job as a trainer, it was almost a
ritual for certain pranksters whose brand of humor eventually
became tiresome to call me up in the middle of the night
to announce that one of my animals had escaped. So that
when between three-thirty and four o'clock one cold winter
morning I received a telephone call informing me that one of
my polar bears had slipped out of its cage and was among
the missing, I decided not to take it seriously. I hung up and
went back to sleep.

The circus was at its winter quarters in Peru, Indiana, at

the time and I was stopping at a local hotel. A shipment of fifteen polar bears, which I was to start training soon, had come in a few days before, and it was one of those that was supposed to have escaped. Only a few days before, I had received a somewhat similar emergency call—from someone who told me he was the night watchman—to the effect that one of my biggest bears had broken loose and was rampaging through the streets of Peru. I fell for the gag, which meant getting out of bed between one and two on a freezing morning and making the three-mile trip from the hotel to winter quarters. There I found all my animals in their cages and everything under control. As I returned to the hotel to resume my interrupted sleep, I felt capable of strangling with my bare hands the first practical joker I could identify as having been responsible for one of these false alarms, or of tossing him into the cage of one of the more vicious lions or tigers in the show's menagerie, or both.

A second call came about half-past four, repeating the mesage about the missing polar bear. I hardly listened this time. The second this sleep-destroyer announced himself as the night watchman I was convinced that I was being hoaxed again. I hung up in the middle of a phrase and notified the hotel's telephone operator that I was receiving no calls until nine o'clock the next morning.

You can imagine my surprise and embarrassment when, on arriving at circus headquarters the following day, I discovered that one of my polar bears had actually escaped. The calls had really come from the night watchman!

"Didn't the night watchman notify you over the telephone that one of the polars was loose?" asked the show's manager.

I nodded blankly.

"Then why didn't you hustle over here and do something about it?"

There was no time for a discourse on practical jokers and why they were responsible for my thinking that my early morning summons was just another of their silly pranks. Even after

I had been bawled out, I half thought I was being kidded. But when I checked up it was obvious that a bear *had* escaped.

But how? It proved to be one of those freakish situations. We were building new, stronger and roomier cages to take the place of an older type that we no longer considered adequate. It developed that one of the older ones was in a state of dry rot, although afterward the caretaker who was supposed to check all equipment insisted at great length that he couldn't tell by looking at it that there was anything wrong with it. He could have by a thorough inspection of the cage, but that's beside the point.

The runaway proved to be Norman, an animal with a wonderful disposition, and the closest approach to a clown I've ever seen in the bear family. I doubted very much whether Norman had actually tried to escape. He was a big fellow, weighing between 850 and 900 pounds, and probably found himself free when he leaned against one of the decayed sides of the cage and it started falling apart.

Under different circumstances Norman might not have left the premises. Captivity had not affected his happy-go-lucky disposition and he was more like a big playful dog than a polar bear. Later on he might turn tough, as so often happens, but now at least he was friendly and manageable.

I believe that if it hadn't been snowing Norman would have been found napping outside his broken cage, patiently waiting for someone to bring him something to eat. He had a hearty appetite and normally would have been too practical to risk missing a meal.

From where he was located in winter quarters Norman would not be able to see that it was snowing. I agree with the zoologists who say that polar bears can sense such things. At any rate, Norman decided to go out and look around.

I routed out a cage boy and we began our search. I armed myself with a chair and a broom. Experience had taught me the folly of using blank cartridges on bears, which do not respond to gunfire as lions and tigers do. The blanks are fired to the right or the left of the big cats—never directly at them—and they can frequently be halted in their tracks by the loud report the gun makes. This firing to one side, it didn't take me long to find out, had no effect whatsoever on an onrushing bear; the animal just kept coming. I imagine most bears could be stopped cold if the blank-cartridge pistol were fired full in the face, but no trainer is justified in blanking an animal in this fashion except when he is called upon to defend himself against an attacking beast that might otherwise maim or kill him. The blast of such a gun smack in the face of a lion or tiger would not save the trainer in a desperate situation of this kind; but it would definitely slow up the animal and give the trainer a little time to figure out what to do next.

Should you happen to be one of those who know how tough the winters can be in the Peru section of Indiana, you have some idea of the type of weather I drew as I set out to find the missing bear. The thermometer had been around the zero mark, and on this particular day it was below.

The ground had been snow-covered for several days, and the boy and I started looking around in the snowy footing for bear tracks. We soon discovered that we had given ourselves a tough assignment, for the ground all around winter quarters was a jumbled mass of horse, mule, camel, elephant, and wagon tracks—not to mention many other varieties. After an hour's hard work, in the course of which our numbed hands and feet kept reminding us of the freezing weather, we found tracks that were unquestionably those of a bear. When we started tracing them, we saw that the animal had circled winter quarters several times before making a break for the open; perhaps he couldn't quite tear himself away from the spot where the other bears were. At any rate, the indications were that he had thought the matter over before he finally decided to take off and do an exploration.

We followed the fugitive's tracks to the bank of the Mississinewa River, which flows into the Wabash. This was a logical destination for an animal that was instinctively a "fisher." Always food conscious, perhaps Norman wanted to see what delicacies he could find for himself in the river.

Whether he did any fishing or not I don't know, but we traced him for some distance up the banks of the Mississinewa. As we followed his tracks we bumped into a man who evidently thought we were crazy—and I must admit we didn't exactly present a picture of out-and-out sanity.

Suppose you met two young fellows who appeared to be wandering aimlessly along the banks of the Mississinewa, one of them (my cage boy) carrying a chair and the other carrying a broom, and suppose the one with the broom suddenly stopped you and asked, "Have you seen anything of a polar bear?" Would you think you were in the presence of the sane or would you have a suspicion that these two figures that suddenly bobbed up out of nowhere with their strange equipment and stranger questions were a pair of escaped lunatics?

I imagine we would merely have further confused our startled-looking chance acquaintance if we had tried to explain that there is nothing like a chair, with its four convenient points for warding off attacks and for keeping an animal at bay, and that the brush part of a broom is ideal for a bear to chew on until he regains his composure. Even a normally good-natured animal like Norman was capable of attacking if in my efforts to catch him I excited him unduly or in any way gave him the impression that he might be punished for his escapade.

"Have you seen anything of a polar bear?" I repeated. The stranger made no reply. He merely stood and stared at us, his astonishment seeming to grow. Then he moved off, crunching his way through the early morning snow without once letting us hear his voice. Looking back at me and the broom I was carrying, he increased his stride until he was almost running.

Again the cage boy and I took up the task of tracing Norman. His tracks were confusing. We trailed him out to the ice of the river and back again. There were several sets of such prints, all of them inconclusive. Indecision, based on unfamiliarity with his surroundings, was indicated.

If the chase continued much longer the bear might encounter people on the way to work; and while the odds favored his letting them alone, there was always the possibility that someone might make the wrong move and antagonize the animal.

These thoughts were uppermost in my mind as my assistant and I followed those hesitant footprints of Norman's. The animal would reach a certain point, backtrack, and then, deviating only slightly from his original course, return to the point he originally had in mind. It was all very bewildering; but there was no doubt that we were on the fugitive's trail, for some of the tracks we found looked fresh.

My back was aching from stooping over mile after mile and giving bear tracks the benefit of my Sherlock Holmes eye. And then, standing up straight to rest my complaining back, I saw the escaped bear straight ahead of us, not more than fifty yards away!

Norman was watching us with friendly interest. His typically keen sense of smell had probably enabled him to pick up our scent and discover us well before we had discovered him.

Having looked us over, he went about his business, which at the moment consisted of standing on his hind legs and throwing his head back and getting the full benefit of the falling flakes. As I approached, he got back on all fours and started throwing snow around in all directions. He seemed to be enjoying himself thoroughly.

I was now fairly close, but this did not seem to bother him. In a number of places the wind had piled up the snow in great drifts, and as I approached to within ten yards of the runaway, he rolled over in one of the drifts and fairly wallowed in it.

I stopped and watched him, not wanting to drive him back any further. Having had a good roll in the snow, Norman started rooting around in it with his nose. I couldn't tell whether he had sniffed something that interested him or whether this was just another of his clownish antics.

I began circling around him, as I thought it was now time to start driving him back in the other direction. He offered no resistance to this plan, being too interested in the snow to be concerned with a mere matter of direction.

He continued to head the right way, then halted in his tracks and turned around and faced me. Next, as if to show me a new trick he had learned, he got up on his hind legs again and started slapping the falling flakes with his forepaws; then once more he threw his head back and let the falling snow—it was now coming down heavily—land all over his face. I've never seen a bear have more fun.

I approached to within five or six feet of him, still carrying my broom. I used it to sweep a great cloud of snow at him, thinking he might enjoy some horizontal flakes for a change, but my playful little gesture seemed to make no impression on him at all. Almost unmindful of my presence, he looked around, and spying another big drift straight ahead, he leaped headlong into it and enjoyed another snow bath.

He made no effort to give me the slip. When we were only a few hundred yards from the animal barn, Norman began traveling at a quickened pace, his interest in loitering seemingly over. My guess was that he was getting hungry. He offered no resistance as I drove him into the animal barn. In fact, he seemed relieved to see it again.

Bears love to swim, and if the sub-zero temperature had not spread a sheet of ice across the Mississinewa, the chances are that Norman would have run off to take a dip and the job of retrieving him would have been much more difficult.

In my absence a cage was made ready for the runaway and I had no trouble driving him into it.

Although it was not yet feeding time, I ordered that Norman be fed at once, and no bear ever enjoyed a meal more.

I've trained and handled plenty of bears—in fact, I once worked the biggest bear act ever shown in America—but I've never known a member of the species to match the brutish feat of Bill, a big brown Russian bear that I was using in a mixed group which included, in addition to him and three other Russians, an assortment of leopards, tigers, pumas, lions and hyenas.

Wild animals that are strangers to one another often develop a quick and sometimes unmanageable incompatibility. That's how it is with bears and tigers, I learned through bitter experience in my early days as a trainer. In my act the bears entered the arena before the striped cats came on and at first did not seem to realize how formidable the tigers were. More in mischief than with any thought of starting a scrap, the bears would reach out for the tigers as the latter entered the ring. Not until they were clawed a few times did my Russian quartet become aware of the dangerous potentialities of the animals they had treated so lightly.

The bears and tigers grew to hate one another. There was a continual growling and snarling when they were in the arena together. Bill was becoming a moody Russian by reason of three successive paw-cloutings and nippings administered by Nellie, a tigress that had no use for bears and made no bones about it. Bill never had a chance to get back at Nellie, but he had a fine opportunity one day to avenge himself on Lil, the other tiger in the act, and he took advantage of it with surprising speed and effectiveness. It was something that had never happened before—at least, nothing like it appears anywhere in the annals of animal training—and perhaps it will never happen again.

Lil was on one of the high seats. It was her cue to stretch out her body full length, her hind legs remaining on the seat, her forelegs resting on a support in front of her. The boy whose job it was to hook this seat in place had been careless and it had come loose. Down toppled Lil, landing right in front of Bill's pedestal. In a split second the bear made a leap for the sprawling tigress, grabbing her from behind by the neck. Bill had one of those unbreakable holds, and he snapped the big cat's neck before she had a chance to defend herself. Lil died a few minutes afterward.

Needless to say, the bear had a tremendous advantage in this brief encounter, but the occurrence astonished me none the less. While Bill was sure to have a big early edge when he attacked under the circumstances described, the chances were a hundred to one against his quickly getting that unbreakable hold. If he didn't succeed in doing this, he was a goner, for tigers are lightning fast and Lil would have quickly brought her claws and teeth into play and made an end of that overambitious bear.

Another thing that surprised me was the way Bill held on. Bears almost invariably, in attacking with their teeth, go in for what I call "series biting." They bite, bite, bite, relaxing the teeth and sinking them in again and again. It was the first and only time I have ever seen a bear bite and hold on. Instinctively, Bill must have known that to let go and try a new hold meant certain death. So he emerged as probably the only bear that ever killed a tiger.

I was puzzled when during the fall of 1963 I found myself thinking back to that awful moment when that Russian bear snapped the tigress's neck. Why should the details of that somber story come crowding back into my mind with such vividness so long afterward?

And then I suddenly realized what the answer was.

I had seen the Moscow State Circus during their tour of the United States in 1963 and had been impressed with the feats of a big, superbly trained Russian bear that did everything except play the fiddle and dance the twist standing on his head.

As I watched him perform, it struck me that there was something reminiscent about his gait, facial expression and general demeanor. He was another Bill!—the spitting image of the big Russian bear that had so quickly destroyed my tigress.

Circus fans frequently tell me that they can't tell one animal from another of the same species. To them, all elephants look alike, ditto all bears, lions, tigers, etc.

To the experienced trainer, as I pointed out earlier, there are very few look-alikes. We immediately detect points of departure that enable us to tell an animal at a glance.

Without this capacity for instantaneous recognition an animal trainer would be unable to function. Lacking it, he would not know which lion, for instance, to cue for which trick. Honest-to-goodness look-alikes don't come along often enough to present a problem.

I was asked by a friend with whom I discussed the resemblance between Bill and the bear in the Moscow State Circus whether the animal from abroad didn't suggest viciousness because he wore a muzzle. A good question, but it had nothing whatever to do with my reactions.

The bear trainer in the Moscow show worked his animals in an open area, not in an arena. The law in practically all states requires that wild animals performing outside an enclosure must be muzzled. I have always performed in an arena, and therefore was never required to muzzle an animal and never have.

I would not get much of a kick out of working a muzzled bear, though I must concede that the one that reminded me of Bill was a fine performer and made a big hit. In fairness to its trainer, I pointed out to my friend that the muzzle didn't exactly make that animal harmless. Bears can do a lot of damage with their claws, although their teeth, set in powerful jaws, are their main offensive weapon.

It was that Russian beast's facial expression, carriage and movements that reminded me of the bear that killed the tiger. Under similar circumstances he would have been capable of the same act of violence as Bill's.

I was having my first season as an animal trainer with the Hagenbeck-Wallace Circus. The show opened with a "spec" (circus language for spectacle), in the course of which a sheik—played on horseback by Mickey McDonald, who subsequently abandoned the ranks of the "heavies" to become a successful circus clown—galloped out on a magnificent-looking horse and sang a mournful song about how he had been betrayed by the girl he had regarded as the lass of lasses.

Mickey had a pretty fair voice and managed to sob out his plaintive story with good effect, after which he would dash offstage and return with the Girl Who Done Him Wrong slung limply across his saddle. Then in even louder and sobbier tones, he called for a pox on all perfidious wenches.

When Mickey made this second appearance, he was followed by a colorful array of circus Arabs—his "court followers," as we called them, though none of us knew for sure whether a sheik held court—and this picturesque retinue would nod sympathetically and even wail their distress when the sheik, achieving new emotional heights, seemed completely overcome by the dirty deal he had received.

The climax of Mickey's song came when he dramatically announced that the faithless lady was not fit to live; for which reason he, the Sheik of Whatnot (I forget the gorgeous billboard name), proposed to toss her to the animules, begosh. Having made that solemn pronouncement, he dashed over to the arena in the center ring where three bears, two pumas and two leopards disported themselves. The sheik, with a final sob about the emptiness of a world so full of feminine treachery, opened the door of the arena and tossed the limp betrayer to the animals.

The lady would then save herself by "charming" the animals. Needless to say, she was an animal trainer, and what she did was to put through their paces these animals that were supposed to tear her to bits.

It was a swell stunt and it brought down the house—when it worked. The only trouble with it was that while the lady who was supposed to charm the beasts was admirably equipped with courage, she was an inexperienced trainer and did not have complete command of her charges. One of the bears sensed this (bears have a faculty for plucking things out of the air) and refused to accept her as boss of the arena, which was rather hard on the lady, who was trying hard and deserved better luck. This particular bear had the effrontery to walk up to the gal night after night and embrace her while she was "charming" the performers in the arena. The result was laughter at a time when the audience was supposed to be thrilled. It just about broke up the spec.

The bear made no attempt to gnaw on the lady who was supposed to subdue the animals in the arena. He just rushed up to her and hugged her, making it impossible for the act to go on until he could be dragged away, which sometimes took a minute or longer. It's always embarrassing when you induce laughter in an audience that's supposed to be on the edge of its collective seat, thrilled to death. For hadn't the circus barker, drawing upon his tremulous voice for his best pitch of excitement, announced in his spiel that the animals in the arena were "all deadly killers?"

I was young enough to be amused by the jeers and catcalls that were mingled with the crowd's laughter. In those days I didn't pay much attention to the circusman's credo that it was the job of the clowns, not the serious performers, to create merriment, that when people laughed at the wrong time they were really laughing *at* you.

One night something happened that prompted me to recommend that our animal-charmer be removed from the act. The bear rushed her so hard he almost knocked her off her feet and then, in what was no longer a comic embrace, gripped her so hard I found it necessary to enter the arena to break his hold. (I had made a practice of watching the act from the safety cage so that I'd be able to help if any of the "charmed" animals became unruly.)

The lady had no control over this bear and in time he

might attack and injure her. I had seen such things happen. By now she was alarmed and glad to be relieved of her role as animal-bewitcher.

Rex Roselli, our producer, who had dreamed up this sequence, refused to let his idea die. He asked if I would be willing to don feminine attire and assume the role. I turned him down. He pleaded. I finally agreed to undertake the part for a few days. Then he would have to find somebody else.

Rex hunted around in the circus wardrobe room (where you could find practically any kind of costume) and came up with a pair of oriental bloomer-like pajamas, a turban and a veil. I have rather prominent biceps and these had to be covered, though I don't recall just how that was done.

I had no trouble controlling the animals. Although their expressions suggested that they were puzzled, they knew who I was because they had picked up my scent.

So there were no embraces from the bear who had made things so uncomfortable for my predecessor as "charmer" of the beasts.

One of the other bears had a habit of assuming funny positions as he sat on his pedestal. He would often sit with one paw behind his head, his feet dangling. He was the last of the group to figure out who I was, and when he did he turned to the bear next to him, removed his paw from behind his scruff, poked his companion and pointed excitedly to me, as if to say, "That's Clyde, chum. What's he doing in that outfit?"

But though I was able to control the animals, Rex Roselli's experiment was not an unqualified success. During my second performance the absurdity of the situation got the better of me and I began doing things that made Sheik Mickey McDonald wonder whether I was ideally cast as his betrayer. I had an irresistible urge to show that I regarded this new development in my career as something pretty ridiculous, and hit upon the idea of tickling Sheik McDonald in the ribs while he was singing his doleful ballad of betrayal.

After two performances Roselli told me I was the worst

female impersonator he had ever seen. My stride was too masculine; I must learn to take daintier steps. And I would have to practice cracking my whip in a more feminine manner.

Rex's dissatisfaction was most pleasing to me. I reminded him that I had agreed to fill in for only a few days and he'd better get busy finding a replacement. Rex and I were friends and that was the main reason I undertook the assignment in the first place.

At the next performance I tickled Sheik McDonald even harder. He got so mad he complained to Roselli. The complaint had the desired result. I was relieved of the role of female impersonator.

Cap Bernardi, a veteran animal trainer, drew the assignment. He was on the payroll in a general-utility capacity, and while he could not dispute that his new assignment was in the line of duty, he was not happy about it. He took a lot of kidding. One day as he lumbered out of the arena in the garb of the lady animal charmer, one of the clowns told him he would have to correct that prize fighter's walk or spectators would start asking for refunds.

Bears, bears, bears. So many bear stories occur to me.

I recall one of my bears that had developed the habit of shaking his forepaws—first one, then the other—up and down. When he did it standing up and facing the audience, children would think he was waving to them and they would wave back, to the delight of everyone.

It was a great laugh-producer, yet it was something for which I had to disclaim credit when complimented for "teaching that bear to wave to the crowd." It was always disillusioning when I told people that that paw-shaking business was just a mannerism of that particular animal. Different animals develop different ones, and most of them are hard to figure out or explain. The bear that seemed to be waving to the crowd often went through the same routine when he was in his cage and there was no one around to see him.

I find myself thinking of Himmy, so called because he was a Himalayan bear.

Himmy made a decision one day to demonstrate that any bear that gave the matter some thought could break up the spec. He was in the arena, in the company of other animals, waiting his turn to go on. This was in the days when our opening spectacle featured an Amazon-like soprano whose job it was to sing the audience into a receptive mood. She didn't sing well, but she sang loud, and this, combined with her commanding appearance—she wore a towering spangled headdress that made her look twelve feet tall—helped her become an effective spec attraction—a big aid in getting the show off to a good start.

On the day to which I refer, our singer was handicapped in her role as audience-conditioner by the unorthodox behavior of Himmy. The main lights that illuminated the show had been extinguished and dim colored lights had been flashed on. The band began to play and our vocalist began to sing. Then all of a sudden the music stopped. Himmy, noticing that the arena door was ajar, (to this day I don't know how it happened) had slipped out of the enclosure and headed for the nearby bandstand, where he grabbed one of the musicians, a chap who played an enormous horn that looped around his neck. When the bear grabbed the horn player, the other musicians panicked, though Himmy was really quite friendly, confining himself to hugging the man he had singled out for his attentions.

But this instrumentalist, undoubtedly remembering occasions when circus bears had clawed and bitten people, let out a yell and broke up the spec by collapsing in a dead faint while his brother musicians scattered in all directions before the "attack" of one of the most harmless bears that ever performed.

Not long afterward Himmy gave us another surprise. Having discovered that it would be a good idea to keep so lively and mischievous an animal where I could watch him until it was his turn to perform, I made a practice of having him tied up outside in the space between the menagerie tent and the big top.

But Himmy was to demonstrate that there is no such thing as a perfect defense against an animal full of energy and curiosity. (For of course, it was impossible to keep an eye on him *all* the time.)

Not far from where Himmy was tied, there was an electric light cable. It had been covered over to keep people from tripping on it. It was the last thing you would expect an animal to be interested in. None had ever tampered with it before. But Himmy was different. He uncovered it and must have started playing with it.

A circus that operates under canvas has to carry its own power plants. Through this particular cable passed the current that lighted the dressing rooms.

Before I or anyone else had a chance to realize what he was doing, Himmy was chewing away at the cable. He bit deeply into it and a few minutes later resembled the latest thing in fireworks, the bear sparkler. Pyrotechnic flashes were flying all around his head. This lent a nice Independence Day touch to the spring night, and quite naturally it was not long before the shock landed Himmy abruptly on his furry bottom.

There he sat, a puzzled expression on his face, regarding this strange new foe. Usually an animal calls it a day when confronted by a situation so completely new that he doesn't know how to cope with it. But not Himmy. Before he could be headed off he scrambled to his feet and attacked the enemy anew, his teeth and claws doing so thorough a job that in a few seconds he succeeded in putting out all the lights in the dressing rooms. This necessitated an emergency repair job, for the show had just started. Many a performer made up that night by candlelight or lamplight.

We were playing in Canada when there turned up in my dressing room a giant of a Canuck wearing what seemed like the world's largest mackinaw. What I recall most vividly about him is that his face and hands were badly scratched.

In each of the big pockets of the mackinaw was a bear cub. They made a charming picture, these baby bears, their humorous eyes and look of innocence suggesting that they were as harmless as toy replicas would be. But I know how frisky bear cubs can be and how much damage they can do with their little claws without meaning to, so I wasn't surprised when the French Canadian explained that the two merry-looking babes whose heads were sticking out of his pockets had given him all those scratches and were daily becoming more unmanageable. Would I like to buy them? I told him I would if the price was reasonable. We talked the matter over and I finally gave him twenty dollars for the pair, five dollars more than he asked. Even so I was getting a bargain.

I'm sure that today this must sound like a minor transaction, although I considered it very important at the time, the purchase price representing nearly 10 per cent of my worldly possessions. I was just beginning to break into the game, and twenty dollars was a lot of money.

The man in the mackinaw explained that he had named his bear duo Murphy and O'Toole after two fighting Irishmen of his acquaintance, both lumberjacks. So Murphy and O'Toole they were thereafter, names which hardly reflected their French Canadian background.

Well, those bears grew up and came to be known as the "justly celebrated" Clyde Beatty Riding Bears, Never Before Viewed by Mortal Man on Any Stage. And a good act it was, too. I had trained Murphy and O'Toole to ride horses, and it wasn't long before they made some of my equestrian friends look like amateurs. But, being bears, they felt it necessary occasionally to do something surprising. So one day Murphy, at the conclusion of his last stunt in the riding act, got it into his head to jump on Jimmy, my boy-of-all-jobs. There was no reason for it except that, bear fashion, he wanted to startle me and his audience. So, instead of leaping to the floor of the arena, purely in the spirit of mischief he jumped on Jimmy, whose shrieks could be heard all over the big top. The frightened boy, crawling from under an assailant who made no attempt to attack him, set a new record for dashing from a circus arena into the wide-open spaces.

The next day, after much effort, I induced him to return to his work, but the incorrigible Murphy again jumped on him. So Jimmy quit, wisely terminating an unpromising circus career.

To one who has worked extensively with them, as I have, bears are an almost inexhaustible subject. Before winding up this chapter I would like to tell one more bear story. It has to do with Mischa, a big Russian bear that I was rehearsing, hoping to break him in as a replacement for an animal I considered too dangerous to keep in the act. Mischa had proved a tough customer but had never shown any signs of downright viciousness. Then one day, without warning, he came hurtling at me, teeth bared, mouth twisted and malevolence in his eyes.

I was beginning to learn something about footwork and I managed to keep a respectable distance between myself and the determined animal for a few minutes. But his forcing tactics eventually resulted in his getting much too close to me for comfort. As he moved in to claw me I ducked and cracked him on the nose with a well-aimed right.

No blow is quite so painful to a bear as a wallop on the nose that has authority behind it. As my fist landed, with every ounce of strength I had behind it, my attacker went over in a heap and turned a complete somersault. Which gave me an idea: a somersaulting bear would be a real novelty.

It worked out beautifully. All I had to do to get Mischa to turn a somersault was to tap him gently on the nose with a whip.

That was the origin of the famous Hagenbeck-Wallace Somersaulting Bear.

People still ask me how I learned to train lions and tigers, and I still reply, although of course it is an oversimplification, "By training bears."

By the time I had learned to accommodate myself to the movements, many of them unpredictable, of a wide variety of bears—polar, American, Russian, Canadian, Himalayan—I had achieved the kind of swift, resourceful footwork without which it is impossible to train the big cats to perform. Needless to say, lions and tigers are much faster than bears, but my broad experience with the latter put helpful emphasis on the need for staying literally on my toes, ready to move swiftly in any direction.

There was a time when animal trainers planted their feet squarely on the arena floor and worked their charges, usually a small group, without moving around much. But when the vogue for young, lively, fast-moving animals became established, these flatfoots vanished from the animal-training scene.

Bears gave me an awareness that nimble footwork is as indispensable a part of the trainer's equipment (in handling *any* kind of animal) as the ability to "communicate" with wild creatures and to convey to them what it is you want them to do in the arena for the benefit of an audience.

Bears also taught me to watch, in handling *all* species, for the animal with the poker face. The inexperienced trainer is overinclined to rely on the instinctive "telegraphing" of their innermost feelings and intentions for which many wild animals are known. The narrowing of the eyes, the twisted mouth, the slashing tail, the ears flattened against the head—these and other outward signs of anger are important to watch. But eventually the perceptive trainer learns that there are animals calculating enough to disguise their feelings—good actors, you might call them, that are really bad actors.

Bears are among the best of the four-legged poker players. For instance Bill, the one that killed the tigress. Bill had made no effort to disguise his dislike of the big cats, but this was more or less routine. Animals that come from different parts of the world seldom like each other. What wasn't routine was that Bill, although he had killing in mind and planned to try to destroy a tiger the first time he found himself in an advantageous position, gave not the slightest sign that such was his intention.

These poker players are the animals that inherently are the most dangerous. The very existence of such creatures makes it necessary for the trainer to keep an eye on *all* his animals, not just the one that roars its displeasure or smashes a leg of his kitchen chair with a vicious swipe of a paw. Therein lies his greatest security.

Years later, after my lion-tiger act had achieved recognition, Louis Roth and I were involved in a wild-animal picture that was being made in Hollywood, he as a consultant, I as a performer. One evening Louis grew reminiscent about the days when I was a bear trainer, reminding me of the many things I learned while working a bear act that gave me the confidence to try my hand as a big-cat trainer. In turn I reminded him that my best break of all came the day a man named Louis Roth decided to take an interest in me.

11. The Big Cats and the Elements

"Two Shows Daily, Rain or Shine" – Working in a Flooded Arena – Thunder and Lightning, Unwelcome Visitors – A Near-Tornado in Toronto – Hurricane Esther Plays a Dirty Trick on Us

On June 2, 1963, our show concluded a ten-day engagement in Philadelphia. Then, having "torn down," we headed with our long caravan of trucks and trailers for Plainfield, New Jersey, where we were scheduled to play a matinee and a night show the following day.

Some time after midnight, as we neared Plainfield, it began to rain. Seasoned troupers take most rainstorms in stride. We are so accustomed to living up to the "rain or shine" commitment in our advertisements that we never give rain a second thought unless it gets out of hand. The big top, our menagerie and side-show tents, etc., are all made of the best grade of waterproof canvas, so usually when it rains our main concern is not whether we can keep the fans dry but whether they will be sufficiently interested to turn out in bad weather.

June 3 was a school day, so in accordance with our policy in such situations we had announced that the matinee would not start until four o'clock. The rain had continued to come down steadily, but by midafternoon had not yet become a heavy downpour. However, because it had rained throughout the night, considerable water had collected in the area where my arena had been set up.

The lot that was made available to us in Plainfield—a big grassy area covering enough acreage to accommodate our show and allow for the parking of spectators' cars—would have been ideal in good weather. To look at it casually you would not be able to guess that great pools of water would be able to collect, when it rained steadily, in the very spot where we had set up the big top. Even the experienced eye is sometimes fooled in this matter of avoiding water retention.

It is standard practice for me to make a daily "footing inspection," as I call it, when we are playing one-night stands. A few hours before our matinee was scheduled to start, I looked over the terrain on which my arena had been erected. It was water-soaked and soggy, and where the surface was slightly concave little puddles had formed. But it would be possible to work the act by dumping enough sawdust over the whole surface, a circular area forty feet in diameter. As it was still raining, more water would seep through, so we delayed the sawdusting of the arena until the latest possible moment.

Not long before the matinee was due to begin, people started arriving. There were children accompanied by parents, and children old enough to be on their own.

It was interesting to contrast the grownups dashing through the wet with the boys and girls leisurely strolling along and chatting among themselves as gaily and animatedly as though the sun were out. Most of the youngsters wore rubbers and raincoats, but even those who lacked this protection didn't seem to be bothered by the bad weather.

A close-up of this kind of support from the public always makes a circus performer determined to go out there and do the best job he possibly can, more or less ignoring the handicap under which he is called upon to play his particular part. If the fans can brave a rainstorm to see us do our stuff, the least we can do is to make an all-out effort to entertain them.

During my footing inspection I had made a mental note of the things I had to remember in moving around on that unreliable surface. Near the entrance to the safety cage from which I enter the arena there was a bumpy spot that I would have to avoid or I might stumble and fall. An animal trainer is in gravest danger when he loses his footing. The surface was uneven in several places and my assistant would have to help me make a careful check so that any pedestals that had a slight "rock" to them were shifted until they were solidly based, and any bad indentations were leveled off with plenty of sawdust.

I'm so used to these terrain inspections that by the time I complete one I have a pretty good mental map of the surface on which I will cue my lions and tigers to perform. It is not often that we are able to rent a field that has a pool-table flatness. Almost always there are imperfections that I must bear in mind, perhaps a few inches of protruding rock. If the rock can be removed and filled in, fine. If not, I must make a point of remembering where it is to minimize the possibility of tripping on it.

Needless to say, I must also remember such things from the standpoint of the animals. They are so sure-footed on almost any kind of surface I needn't concern myself about the possibility of their stumbling. But there are moments in my act when an animal is called upon to get over on its side; and since their movements are quick and precipitate, it would be possible for a lion or a tiger to bruise a rib or a thigh in the swift execution of a cue.

Things went fairly well during the matinee. The lion whose job it is to roll a big steel cylinder across the arena, meanwhile maintaining his balance on top of it as he maneuvers it with his feet, found the going tough. This animal loves that assignment and normally executes it with great zest. But that day it was difficult for him to get the cylinder started and keep it in motion. Its sheer weight, plus his own (five hundred pounds or more), severely complicated the problem on so soggy a surface.

After getting the cylinder started and rolling it a few feet the animal would look straight at me, his expression suggesting a combination of bewilderment and frustration. I spoke to him softly, seeking to communicate that I understood his problem. There must be no urgency, no suggestion of impatience on the part of the trainer in a situation of this kind, to avoid the possibility of getting the animal rattled.

My cylinder-roller rested on his perch for half a minute, then resumed his efforts and managed to move forward four or five feet on what was becoming a more and more uncertain surface. Then I signaled him down. Normally he rolls the cylinder the full diameter of the arena, but nothing approaching this was indicated that particular day. He gave me a benign look as I cued him off the cylinder back to his pedestal.

In a situation of this kind there is much room for exploration by students of animal psychology and behavior. Long years of experience had taught me how far I could go in working that willing but somewhat frustrated animal. I knew just when to quit. And when I did, that benign look I mentioned practically amounted to his saying, "Thanks a lot."

I doubt very much whether in the early days of my career I would have been able to gauge as accurately when to cue that lion off the cylinder. In time you make the very simple and obvious discovery that what is best for the animal is also best for the trainer. Because an animal that is pushed too hard in a situation such as this one is capable of anything. One of the possibilities is that he might turn on the man who is expecting too much of him.

When you are young and comparatively new to animal training, your only thought is to make audiences happy regardless of the circumstances. Experience has a way of putting things into perspective. The more you learn about the game the more you find yourself thinking in terms of what is best for the animals and adjusting to circumstances in a manner that sometimes means putting on a show that is less exciting than you would like it to be.

One of the decisions I had to make that day was whether or not to work my rollover tiger, one of the high spots of the act. This animal usually does two series of rolls. After the first series that afternoon in Plainfield the tiger was covered with sawdust that it had picked up. Tigers are neat animals and have the same passion for personal cleanliness that one finds in a much smaller member of the feline family, the ordinary house cat; and that particular tiger, realizing his dampened fur had picked up some foreign substance, shook himself in an effort to get rid of the sawdust. He looked up at me almost apologetically as if to say, "I wish I didn't have to look like this in front of all those people."

The rain continued all afternoon and then increased in intensity, becoming a heavy downpour early in the evening. There was now considerable water in all three rings of the big top and more seeped in as the deluge continued. The sawdust that we kept shoveling in had too much water to combat and it would be difficult to put on the show. The main difficulty would involve my act, because it's pretty ticklish business to get animals to perform on so treacherous a footing.

One decision I quickly made. There would be no rollover that night. It's one thing to get a tiger to do this stunt on a soggy surface, as I had done at the matinee; it would be quite a different proposition to try to bring it off in several inches of water.

I got through the evening by putting extra emphasis on tricks and tableaux that can be exhibited on pedestals—for instance, I cued my "stand-up lion" that raises up on his hind legs, his front legs stretched straight upward until he looks a mile high, to do this stunt—(which is very popular, especially with children, who sometimes tell me they try to do the same thing with their dogs)—over and over again. The big lion I used for this bit was glad to cooperate, as he seemed to enjoy stretching out full length, being one of those animals that love exercise.

My cylinder-roller surprised me by making it plain as could be that he wanted to perform, soppy footing or not. But perhaps I should not be surprised by anything that lion does. He's a ham actor if I ever saw one. Maybe he had it figured out that he would get more applause if he maneuvered his circular steel perch across the little lake that was forming in the arena. Or am I endowing that animal with reasoning powers he did not possess? In *The Expression of the Emotions in Man and Animals,* which has been properly described as "brimming over with everyday testimony of the kinship between man and animals," Charles Darwin makes some rather startling reports on the mental processes of wild animals. I have reported far less surprising examples of big-cat thinking to friends, who occasionally seem a bit incredulous.

I am glad that there is so much activity today in the field of animal psychology and that so many men of reputation are trying to learn more and more about what goes on in the minds and emotional apparatus of animals, both tame and wild. Years ago I said in an interview that while it might seem like reaching for the moon, I felt that some day we would achieve close communication with wild animals and learn how to exchange thoughts with them on a systematic basis. Since I made that statement, man has decided that the moon is quite reachable and I am becoming more and more optimistic about fairly full-scale communication with animals.

In the introduction to the latest edition of the Darwin book just mentioned, the following appears:

"The modern trend in biology is towards an increasingly greater stress on the behavior of animals. . . . It is becoming noticeably popular to forsake the stuffed skin, the mounted skeleton, and the animal preserved in alcohol. Instead there is a desire . . . to observe the animal as a living being. Although we have progressed considerably in such studies since Darwin wrote, he was a pioneer and the modern works on animal behavior can be more readily understood by re-tracing the early trail he blazed. . . .

"Wherein lies the importance of Darwin's work, and why need we concern ourselves with animal behavior and emotions?

"The simple answer is that unless and until it is more generally realized that man has a oneness with the animal kingdom in the expression of his emotions . . . and that the great part of human behavior is basically emotional, approach to many urgent social problems will remain distorted."

I have no illusions about the contribution an animal trainer can make to the science of animal behavior. But perhaps a useful purpose can be served by reporting some of the phenomena I have observed in the arena over a period of many years, with the thought that possibly some of it may have a bearing on this or that aspect of animal psychology or here and there throw light on a behavioral problem involving the big cats. The scientists are better equipped than I to decide what, if any, significance my observations have.

Now and then in working an animal on a muddy surface I get spattered. Once a pawful of mud momentarily blinded me and I almost lost control of the lion I was trying to force back to his pedestal, having decided not to ask him to do his stuff on a surface that kept worsening due to under-tent seepage during a heavy downpour. As the animal took a swipe at my chair, the mud flew in all directions.

A few times I have seen expressions on the faces of lions in situations of this kind that convince me that, if they weren't deliberately throwing mud at me, they *were* enjoying throwing the stuff around.

Full-grown lions are sometimes as playful as cubs. This characteristic is best observed during an exercise run. A big adult lion—they are usually exercised singly—has been known to play as enthusiastically with a rubber ball tossed into the arena as his four-month-old son might. I recall one that got the fun started by nudging the ball gently and letting it roll a short distance. Then he stalked it and pounced on it. To vary the proceedings, he dealt the ball a tremendous clout that sent it ricocheting off the bars in all directions until it finally came to a halt. Once when one of my lions belted the ball in this fashion, it got stuck between the bars. In his effort to dislodge it, he pushed the ball through the bars and it landed outside the arena. That lion—a five-hundred-pounder—set up a howling that made me think of a child who had let a favorite toy get away from him. The animal was not consoled until the ball was tossed back into the arena where he could start playing with it again.

I recall an instance of a lion playing with a ball that suggested he was trying to figure out what made it bounce. This, of course, was just an impression, perhaps fostered by my experience with lion curiosity and possibly by my reading too much into the way he seemed to be studying the ball every time it took a hop.

I have long felt that something can be learned about big-cat psychology by studying the behavior of lions and tigers under varying weather conditions, also their reactions to such basics as light, darkness, fire and a few others.

Of course, much that happens in these areas takes place suddenly, and at times there are dangers involved that make it necessary to concentrate on staying out of trouble. This can prevent the trainer from observing significant developments that are unfolding right under his nose. I've caught some of these developments—occasionally they seem to offer worthwhile insights into animal behavior—but I'm reasonably sure I must have missed many others.

One of the most serious hazards as far as the weather is concerned is a sudden electrical storm while the trainer is in the arena with his animals. My narrowest escape in a storm of this kind took place at Greensburg, Pennsylvania, a number of years ago when I was with the Hagenbeck-Wallace Circus.

Several times my big cats and I had escaped an experience of this kind by ten to twenty minutes. In Greensburg I was putting on my act when such a storm started, but missed by seconds a bolt of lightning that struck the arena.

I was playing a matinee on the day to which I refer. There had been no indications up to the time I entered the arena that the heavens were planning an electrical display; so I gave no more thought to weather conditions in Greensburg, Pennsylvania, than I did to those in Needles, California, or Troy, New York, or any other place you can think of.

Without warning, after I had completed a little over half my act, the arena suddenly grew dark and I could hear the loosened poles of the tent structure bobbing up and down—an unmistakable sign that a heavy gale is blowing. I could have looked around and gathered a few confirming details, but it was up to me to keep my eyes on my animals.

I didn't like the way my top-mounter was behaving. He was fidgeting on his seat and nervously slashing his tail back and forth pendulum-fashion. With typical lion curiosity he looked around in every direction in an effort to figure out what was going on. The noise made by the loosened tent poles seemed to bother him, but this was quickly drowned out by a tremendous clap of thunder which brought the animal to the edge of his high perch. He seemed on the point of leaping down. I got his attention with a crack of the whip and cued him back where he belonged.

I know no better example of instantaneous reaction to a given situation than the restlessness the creatures began to show the very second the arena darkened. At once they grew hazy about cues and showed an unresponsiveness that could be attributed only to the sudden change in the weather. Some of them became almost uncontrollable, including a beautiful tigress named Venus, a normally easygoing animal. I was getting ready to put her through the rollover stunt in a half-darkened arena when there was another great clap of thunder.

I had tremendous difficulty in prevailing upon Venus to leave her high seat for the floor pedestal from which I cue her for the rollover. I used all the persuasiveness at my command, and just as she was moving her paws over the edge of the seat-top by way of indicating that she had finally made up her mind to perform, there was another blast of thunder that sent her cowering back. In fact, she withdrew so hastily that she almost went toppling off her pedestal, righting herself only by an effort of will.

Venus had my complete sympathy. I don't like electrical storms any more than she did. But there was the audience. A crowd gets restive under the big top when thunder and lightning start, and the surest way to make them even more so is to show by your conduct as you perform for them that you are worried too. That's always been an excellent way to start a rush for the exits. The confident manner is a great tranquilizer.

As the rumble of thunder continued, I made a quick decision to finish the rollover business as swiftly as possible and skip the rest of the act. Having cued Venus to leave her pedestal, I felt it would be bad psychology to give up. It would have made an uneasy audience more uneasy.

Overhead, I could see the dislodged tent poles swinging crazily in all directions; in fact, a quick glance upward convinced me that the situation was becoming serious, for a blow from one of these heavy poles could kill a spectator. I feverishly resumed my efforts to coax Venus from her pedestal, finally managing after much effort. My analysis of her reluctance is that it was based on bewilderment and the feeling that she had to re-evaluate many factors, including me. Normally the most cooperative of animals, she was now confused, and this resulted not so much in a refusal to do my bidding as it did—and here I am relying on years of observation rather than incontrovertible proof—in an undermining of her confidence in me. In other words, I believe she wasn't resisting so much as she was trying to figure out whether I knew what I was doing.

After what seemed a long, long time and may have been only half a minute Venus came scrambling down to the floor of the arena and began stalking me as a prelude to doing the rollover.

The lights in the big top began to behave queerly as I gave Venus the soft whistle cue by means of which I got her to start moving toward me. As the lights dimmed, flickered and brightened, only to grow dim again, it wasn't hard to guess that the storm had damaged our power plant in some way. The animals ranged on seats around the arena grew more and more restless as the lights continued to flicker. Most of them were now on their feet as if preparing to spring from the pedestals.

I had just gotten the apprehensive Venus started on the first stage of the rollover stunt when the thunder, which had momentarily lowered its voice, exploded in its most deafening boom. I got Venus to do one token rollover—and that was that. Usually I called upon her to do several of these body revolutions, getting her closer and closer to me with each roll. But this was no time to strive for effects.

The rollover completed, I had a plausible windup for the act, for there is a certain conclusiveness about this trick. To many spectators it would seem a natural finale. I signaled to the boy at the door to let the tigers out. He seemed puzzled, and for a few seconds stood as if in a trance. Having become accustomed to a fixed routine, he now expected me to put my hurdling lions and tigers through their paces, since this normally followed the rollover.

"Let 'em out!" I yelled. The boy rattled the door and opened it and the animals started jumping from their pedestals and leaving the arena.

As I reached the safety cage and looked around, I realized that conditions were even more serious than I had thought, and I congratulated myself on cutting my act short. The big top was ballooned out and more and more wind was getting under the canvas. I was afraid we were going to suffer that

Facing the Big Cats

worst of all circus calamities, a blowdown. Outside the wind was howling and overhead the loosened poles were swinging more wildly than before. Spectators were frantically ducking as circus hands strove to grab the flying poles.

The animals were now out of the arena and in the tunnel, being fed back into their cages, when there came a great torrential downpour—practically a cloudburst—accompanied by more booming thunder and an ominous crackling which those who were outside and witnessed told me lit up the sky for miles around. A freakish bolt of lightning hit the arena—obviously it started contact from some higher point—and for a second or two I could hardly believe what I saw; and the same must have been true of my circus associates and the huddled spectators. The arena, during this brief and awful moment, looked as if it were on fire. Each bar seemed to have jagged flames shooting from it. Then the entire front section crashed to the ground.

Then, as quickly as it came, the fire flashed out and we were in semi-darkness as the electric lights began to flicker again. Some of them gave off a faint, faltering light—the rest, weary of this game the elements were playing, gave up entirely.

If I had not cut my act short, I would have been inside the arena with my lions and tigers when lightning struck and set the metal enclosure ablaze, and I shudder to think what might have happened.

That bolt of lightning traveled weirdly. It had no effect on people who seemed near enough to be hurt, and it knocked down others who seemed to be more safely located, including a group of performers from our Wild West unit who were waiting to go on. They were rushed to the local hospital. Five of the ushers were badly shaken up. Two of them were quickly revived, but the other three had to be carried out to the medical tent, where Dr. Cox, the circus physician, worked on them and brought them around.

Old circus hands—men who had been in the business for years and had lived through storms that had caused all kinds of trouble, including blowdowns—said they could recall nothing comparable to that freakish lightning bolt at Greensburg, which diffused itself so peculiarly and knocked down several people but actually injured no one.

Fortunately the storm spent itself quickly and we were able to quiet the audience and go on with the show. Danny Odom, our manager, stood by like the valiant captain of a ship in distress, and I attribute to his coolness and quick thinking the fact that no one was injured. A few people suffered from fright, but they were normal again when our clowns, doing an inspired job, swung into action and started the audience laughing.

I'll never forget that picture of Odom grabbing flying tent poles as he issued commands all over the place. Not many minutes after the lightning struck the arena and I was recovering from the shock that accompanied my thoughts of what might have happened if I had been in the arena with my lions and tigers when that bolt hit the bars, I found myself beside Odom, grabbing unruly poles that swung down near spectators. I don't remember how I got there, but there I was obeying his commands, along with scores of others.

I find it interesting to study the behavior of the big cats in an arena that is barely usable after a heavy rain.

I recall one such situation in which some of the lions, before stretching out on the ground in the laydown, looked around for dry spots. The first six animals to be signaled down from their pedestals found such places and reclined as cued.

The footing that day was peculiar. The arena was about half near-dry to dry, the rest had places where water had collected. The remaining four lions to be cued down were reluctant to lie in these sloppy areas. One by one they looked up at me as if to say, "Mind if I remain standing during this formation?" And I let it go at that. The use of forcing tactics in an effort to get them to lie down in those puddles would have been a mistake. There are times when it is best to let them do what comes naturally.

Lions and tigers are at home in the water. Both are swimmers, and tigers especially strong ones. Both prefer an honest-to-goodness plunge into a real body of water to reclining in a few inches of mucky dampness.

The big cats know that if they recline on sloppy terrain they will get a good hosing after the performance, an experience they enjoy. Sometimes a lion or a tiger, after looking at a soggy area in the arena where he would be called upon to stretch out for the laydown, will, after seeming to reject it, make a sudden decision to lie down there after all. And I have wondered more than once whether the animal had changed his mind because he suddenly remembered that if he got muck all over him, later on he would have all that fun when it was being hosed off. We often strike warm weather during our summer tour and there is nothing a lion or a tiger enjoys more at such a time than a stream of water played all over him. When the weather is extremely hot we give the cats a hosing to cool them off; the ones that need de-mudding merely earn an extra dividend.

A few years ago in Toronto an exceptionally severe storm necessitated our calling off our opening performance, a matinee. The heavy downpour almost amounted to a cloudburst and the wind reached tornado velocity. The big top took so bad a beating that for a time we thought we were in for a blowdown. Late in the afternoon the storm subsided, but the wind continued to blow with sufficient force to create serious problems. Our sponsors wanted us to appear that night if we could do so without jeopardizing the safety of spectators or performers.

Our answer was that we could put on a performance if certain precautions were observed. Our chief difficulty was that the wind still had enough velocity to billow out the big top with the possibility that the stakes that held the guy ropes in place might be uprooted. When anything of this kind happens it is hard to prevent a blowdown.

What we needed was a windbreak, and we created one by

surrounding the big top with heavy trucks and trailers. But even this measure was not sufficient. We were located on a lot that had not permitted us to drive the stakes down far enough for maximum safety in a situation of this kind—so one by one we pulled up the stakes and fastened the guy ropes to the big trucks.

The center ring was flooded and it was obvious that even the great quantities of sawdust we had dumped into the arena to improve the footing had accomplished little. Hay was also used in an effort to create a more reliable surface, although I never considered this more than a makeshift. When it packs down, hay gives you a more solid footing, but even when you move on it with extreme caution you run the risk of getting yourself snagged in the long strands. I once tripped and fell when my shoes got tangled in some matted hay. But when your assignment is to put on a show under near-impossible conditions, you're willing to try anything.

After testing the footing I decided that I would have to dispense with tricks that had to be performed on the floor of the arena and try to get by with lesser examples of animal training that could be performed by pedestaled cats. It amounted to what we call "walking through the act." Our sponsors were understanding people who realized this was the best we could do.

My principal recollection of that evening is the expression on the face of Sabre, an extraordinarily intelligent rollover tiger. Not sure what my intentions were, he walked slowly around the arena after he had splashed his way in through the tunnel. He seemed to be inspecting the footing and trying to find a dry spot. Satisfied that there was no such thing, he gave me a devastating look of disgust. It was as if he were trying to communicate: "You ought to have more brains than to think I'd roll over in *that*."

On another occasion Sabre had done the rollover on a soggy surface but under conditions that were better. The layers of sawdust we had sprinkled over the slightly muddy terrain had provided a fairly good footing. But when Sabre did the roll-over, the sawdust clung to his coat in heavy clumps, and the look he gave me that day wasn't complimentary either. His reproachful eye reflected his feelings as he gave himself a series of shakes in an effort to free himself of that obnoxious stuff his coat had picked up.

In the fall of 1963 the Clyde Beatty-Cole Bros. Circus was touring Texas. We had played two performances in Galveston and our next stop was Texas City. We had hardly arrived when the local authorities advised us that we'd better be pepared to remain there until further notice. We were directly in the path of Hurricane Esther and there was no likelihood that we would be able to keep our scheduled engagements for several days to come.

The heavy downpour bogged us down in a foot and a half of water. To keep the howling gale from overexciting the big cats we created a circular wall of trucks around them, using the windbreak principle described earlier. We couldn't very well silence the gale, but we could at least break its impact.

Luckily we had an adequate supply of horse meat, which meant that the big cats would be fed. We have a special refrigerated truck that accommodates five thousand pounds, and it was almost full, so we had enough to feed my act for at least ten days. En route it is not always possible to buy the quality I use—government-inspected—so we always fill the truck when this grade is available.

There was no way of exercising the animals. For five days we were bogged down in Texas City and throughout that period my lions and tigers supported one of my pet beliefs: that animals in good physical condition will exercise them-selves when the trainer can't turn them loose for a run in the arena. These exercise runs are important. Combined with the limbering up provided by two performances a day, they keep my cats toned up.

An animal whose muscle tone is good has an instinctive

urge to move around even in a small enclosure. As cages go, mine are roomy, but they provide nothing like the opportunity the cats have for exercising in an arena whose diameter is forty feet. For five days those lions and tigers exercised themselves by pacing back and forth.

Now and then they also stood up against the bars, bracing themselves with their forepaws, which enabled them to get a good stretch. The lions, typically more inquisitive than the tigers, also used this as a means of trying to figure out what was going on. After an unrewarding look at the wall of trucks straight ahead, they kept twisting their heads around in a determined effort to see what they could see to the right and left.

It seems appropriate to include, in a chapter dealing with wild animals and the elements, a story about their reaction to fire.

When I first joined the Gollmar Brothers Circus, we had winter quarters in the outskirts of Montgomery, Alabama. Some time later we were on our way to our new base at Peru, Indiana, where our show would change hands and become known as the John Robinson Circus.

The night before we were to leave I had loaded my big cats on the cars—leopards as well as lions and tigers in those days—and left for town, four miles away, to see a show. (That's what an off-duty showman often does.)

When I returned, about midnight, I went to bed in my quarters in one of the cars. And soon I was fast asleep.

My hand chanced to touch the window of my lower berth and I awoke with a start. The glass was hot. Looking out the window I could see a fire. The elephant car was ablaze.

Fortunately the car was empty. It was an established practice not to load the elephants until we were ready to depart. They are more manageable en route if they are not confined any longer than is necessary.

The big cats, in flatcars within full view of the flames, had set up a great commotion, and I imagine it was a combination of the noise they made and the hot window that woke me.

My lions, aroused by the blaze and the stench of heavy smoke, set up a mad roaring. The tigers and leopards joined in and the result was a deafening din. The more terrified of the animals flung themselves at the bars of the cages.

Circus hands, dragged out of bed, began arriving, some of them still dressing as they reached the scene. We got some heavy chains and, with horses and elephants tugging away, succeeded in hauling the burning car to a place on the tracks where it was not likely to set fire to anything else. But even after the flames had been extinguished, some of the big cats continued to hurl themselves at the bars. The smell of smoke persisted and apparently they weren't satisfied that the danger was over.

All of us have heard stories about people who bring off superhuman feats of strength in grave emergencies. I learned that there is the wild-animal equivalent of this phenomenon. The evidence was impressive. Normally it was impossible for a lion or tiger, however big and powerful, to bend the bars of the type of cage we used in those days without first weakening the oak baseboard. When I had a chance to study what happened that night I found that, while some of the cage bars had actually been bent, no damage had been done to the hardwood two-by-fours in which the bars were sunk! The pattern of attempted big-cat escape in those days (before today's all-metal cage) involved the animal's first scooping into this hardwood with its claws until it had loosened the bars at their base before attempting to bend them.

This was the first time I had seen cage bars bent on a straight desperation basis—and I haven't seen it since.

12. Big-Cat Catchall

How Good Are the Memories of Lions and Tigers?
– When You Are in the Arena Performing and the
Lights Go Out – Performing in Street Clothes – Do
the Big Cats Have Color Vision? – How Would You
Bet If You Could Witness a Fight between a Lion
and a Tiger? – The Last-Day Jinx – Leopard-Hyena
Episode – And Other Oddments

People are so used to the idea that "elephants never forget" that it comes as a surprise to them that other animals have
fabulous memories too. Having observed elephants in every
circus with which I have appeared, and having trained many
of them myself, I am in a position to support the argument that
elephants have a fantastic capacity for remembering.

I am also in a position to state—and this is based on even
closer observation—that many of the big cats have remarkable
memories too.

For instance, there was Big Nellie, a lioness known for the
"spin" I had taught her. She had become letter-perfect in the
business of whirling around and around like a kind of leonine
top. She enjoyed spinning so much and she overdid it to such
an extent that there were times when her hindquarters became
sore from her exertions. When this happened she developed
a limp and I would take her out of the act until she got over
it. But nothing could curb her enthusiasm for this twirling

routine and a few weeks later she would be hobbling about again. A healthy, well-built animal, she nevertheless seemed to put too much strain on certain muscles when performing this trick.

Although I found Big Nellie manageable, some of her co-performers did not. She had a way of getting into grudge fights, and I figured that if one of the animals with which she was feuding decided to attack while she was limping back to her pedestal, she would be at a serious disadvantage. So, although Nellie was a spectacular performer whose talents never failed to please audiences, I decided to discontinue her as a spinner and substitute an understudy—(I always have one handy as a replacement where a featured stunt is involved)—a male who was not quite as spectacular but who was a calmer animal and could be counted upon to do this trick without knocking himself out.

Two years passed, and in that time Nellie gave no indication that she had the slightest recollection of her old specialty. Then one day during a matinee at Madison Square Garden, in backing away from another animal, I accidentally gave Nellie her long unused cue. Instantly she was off her pedestal and coming toward me. I braced myself for what looked like an attack, pushing the kitchen chair far in front of me to fend her off. But Nellie was only trying to obey me. In leaping off the pedestal and bounding toward me she was trying to perform, not attack. Around and around the arena she whirled with as much zest as ever, until, after a few futile attempts, I managed to cue her back to her seat.

At the night performance that same day I determined to find out everything I could about Big Nellie's unexpected spin two years after she had last performed this stunt. Although in those days I was not as deeply interested in the mental processes of the big cats as I am today, there are a few categories in which my interest dates back to my earliest days as a trainer. One of these classifications has to do with the question of how much dependence I could place on the memory and re-call of the big cats.

The more you learn about this subject the more efficient you become as a trainer. For instance, in breaking in a new animal you have to learn what is the right daily dose of in-struction. If you err on the side of underplaying, you can be so superficial in those early lessons that your trainee—lion or tiger—will not pick up enough knowledge that will stay with him until the next lesson. On the other hand, if you overdo—that is, if you try to get your four-legged pupil to assimilate too much in any one training session—you merely confuse the animal, he learns nothing and you have to make a fresh start.

Two questions were uppermost in my mind in connection with Big Nellie and the experiment I planned to conduct that night. Had this lioness, on her own, had a freakish recall that sent her into that spin after so much time had elapsed? Or was I right in my assumption that I had accidentally given her her old cue?

I was preoccupied with a number of pressing problems at the time and therefore my diagnosis of the situation had to be a guess—an educated guess, to be sure, but I wanted some-thing more to go on before I decided that this was an example of total recall after two years, which at least to me was a wholly unprecedented phenomenon.

With the animals well spaced out to give Nellie plenty of room in case she responded again, I deliberately gave her the cue which I figured I had accidentally given her in the after-noon. She immediately went into a frenzied spin, this time exceeding even the pace and enthusiasm of her afternoon performance. She was spinning so madly it was difficult to get her attention, and it took every resource at my command to bring her out of it.

Annually a circus of any size publishes what is known as a "route book." Actually it is a log of the whole season. There is an entry dealing with each town we have played, and if any-thing of an unusual nature happens a special notation is made.

In our route book for 1960 the following appears on page 41:

"Played three days at Montreal, Quebec—July 15, 16 and 17. On Friday, the first night of the engagement, the lights went out in the middle of the Beatty act. Only light on was in the connection at Louie Gustoff's novelty stand. Walter Kernan, Cole Show Joe and Louie picked up the stand and rushed to the arena, and with only this light Beatty finished the act to thunderous applause. Performance continued when lights were restored after cat act."

Circus crowds are generous. They frequently applaud a performer for taking the only course that is open to him.

When the lights went out that night in Montreal, the sound-est of the alternatives open to me was to continue doing my act. When I took this position afterward in discussing the matter with friends, they seemed puzzled. How, they wanted to know, could the animals see to perform?

Since the lions in my act outnumber the tigers, I dealt with them first, pointing out that in years of experience with them I never ceased to be amazed by the acuteness of their vision at all times. As to the situation that developed when the lights went out, this was no problem for the lions. In support of this I quote the following from *The Book of the Lion,* an authorita-tive work by Sir Alfred Pease:

"Lions see exactly what they are doing at night, and the blacker the night the easier they seem to find it to pursue and kill their prey."

How about the vision of tigers in the dark? I have always had reason to regard it as excellent. In the comprehensive *Who's Who in the Zoo,* a group project prepared under the supervision of distinguished zoologists, we read that the tiger does most of his traveling and prowling at night. Since this necessitates—in India and Sumatra, where he is most fre-quently found—the avoidance of terrain where a surprise attack would put him at a disadvantage, we can safely assume that the big striped cat knows what he is doing in the dark.

It was I who was at a disadvantage in that dim light in the arena, although I could not afford to let the animals realize that I had such a problem. Even with a trickle of light from the bandstand, where the current was freakishly unaffected, I wasn't able to see much, and I don't mind admitting that I waltzed through the rest of the act.

Asked why I did not signal the cage hand who operates the arena's entrance and exit door to open it and let the animals out, I gave these reasons: first, you get used to the idea that the audience is there to see you perform and almost instinctively you keep the show going if it is at all possible. A second factor in such a situation is that animals are creatures of habit. If in cuing them out of the arena too suddenly one bumped into another, a fight could easily ensue that would involve greater hazards for all concerned than finishing the act in a semi-dark arena. A pugnacious member of the big-cat family, when one of his fellows collides with him, sometimes decides he is being attacked, and anything can happen as a result.

There was no heroism involved in my continuing to perform under the circumstances described. It was the soundest move I could make. Discretion is still the better part of valor.

Tom Fitzpatrick is the superintendent of the sixteen-man Electrical Department of the Clyde Beatty–Cole Bros. Circus. This department is one of our most important, as 95 per cent of our engagements are under canvas and we therefore have to carry a series of mobile electrical power plants from town to town to supply the juice for the tented city we erect and tear down almost nightly.

With three or four managerial exceptions, no one seems to know that there is a Mr. Fitzpatrick connected with our show, and practically every one of our employees would give you a blank look if you asked for such a person. This is because the head of the Electrical Department has become known to one and all—including the few who know there *is* a Tom Fitzpatrick—as "Kilowatt." The name has stuck and no one would think of calling him anything else.

Now and then Kilowatt calls on me in the house-trailer that serves as my home during the circus season, to reminisce over a bottle of beer. One day during the spring of 1963 we were having such a visit when something I said reminded him of the time a member of his staff accidentally pulled the wrong switch while I was in the arena performing.

The result was a heavy overload of power, and electric lights started popping all over the arena—the 8000-watters directly overhead, the 1000- and 1500-watters, and then the great band of multicolored bulbs of average size that encircle the whole arena near the top. The small bulbs cracked without much noise or fanfare, the next larger ones sounded like a series of firecrackers going off at an Independence Day celebration. The biggest ones—the 8000-watters—sounded like muffled cannonfire as they exploded.

The reaction of the animals was a good example of the difference between lions and tigers. The lions, with typical curiosity, kept looking up as the bits and pieces of the shattered bulbs fell to the arena floor. Astonishment was written all over their faces as they took turns at giving me a sort of what's-*this*-all-about look.

The tigers, on the other hand, were merely fretful. As the bulbs kept popping they moved about nervously on their pedestals, but their curiosity seemed blunted and they seldom looked up for a good view of the spectacle that the lions found so absorbing, the exploding of the lights one by one. To the tigers, those overhead popping sounds were an annoyance; to the lions, the whole development seemed fascinating. The composite tiger expression seemed to say, "What kind of low-down trick are they pulling on us *now?*" The lions evidently regarded the whole business as a game, and as bulb after bulb cracked and fell they kept gazing upward with the deepest interest, after which they looked at one another with a kind of puzzled amusement, then looked over at me with an air of expectancy as if they were ultimately counting on me to communicate to them some idea of what was going on.

There is something about a tiger that gives most people the impression that he is more imaginative than the lion. Early in the game I vaguely had that feeling myself. Experience has taught me that the reverse is true.

In the early 1950s I was playing a two weeks' post-season engagement in Detroit under the auspices of the Shrine Circus, which was so ably managed by my friend the late Eddie Stinson.

One night I got into a poker game that lasted until three or four o'clock in the morning. I was staying at the Fort Shelby Hotel, which is about eight miles from the Coliseum, where the Shrine Circus was showing. Before retiring I left word with the telephone operator to call me at noon, which would give me plenty of time to be on hand for the matinee.

I was awakened by the telephone from a happy dream about a poker game in which I was drawing straights, full houses, four of a kind and even royal flushes. It seemed to me that this call came about ten minutes after I had gone to bed, but it developed that I was wrong.

It was Stinson who was calling. He wanted to know if I was sick. I told him I felt fine. Why did he ask such a question? He explained it was almost time for me to go on at the matinee. They were holding up the show for my arrival. He reminded me that February was a cold month in Detroit, that the Coliseum was unheated and that the show girls who appeared in the spec and other acts, many of them scantily clad, were standing around shivering.

I looked at my watch and groaned. It was hours past noon. The telephone operator had forgotten to call me and I had overslept.

This was a Saturday matinee, to which the public-spirited

Shriners had invited hundreds of children, many of them from orphanages—which of course made me feel all the worse about being late. I felt better when Stinson informed me that the Police Department was sending a squad car to pick me up.

When I arrived at the Coliseum I made a quick decision to work the act in my street clothes. If I took the time to change to my regular arena outfit, I would further hold up the show.

So, for the first time, I appeared before an audience without the uniform I adopted years ago and which has become a sort of trade-mark—white jodhpurs and white shirt. I removed my coat, grabbed the blank-cartridge revolver, whip and chair a waiting attendant handed me, and dashed into the arena.

I had no trouble getting the animals to perform, which seemed to puzzle some of the circus fans and a few of my associates, one of whom expressed astonishment that the big cats accepted me so readily as their trainer. For after all, I was wearing a blue shirt and dark gray trousers, an outfit that was unfamiliar to them.

Recently I read a zoological work that states flatly that the big cats do not have color vision. I have had experiences in the arena that make me wonder if this is so. If that book is correct, it would explain the animals' indifference to the colors in which I appeared that day.

I have my own idea of what the situation was. My lions and tigers performed as usual because they picked up my scent. My unfamiliar garb in no way interfered with my giving them the cues with which they were so familiar and to which they so readily responded.

When my animals are not performing they are on exhibit in the spacious tent that also houses elephants, camels, giraffes, monkeys and other members of our traveling zoo. No matter how many people are milling around in front of the lion and tiger cages, if I happen to be making my way through the crowd the big cats react immediately. They start trying to find me in the throng. To get a better look, some of them rear up on their hind legs with their forefeet against the bars and follow me with their gaze until I am no longer in view. In other words, they have picked up my scent.

Lion or tiger? Which is more formidable? People have been asking me that question for years. I doubt whether it will ever be answered to the complete satisfaction of everyone.

Countless circus fans have tried to draw me out on this eternal theme. So have friends and animal dealers and an assortment of people I meet in connection with my work. As often as not, the person who raises the question has a definite opinion of his own—usually one that is strongly held—and occasionally I find myself involuntarily dragged into an argument regardless of how cautiously I express views that are based on long experience.

Centuries ago when the lion roamed far and wide in southern Asia, there must have been clashes between lions and tigers. But nowhere is there any record of any such encounter. I once commissioned a talented researcher to see what he could find on the subject, and I am satisfied that nothing has been recorded.

Today lions are African, tigers Asiatic (although the lion of India is not wholly extinct). According to New York's Museum of Natural History, a few Asiatic lions are left—the figure they give is approximately two hundred—in a protected reservation in the Gar Forest, an area of about four hundred square miles in Kathiawar. But the protection is so rigid that there isn't the scantest possibility that one of these lions will ever encounter one of India's many tigers.

Lions and tigers have an instinctive dislike for one another but can be taught to perform together. This is one of the major aspects of the big-cat trainer's job.

But if a lion and tiger met in open country, there would be no one to keep the peace and a battle would undoubtedly take place. What the result would be is anyone's guess.

If what I have witnessed in the arena applies to an encounter in the open, the tiger would try to get away. The lion would pursue him and try to engage him. In an enclosure—and this is based on forty years of observation—the lion is almost invariably the aggressor and the tiger habitually tries to avoid him.

There are exceptions to this. I have seen a male tiger pick a fight with a lioness—(this gives the striped cat a big weight and measurement advantage, and besides the female lion has no mane)—and I have seen the tiger quickly rout the lioness. But the fact remains that in the big-cat world in which I operate the male tiger avoids the male lion.

I can cite a few instances of male tigers whipping male lions, but I can't think of one such case where the tiger didn't have a distinct advantage. I also recall a case where a tiger had a marked advantage and lost the fight. I'm thinking of a big powerful tiger, normally fearful of lions, who saw an opportunity to grab one from behind. The tiger sank his teeth in the lion's shoulder, and the lion, the victim of shock, slumped to the arena floor. I've often wondered whether this was pure shock or whether there wasn't an element of strategy—a kind of bluffing—involved in the lion's winding up on his stomach, stretched out full length and looking as if he were submitting to his attacker.

The tiger, with all the force behind his tremendously powerful jaws, seemed to be clamping his teeth down even harder; then, seemingly thinking he had won the fight, he relaxed his jaws a little. So quickly I could hardly follow it, the lion shook himself loose, scrambled to his feet and wielding his right forepaw as though it were a club, struck the tiger with great force and sent him banging against the bars of the arena. If the blow from that huge, powerful paw had hit the tiger on the neck, which was what the lion was aiming for, it might have snapped it. The fight was over. The tiger never again wanted to tangle with that lion—in fact, did everything he could thereafter to avoid the maned cat short of hiding behind a pedestal.

Everything that has been written on the subject of the tiger versus the lion in hypothetical combat in open country has had to be in the realm of speculation. At least my own particular brand of speculation is based on many years of observation of the two species at close range in the arena. The tiger's fear of and respect for the lion has developed into a pattern so fixed that it has become my main prop in handling these two biggest of the big cats and in keeping warfare down to a basic minimum. It is responsible for many of my policies. For instance, I send all my tigers out of the arena as soon as they have finished performing, instead of keeping them on their pedestals as "background," and they never seem to be able to get away from the lions fast enough. In the last part of my act I work lions exclusively.

The lion seems to have no fear of the tiger. Seated next to a tiger, the lion is composed. The tiger, on the other hand, is usually nervous and apprehensive.

The tiger, lashing out furiously with his great paws and snarlingly baring his awesome teeth, suggests the last word in destructive power; yet there are times when he reminds me of a boxer who fills the air with gloves, striking countless blows yet incapable of scoring a knockout.

I should add that in making this point I am thinking of the tiger versus the lion. For of course the tiger knows how to score a knockout—but not against the lion. In his jungle domain, where there are no lions to worry about, he is supreme.

I have heard hunters say that tigers are smarter than lions. What they mean, when you get down to the details, is that the tiger is a more elusive target. I can't offer any firsthand opinions on the significance of this as I do not believe in killing animals and therefore do not hunt, although I have no holier-than-thou attitude toward those who do. Since I am not a hunter, I am forced to concede that my own conclusions are not based on opportunities for observation in the field.

Big-game hunters of my acquaintance, and others whose books I have read, are in complete agreement that it is harder to track a tiger than a lion. Therefore the tiger is smarter than the lion. Maybe.

One of my friends who has hunted the big cats—tigers, lions and leopards—insists that the tiger has a quicker brain than the lion, and is in fact the smartest of the big cats. "Clyde, let me tell you about the time . . ." Then comes the familiar story of how the tiger takes to cover at the first sign of the hunter while the lion—"the idiot!"—allows himself to be "tricked" into open country.

The lion, as I have pointed out, has an insatiable curiosity. Martin Johnson once told me that on one of his movie expeditions to lion country in Africa, as many as twenty lions, curious about his automobile, came out to inspect it when he and his wife Osa Johnson stopped somewhere in open country. "We could have knocked off a dozen of them if we had wanted to," Martin said.

The lion sometimes pays a big price for his curiosity, but that does not mean he is an "idiot."

The lion is an exceptionally intelligent animal. Pharaoh, in my present act, has actually shown me how to improve my finale. Other lions have conveyed to me how something can be done better than I had planned it.

The tiger, also intelligent, does not seem to have the lion's capacity for calm analysis and appraisal. This puts him at a disadvantage in a fight with a lion.

Nevertheless, a big majority consider the tiger the most formidable of the big cats. I have conducted informal polls on the subject and it always comes out the same way. People believe about three to one that the tiger is more than a match for the lion.

Most writers seem to share this view, including William Bridges, who in *Wild Animals of the World,* a popularly treated and handsomely illustrated wildlife encyclopedia, writes:

"The tiger and the lion are the two biggest members of the cat family and there has been much argument as to which is the more powerful. Experts are inclined to think the tiger is."

If anyone qualifies as an expert, William Bridges does. He is curator of publications of the New York Zoological Society, an accomplished naturalist and a familiar and respected figure in his field.

Psychologically the public has been conditioned to accept the tiger as the mightiest of the big cats. Whole books have been written about him as a man-eater, and in wild-animal motion pictures he seems more formidable than the lion, somehow suggesting a greater savagery, with more latent power.

You seldom see a tiger with a benign or kindly look. This is a quite common expression among lions. In repose the average lion has a much gentler look than the average tiger, and this has a tendency to give people the wrong impression. You have to live with these animals, as I do, to appraise those expressions for what they are worth.

Much has been written about the protection a lion's mane provides. The tiger has no such protection. But I have always thought this advantage is more psychological than real. The tiger's respect for the lion—which sometimes is based on what I consider to be out-and-out fear—provides far more protection than the latter's mane. The tiger's previously mentioned avoidance of the lion takes on so definite a pattern that the lion, aware of it, has a feeling of superiority which becomes an advantage against a less confident adversary.

As to the question of weight, a full-grown tiger (Royal Bengal) and a full-grown lion are about a stand-off. The lion would have a weight advantage over the smaller Sumatra tiger. On the other hand, the average full-grown Siberian tiger would outweigh his lion equivalent. (There are, of course, exceptions to all such statements. For instance, Pharaoh, mentioned earlier, is an unusually big lion and would probably equal the weight of the biggest Siberian tiger.)

Both species are remarkably fast. In open country lions rush upon their victims at a speed which may exceed sixty miles an hour for a distance of about one hundred yards. They cover as much as forty feet with one spring. The tiger is equally fast and, in a confined area like my arena, is a bit lighter on his feet, which gives him a slight edge in maneuverability.

If it were possible to walk into a stadium and witness a fight between these two most powerful of the big cats, first placing a pari-mutuel bet on the outcome, I would put my money on the lion. I would be backing a belief that he would win through a combination of superior power and tactics designed to get the tiger to wear himself out. The lion would fight calculatingly, and one of his objectives would be to conserve his strength. One of several ways of accomplishing this would be to avoid becoming paw-weary, a condition that would handicap him as much as arm-weariness depletes a boxer.

To give you an idea of the force with which a lion can strike, I cite the fact that this big cat, whose favorite prey is the zebra, can break a zebra's neck with a single smash of one of its heavy paws.

Paw-clouting is one of the favorite methods of attack of the big cats. It is their form of boxing. Sometimes, as shown in illustration number twenty-seven in the photo section, they raise up on their hind legs when they deliver these blows, which can be shattering when they connect. A miss can be shattering too—to the animal that misses. A series of such misses can bring on the paw-weariness referred to. From my own observations, the tiger misses much oftener than the lion and therefore is likely to tire faster. By the same token, the tiger leaves himself "wide open" more frequently than the lion.

On one of my movie-making excursions to Hollywood, one of my toughest lions (Sultan the First) was in a scrappy mood —perhaps disliking the role of motion-picture actor—and one by one took on and whipped every tiger in my act. It was an amazing performance since my entire entourage consisted of big, young, powerful animals. So these were not pushovers that Sultan defeated. This remarkable lion, feinting like a clever boxer and making his opponent miss, would then send the off-balance enemy sprawling across the arena with a tremendous clout.

I don't cite this as typical. Sultan was in a fighting mood such as I have never observed in *any* other animal and he was unbeatable. I have never seen a lion strike with such fury and I have never seen so many fights wind up so swiftly.

Occasionally I am told that I am prejudiced on the subject. If I am, it is a prejudice born of experience. The sum total of what I have witnessed in the arena tells me over and over again that the lion *is* the "king of beasts." Or at least the mightiest of the big cats.

In clashes between animals there is the equivalent of what in the prize-fight world is known as a lucky punch. I know of a case recorded in a turn-of-the-century book on animal training in which the author tells about a tiger that quickly routed a lion, killing him in a few minutes. The circumstances surrounding this fight suggest that the tiger scored a lucky punch, attacking suddenly and without provocation, which enabled him to catch the lion off guard and practically win the fight before his opponent had a chance to formulate a battle plan.

One of the superstitions of the circus world is that the last performance of the season is jinxed. I'm not superstitious, but I must admit that the big top has known many closing-day accidents and disruptions. I was involved in one of them. It happened in Shreveport, Louisiana, where I was appearing in the featured animal act with the Hagenbeck-Wallace Circus.

As usual, several of my friends in the circus warned me to exercise extreme caution during that final performance. "You've got to be on your guard 200 per cent on jinx-day," was the extravagant warning of a veteran equestrian who proceeded to describe a bad spill he had had on the final day of the season a few years before. Then he added the harrowing details of another last-day accident—an almost fatal one—a performer with another circus, a friend of his, had had.

One of the best of my big cats was a lioness named Babe,

who was trained to make a leap for the door as I made my exit at the conclusion of my act. It gave the performance a spectacular finish.

All went well with my act. The animals responded beautifully to my commands and the repeated volleys of applause attested to the pleasure of the audience. The act over, I started moving backward toward the door and it was a hundred-to-one shot that I had bested that last-day jinx. Babe came loping toward me, stopped as she picked up her cue, and poised herself for that windup leap. The stunt was so timed that as I opened the door and put it between me and the occupants of the ring Babe would bang against it and slam it shut with the force of her forward thrust, giving the impression that I had got out none too soon. This type of showmanship is an essential part of any good animal act. It's the sort of thing people remember and tell their friends about.

As a safeguard against grabbing a section of the steel cage itself, instead of the door whose bars were painted an identical black, I had long before hit upon the scheme of having three of the bars of the door painted white. This was an excellent guide for the eye. I could look over my shoulder as I backed out of the arena and know just where to grab the door to make a hasty exit. Perfect timing was essential, for Babe was a well-trained animal and if I did not get out of the ring on schedule it meant meeting that charge. And that, in turn, meant trouble.

Babe came on toward me to do her stunt in the regular way. Having completed my backward trip to the exit, I reached for the bars. My heart sank as they failed to give. . . . Funny . . . those white bars didn't stand out as they used to. . . . Frantically I tugged away. The bars held firm. I gave another panicky yank, holding my chair out firmly to meet the charge in the split second it took me to realize I was trapped.

With a powerful sweep of the paw the onrushing Babe knocked the chair out of my hand, smashing one of the legs to splinters. I blazed away with my blank-cartridge pistol, momentarily stopping her, then made a dash for a big pedestal near the door and got behind it. Bredo, a five-hundred-pound male lion, came tearing after me. As I slumped down behind this protective barrier, my new assailant came at me from the right side. To protect my face, I threw up an arm.

At this point I was saved by Equestrian Director Alan Hauser, who was keenly interested in wild animals and always watched my act. Grabbing a pole—one of the prods kept handy for emergency use—he quickly slipped it through the bars, beating my assistant to it. My assistant at once joined Hauser in poking away with a pole and they soon drove the animal off.

I had concentrated so exclusively on Bredo's movements that I had momentarily overlooked Babe, who now, having recovered from the "blanking" I had given her, made for me from the left. She dug a claw into my leg as once again Hauser came to my aid, but she did not dig deeply enough to cause serious injury. She, too, was driven off by the men with the poles.

What had happened when I reached for the door the first time was that my eye played a trick on me. The season nearly over, the once white stripes that had always served as my guide were now more of a dirty gray. The light had hit them peculiarly, they had not stood out sufficiently, and in my haste I had grabbed the wrong bars.

In fiction tales I have read about the wild animal that is so devoted to its master, an animal trainer, that it stays awake nights trying to devise ways and means of helping the boss. I can cite remarkable examples of cooperation provided by some of the animals I have trained, but I never could be as sure as the fiction writers seem to be that the beasts were motivated purely by a desire to lighten the boss's load.

I find myself thinking of Rama, one of the leopards in a curiously mixed act I once worked.

But perhaps I'd better begin at the beginning.

The act I presented in those days was indeed a strange assortment—lions, tigers, leopards, pumas, bears and hyenas.

My love for wild animals does not extend to hyenas. Perhaps I recalled too vividly what I had read about them as cowardly camp followers of lions and other beasts of prey. I also knew that in India hyenas had a long record of dragging human bodies from graves and devouring them. For carrion is a delicacy to the hyena, and for this and other reasons it is hard for the animal trainer to muster any enthusiasm for the species.

"Chubby" Gilfoyle, a great trainer in his time, was my boss and mentor and I never had a better friend or teacher. He had handed me this group of animals and taught me how to make them function as an act, and I was determined to make the best of it, hyenas and all.

The most important thing I had to remember in working with hyenas was that they have tremendously powerful jaws and teeth.

In their native habitats these queer creatures have an unsavory history. The hyena never confronts its prey. It is known for its practice of suddenly jumping out at a domestic animal —horse, colt, cow or calf—causing the animal to flee as it emits the weird-sounding cry which has earned it the nickname "laughing hyena." It slays its fleeing victim with its irresistible teeth, invariably attacking from behind. Those teeth, set in jaws that have the strength of a steel vise, are powerful enough to snap the bones of an ox. A sick cow that is unable to flee escapes attack, for the hyena dashes off in fright when an intended victim stands its ground. The records show that in India and elsewhere the hyena also attacks small children.

Several times my hyena trio attacked me while I was giving them a workout in the arena, always aiming for my shins. (I never let them get in back of me, so they were unable to indulge in the luxury of attacking from behind.) No damage was done, as I had taken the precaution of wrapping several layers of heavy close-mesh chicken wire around my legs,

Gilfoyle having warned me about the hyena's fondness for snapping shinbones.

One day a member of the hyena trio almost messed up the sequence of my act by forgetting to enter the arena or deciding not to—I didn't know which. At any rate, he lingered behind after the other two members of his species had trotted into the ring through the tunnel.

The leopards entered the arena next and an astonished audience was treated to the sight of one of the spotted cats—Rama—carrying the reluctant hyena into the ring. Rama practically deposited the delinquent at my feet!

That leopard was a friendly type and I always thought he liked me, but I never could convince myself that this was one of those cases—in the best tradition of wild-animal fiction—where the animal that loves its master figures out a way of proving it.

Leopards have an instinctive distrust of hyenas—in fact, they have a strong dislike for them—and I figured that Rama was expressing his contempt for hyenas rather than his love for me.

A few years ago I was asked to "drop everything" and, as a public service, help a roadside animal farm capture an escaped lion. The frantic proprietor was sure that "by now the animal has wandered off a great distance." He wanted me to help organize searching parties to roam far and wide in quest of the fugitive after I had instructed them in procedures and precautions.

Playing a hunch, I urged the overwrought proprietor, who had reached me on the telephone, to start looking for places *near* his premises that the runaway could, if so inclined, use for hiding out until it decided what the next move was. I figured that this lion, bewildered by his new surroundings, whatever they happened to be, and not knowing what to do as he grew hungrier and hungrier, might gravitate back toward the animal farm. At any rate, it was my guess that he hadn't wandered very far away.

It doesn't always work out this way—for the only predictable thing about wild animals is that they are unpredictable—but the law of averages, as it pertained to what others and I had experienced in similar circumstances, gave me the feeling that my recommendation should be given a fair trial before I could be expected to get actively involved in this lion hunt.

It developed that I had made a good guess. Not many hours after I had received that frantic telephone call, the runaway animal was found in an old barn—it was dilapidated and had been abandoned—located not more than a quarter of a mile from the place of escape, and the fugitive didn't offer much resistance to the attendants from this roadside menagerie that had been sent out to track him down and recapture him.

When a bear is a practical joker, he works at it pretty hard.

When I operated my between-seasons show and menagerie at Fort Lauderdale, Florida, I exhibited bears and tigers in adjoining moated grottoes separated by a thick wall. The moat gave them a chance to take a dip when they felt like cooling off.

The wall did more than keep them apart; it prevented them from seeing each other. But each picked up the other's scent, so the bears were keenly aware of the tigers and vice versa.

Animals such as bears and tigers, in the higher-intelligence category, like to keep their minds occupied. This is especially true of the bear, who enjoys busying himself with whatever happens to amuse him most. Sometimes it takes the form of seeing whether he can dupe some other animal.

One of the bears discovered that the layer of thick wire matting that covered the underwater separation bars had come loose and fallen off. This gave him an idea. He began slapping the water at the point where the bars were now exposed, for the purpose of attracting the attention of the tigers.

The first of the cats to respond was one I had named Sumatra, after his native land. He had been renamed Porky by one of the cage boys because, more than any other tiger in that group, he enjoyed slopping around in the muckiest part of the moat. While all tigers like the water, few of them are wallowers.

Porky—the name stuck—was more than a mere wallower. He was an enthusiastic one and frequently rolled in the mud where it was thickest and sloppiest until he looked like an old pig.

One day that prankish bear, having had no success in luring a tiger to the bars, slapped the water with increasing intensity at a time when Porky happened to be rolling in the mud near the wall.

Porky stopped wallowing and went over to investigate. His sense of smell told him that there was a bear very close to the wall separating the two species.

The slapping continued. Porky bent over and took a good sniff. Why, that bear must be even closer than he thought. Perhaps this was a chance to reach over and grab him. An earlier probe had revealed to him too that the wire mesh was down. What an opportunity!

The slap-slap-slapping on the other side continued, creating ripples on the tiger's side of the water.

Porky, fooled by the trap the bear had set for him, reached a paw through the underwater bars and made a grab for the bear, who was expecting just such a move. Before the tiger could withdraw his paw, the bear had nipped and clawed it. Howling his rage at being hoodwinked by this dodge, Porky made up his mind to get even the first chance he got.

A few hours later that impish bear was again slapping the water to attract attention. Slowly and deliberately Porky stalked over until he was less than a foot from the uncovered bars. Eyes on the rippled water whence the slapping sounds came, he stood poised as if preparing to pounce, although it's pretty hard to pounce on something below water you can't see.

It had to be a one-paw pounce, if you can imagine such a thing—and when he reached down to grab any grabbable part of the water-slapper, the alertly watching bear again grabbed Porky's paw between his teeth and gave it a quick, authoritative bite.

After a few more attempts Porky gave up and another tiger gave it a try. He too set up a loud howling when the bear grabbed his probing paw and clawed it.

I got a workman to cover those underwater bars with a heavier and sturdier wire mesh and saw that it was installed so that it would remain in place—and it wasn't until then that the frivolous bear stopped playing his game of Dupe the Tiger.

A bear is hard to outwit in a situation of this kind. He starts with a plan and sticks to it. The expression on that animal's face as he went about setting his trap for tigers with his water-slapping routine convinced me that when it comes to wiliness tinged with humor, you can't beat a bear.

During an engagement at Madison Square Garden in the 1930s one of our attractions was a group of women from Ubangi in west-central Africa whose thick lips protruded so far (sometimes as much as ten inches) they soon became an item in Bob Ripley's "Believe It or Not." In their striking native garb and wearing enormous brass rings in their ears, the Ubangis soon became known all over New York, and before long, with the aid of colorful and somewhat inventive press-agentry, from coast to coast.

The Ubangis were deeply interested in my act and seldom missed it. The particular engagement to which I refer lasted a whole month, so they had a chance to become completely familiar with everything I did in the arena. They had never seen me perform before, and it amazed me to see how quickly they familiarized themselves with every detail of the different tricks and formations, and with my every movement in the arena.

Their interpreter—they didn't speak a word of English—

told me that they had decided I must be some kind of god. No ordinary mortal, they insisted, would be able to step into an enclosure with so many lions and tigers and come out alive.

They didn't know much about tigers, which are Asiatic, but like all Africans they knew and feared lions. There weren't many people on their continent, whether they lived in lion country or not, who hadn't heard of the depredations of the big maned cats.

Americans are familiar with man-eating tigers, but not many are aware that lions have a long history of invading African villages and carrying off natives.

According to the Ubangi interpreter, these women had a consuming curiosity about the "wonderful spell" I cast over the animals that robbed them of their powers of resistance and made them so "frightened" of me. I asked the interpreter to tell these flattering ladies that they wouldn't be so sure the animals were afraid of me if they could see how rebellious they frequently were in training quarters. Why, only a few weeks before this engagement started, a young lion, a newcomer to the act, seemed wholly unaware of the "spells" I cast, kept lunging at me so hard that I ducked behind a pedestal and from there sought the security of the nearby safety cage in a few swift strides. This was hardly the behavior of a "god." I also requested the interpreter to tell his troupe that my animals had sent me to the hospital many times, that one of these attacks had put me out of action for three months and almost ended my career, and that apparently someone had forgotten to tell these rough, tough playmates of mine that I was a divinity.

I watched the Ubangis as he translated my message. The first thing I knew they were shaking their heads and looking at me with complete disbelief. Then one of them said something that approximated:

"The young god should not hold back his secret. If he will tell us how he casts his spell, we will give the information to our families and friends when we return home and the news

will spread and spread and soon everyone in Africa will know
how to make the mighty lion powerless and we will no longer
live in fear of him."

When I insisted that I was an animal trainer, not a sorcerer,
they again registered total disbelief.

They kept visiting me and continued to address me as a
god, and even did incantations over me such as magic-makers
rate in Ubangi, hoping to get me to cough up the mysterious
formula that made my hypnotics possible.

Despite their stubbornly held belief that I was a god, I
liked these African women and regarded them as friends.
They seemed pretty weird at first glance, but when you got to
know them you discovered their appealing dignity and child-
like charm.

There were so many of these Ubangis that they couldn't all
get into my dressing room, so usually a delegation of anywhere from three to five called on me at a time (although I
had met the whole group a few times at rehearsals). Such a
delegation was waiting for me outside my dressing room one
day when Martin and Osa Johnson dropped in to see me,
Martin remarking, "Your girl friends are waiting for you outside."

I told the Johnsons the story of my experiences with the
Ubangis, explaining that I was now a god and henceforth
expected to be addressed with less familiarity. No more of
that "Hello, Clyde!" stuff, I cautioned. They promised to think
the matter over and address me in a more exalted manner the
next time they called.

I took a lot of kidding in those days about the Ubangis.
One day John Ringling—the beloved "Mr. John"—told me I'd
better watch my step or I'd wind up with a Ubangi wife. If
the irrespressible Dexter Fellows had heard Mr. John's remark he probably would have planted a story along that line
with one of the newspapers. One of the highlights, I imagine,
would have been an announcement that after our honeymoon
my bride and I planned to establish in Ubangi a school for

teaching the natives how to put the hex on the Mighty Lion, send him into a trance and then hypnotize all the evil out of him.

Another year we featured a group that were billed as "The Giraffe-Necked Women of Burma." Some of them had necks a foot long, around which they wore layers of metal rings reaching from the base of the neck almost to the chin.

The "giraffe-necks," as we called them, were as interested in my work as the Ubangis and liked to watch me perform, but not because they considered me a god. Like the rest of the show, they regarded my work as a form of entertainment. But since animal training interested them as a spectacle, they frequently watched my act and—also through an interpreter—asked questions about it, some of these queries indicating that they were keen observers. And when they thought I was taking too many chances, they cautioned me to be more careful.

These giraffe-necks were every bit as friendly as the Ubangis, but instead of trying to feed my soul they offered food for my stomach—grasshoppers. Yes, grasshoppers. These insects were their favorite food and when we toured the states where the really big ones abound—Kansas and Missouri, for instance—they subsisted on grasshoppers alone, seemingly unable to get enough of them. They toasted them over a fire made of small sticks, dangling them over the flames by their hind legs.

They were disappointed that they could not get me to join them in these grasshopper roasts. They made their offerings frequently and after a while I began to run out of excuses. One day, when they were at their most appealingly persuasive in their efforts to get me to eat some of their toasted grasshoppers, I almost broke down and accepted. But I was due to perform in a matter of about twenty minutes and the thought of trying to work the big cats with a stomach that might be rejecting grasshoppers made me change my mind. The giraffe-necks practically wailed their disappointment.

Their most concerted effort to convert me to grasshoppers came when we hit a section of the Midwest where these delicious insects, they enthusiastically announced, were every bit as succulent as the ones to be found back home in Burma. When I resisted these jumbos, which they brought into my dressing room for me to see and admire, they decided I was a lost cause. But not before they had used a lot of persuasion. One of them—a woman who in her own way was as imaginative as the Ubangis—insisted that grasshoppers were more than a food. They brought good luck and if I could get used to eating them regularly I would be protected against misfortune forever, including accidents in the arena. I would never again suffer a scratch.

When they finally realized that I could not be budged, they gave up. But the giraffe-necks and I remained good friends. Once I found some enormous grasshoppers jumping around in the circus wagon I used in those days as a dressing room during one-night stands. I caught a few of them, put them in a paper bag and sent them to the giraffe-necks as a token of good will. This made us better friends than ever.

A magazine article published several years ago describes in graphic detail "Beatty's strategy of watching the crowd for clues to hazards behind his back." The article, a sound one in most respects, told how I scan the faces of people in the audience for signs that a lion or tiger "is about to attack this well-known trainer from the rear." This interpretation was developed in considerable detail, all of it interesting but none of it recognizable as fact.

To begin with, it is essential that I keep my eye on the big cats from the second I enter the arena to the second I leave. Even if I had the time and the inclination to study the faces of the spectators, it would be of no help to me. I am too far removed from them to be able to read individual expressions.

Once the scream of a spectator saved me. It was so piercing, so real, that I instinctively ducked and as I did a tiger went sailing over my head. Needless to say I was grateful. But this, I should add, was in no sense typical; it was one of those once-in-a-lifetime occurrences.

Although the audience may not realize it, I know what is going on behind my back practically all the time. I move around in such fashion that seldom do more than a few seconds elapse without my knowing what is taking place in back of me. If out of the corner of my eye I spot an animal that is standing on his pedestal when he should be seated, I lose no time getting him to sit down. It is possible that he is standing merely to stretch his legs, but there is also the possibility that he is preparing to spring. I can't afford to guess which it is going to be, so I must get him off his feet and back in the seated position that enables me to relax and go about my business.

On those rare occasions when I happen to miss something potentially hazardous that is going on behind me, an attendant outside the arena quickly tips me off.

Needless to say, there is no such thing as absolute insurance against attack—or I would not have wound up in the hospital so many times—but there is a way of minimizing such dangers. I believe I have worked this out reasonably well, with the result that I have sustained far fewer injuries in the past ten years than during any similar period of my forty-year career. There is no more shopworn saying than that experience is the best teacher, but it is true nevertheless.

In Chapter Seven I tell how, in the rollover, the tiger performing this trick comes toward me in a very slow, deliberate stalk. One of the best animals I ever trained to do this feat was the big handsome Sabre, an exceptional performer and a most cooperative one. He had become so good an actor that now and then there were people in the audience who thought he was about to spring at me. Once during such a moment a woman emitted an ear-splitting shriek. In one of those developments that fix themselves permanently in a man's memory, Sabre turned around in the direction whence the cry came—the first and only time he ever permitted a spectator to interrupt his assignment—and cast what I interpreted as a friendly though pitying look in that direction, as if to say, "I'm not going to hurt him, you nervous Nellie. I wish you wouldn't confuse us." After which he looked back at me, picked up his cue, lowered his head and advanced toward me in that crawling, protracted stalk in which he kept himself so low his stomach grazed the arena floor, then executed a series of perfect rollovers.

Several books on wild animals published in recent years give varying figures on the weight of lions and tigers. The maximum weight listed for either species is five hundred pounds. One of these volumes qualifies the figure slightly by saying "500 pounds and occasionally a few pounds more" (this in a reference to the Royal Bengal tiger). I have trained several Royal Bengals that weighed well in excess of five hundred pounds, and I have worked a number of lions that weighed between 550 and 600 and, in a few instances, a little over the last-named figure.

The heftiest member of the big-cat family I have ever seen was "Louis the Great," a massive black-maned lion that weighed eight hundred pounds. Because he was a freak, he was used purely for exhibition purposes. Actually, Louis, who suffered from obesity, was the leonine equivalent of the fat man in a circus side show.

Now and then I acquire a lion that reveals gluttonous tendencies, though fortunately I have never been stuck with one that could begin to match Louis' appetite. Once—and this was unusual—I had four lions in my act that bolted their meat as fast as they got it. Later they regurgitated it and tried to eat it again. This partly digested meat was not good for them, so the attendants had instructions to remove it immediately from the cages.

As time went on I learned that the only way to cope with the overrapid eater of the big-cat world is to feed him meat that has to be chewed off a bone. This slows him down considerably, especially if he is not given all his meal at once.

Air freight has revolutionized the transportation of the big cats from the compounds of the dealers in foreign lands who have them for sale. Not many years ago, to cite just one example, all tigers that arrived in this country from India and Sumatra traveled as deck cargo on slow freighters.

The trip across the Pacific on these leisurely carriers took anywhere from six weeks to two months, and in rough weather the animals had an uncomfortable time. Some wild animals, earmarked for zoos, circuses and dealers, still reach this this country by water, but the tendency more and more is to fly them. They arrive in better condition. Ultimately they will all be flown in.

Many years ago during a Philadelphia engagement I entered the enclosure where my animals were lined up in their cages to look them over before a performance. The cages are always roped off and there are signs—one of them dangling from the middle of the rope—that read "Keep Out."

On this particular day a boy of about twelve had chosen to ignore the signs. He had slipped under the rope and was standing dangerously close to one of my biggest and toughest lions. I ordered him to leave, or so he tells me. I've had so many similar experiences all over the country with so many youngsters that I can't distinguish one such set of circumstances from another.

That Philadelphia boy, now a man in his thirties, even remembers what I said: "Hey, you, get out of there before I throw you out! Do you want to lose a hand or an arm?"

Once again I was in Philadelphia (now an annual eleven-day engagement). This was in May 1963. A tiger had gotten into a scrap and needed to have one of his thighs stitched up.

I called a friend at the Philadelphia Zoo and asked him to suggest a good veterinarian. He recommended Dr. Lee Rubin of that city. I telephoned Dr. Rubin and he came over and did the job. When he had finished, he told me about my having chased him away from the lion's cage many years before and gave me his recollections of the incident. Needless to say, we had a good laugh over it.

Early in life Rubin had developed a love of animals—tame and wild—and on that particular day he was trying to get a good close-up of my lions and tigers. It was no accident that he became a veterinarian. He was headed in that direction from his boyhood days.

On that visit a few years ago as a veterinarian Dr. Rubin was unlucky enough to see me lose my temper again, although perhaps I should point out that again there was a certain amount of provocation. (I like to record these moments of irritability to confound old friends who over the years keep telling me that I am too "easygoing." It's amazing how many of them have hit upon the same adjective!)

A lion of which I had grown very fond—Buddy, one of the most lovable rowdies I have ever trained and a spectacular top-mounter—had developed cancer. He was no longer a performer, having been retired to the menagerie after a little over five years in the arena. An operation having accomplished nothing, and the veterinarians who examined him having confirmed my feeling that the animal must be suffering great pain, I had no course open to me except to take the advice of these professionals and have the animal put out of his misery in the quick and merciful manner recommended.

I felt badly about the impending passing of Buddy and thought it best that the end should come quietly about an hour after an evening performance of the whole show when the tents would all be deserted. But word had somehow leaked out about my plan, and when Dr. Rubin and I stepped into the menagerie tent where Buddy's cage was located, we were greeted by quite an audience. This business of making a carnival of the death of an animal I loved upset me and I'm afraid I said some harsh things as I asked the crowd to disperse and take its morbid curiosity elsewhere.

What next for a man who has been in this animal-training game for forty years?

I would like to acquire and train a white tiger, the rarest of the big cats. According to the distinguished Theodore H. Reed, D.V.M., director of the National Zoological Park at the Smithsonian Institution, only nine of these rare animals have been reported during the past fifty years. There is only one in captivity in this country, and it is to be found in the zoo which he heads.

"Exotic coloring and magnificent physique," Dr. Reed writes, "make this a tiger without peer. . . . The stripes are black, shading into brown, but the main coat is eggshell white instead of the normal rufous orange. . . . The ice-blue eyes are peculiarly aloof."

Dr. Reed states that he had first heard of "the white tiger of Rewa" through Ralph S. Scott, a Washington attorney who had seen one on a hunting trip to central India. Scott thought that one should be exhibited at the National Zoological Park. Later he interested John Kluge, president and chairman of the Metropolitan Broadcasting Corporation, in purchasing a white tiger "for the children of the United States."

With the aid of Mr. Scott, who is a good friend of mine, I negotiated with the Maharaja of Rewa for the purchase of one of his white tigers, the only ones now extant. Scott had paved the way for the National Zoological Park's negotiations and he volunteered to do the same for me. I welcomed his offer, as he has the friendliest kind of relationship with the Maharaja.

I agreed to the asking price of $10,000 for one of His Highness's rare cats and sent the money. Subsequently there were some unexpected developments, which need not be detailed here, the deal fell through, and my money was returned with a pleasant and puzzling letter. But I am still hopeful that a resumption of negotiations will prove successful.

The National Zoological Park experienced great difficulty in getting its white tiger out of India after negotiations had been completed and it looked for a time as if the transaction would be called off. Almost at the last minute objections from powerful political sources were raised to letting one of these tiger rareties out of the country; and it was not until President Eisenhower (toward the end of his second term) interceded that the deal was reinstated.